SILENT SCREAM

Charles Bronson

With

Stephen Richards

Mirage Publishing

A *Mirage Publishing Book*
Publishers of Investigative authors

New authors welcome to submit manuscripts

New Hardback

Published in Great Britain
By Mirage Publishing 1999

A CIP catalogue record for this book
is available from the British Library.

ISBN 1 902578 08 2

Mirage Publishing
PO Box 161
Gateshead
NE8 4WW
Great Britain

Printed and bound in Great Britain by

C P Print Ltd, Swalwell, Newcastle upon Tyne, NE16 3DJ

© Cover designed by Artistic Director: Sharon Anderson

Foreword by Dave Courtney

Hello, my name is Dave Courtney; you know the one, the cocky bald headed bastard that's on TV all the time. I first me Charlie while in the Special Unit at Belmarsh prison in 1996 and I don't think I've ever come across such a powerful human being in my life! I was pleasantly surprised to find that he was a very intelligent, witty and funny man indeed. Although an extremely serious man at times he is the sort of bloke, that if you were lucky enough to be a friend of his then he would do anything in the world for you. But if you were someone that's been silly enough to cross him he would make it his duty to even the score.

To be honest it wasn't love at first sight between Chas and me, but I now class him as a very close friend of mine. So close that I've since done interviews with him for '*Front Magazine*' and taped him singing 'What a Wonderful World' for a phone-in slot also in '*Front Magazine*', and he can fucking sing as well!

Even the strongest of people get low days when inside and you feel left out of it all and forgotten, a letter always puts you back on the right track to tackle the day. So to my pal, Charlie, I'd like to say you're far from forgotten and everyone out here is gunning for you.

Stay Strong my friend,

Dave Courtney

For Loraine

I swear I saw you walking in the air
And then I knew you were my angel

Introduction

Kenneth 'Panda' Anderson
(The Original Geordie Mafia and film adviser)

"Charlie is a good, good fellow, a tough guy not just in strength but within. I don't know how he's survived solitary for 22 years! Charlie isn't mad. They wouldn't beat Charlie up, as they know he can take it, they would wind him up mentally, which is worse. The screws would have knocked Charlie down many times, but he wouldn't have left his head down, it would be back up, he would not bow down to them and that's what the screws hate. I have respect for him, he wouldn't hurt women or children and he was a funny fellow. At Full Sutton a football game was going on and Charlie ran around the pitch with a guy on his shoulders and he had the corner flag in his hand. He lasted the full match including half time –it was funny. Charlie is a very loyal person."

Dave Courtney
(Respected face of the underworld, voted Rave Promoter of the year, TV personality, author, businessman and the press say he is: 'The Monarch of the Criminal Underworld'

"I believed that journalists were writing from a none biased point and that they left you, the reader, to make your mind up but this is not the case. So unless they can write bad things about criminals they don't want to, they only want to print mad things about Charlie. His book will even it up, it will also show what Charlie is really like, not the garbage some of the papers print. I believe Charlie has left his past at being an armed robber and he is also being held in prison as an example to others not to do the same. I admire his staunchness. All of the faces have a lot of respect for Charlie. Ron Kray said, 'That man is one right proper handful and you can't do anything better than have that man on your side and you wouldn't want him as an enemy', coming from Ron that's something! If Charlie is a friend then he'll defend you if right or wrong. He's a very witty, charming and talented fellow, his poems and drawings are very good. Charlie has to show he can handle himself in the environment he's in or people will walk all over him. Charlie definitely has a very good book and film in him and Charlie would come out of prison as a celebrity."

Andy Jones
(Owner of 'Crime Through Time' Museum, Newent, Gloucester)

"I like to give Charlie respect along with others like the Krays, etc. by having them in my museum. I think Charlie is a very highly intellectual person, but he has been very badly treated. Many people comment on how good his work is, which is on show in the museum. He may be aggressive by nature, but you can see the gentle side of him in his art. The system has let him down; he needs to be understood and not to be locked up for 22 years in solitary. He needs assistance to help him; it is not right to cage him like an animal. I am honoured and proud to have Charlie in the museum with his artwork. I hope Charlie will be able to come one day, with his mother, to visit the museum and see what's on display. I would like him to come out for a day to visit the museum, even if it takes 200 guards. I would gladly shut the museum for that day."

Jan Lamb
(Close friend of Reg Kray, personal friend of Frankie Fraser, poet, author, and Charlie's ex-girlfriend, Road to Justice and Victim Support worker)

"I first met Charlie through a mutual friend on the Isle of Sheppey in 1992. We got on right from the beginning as we both have the same sense of humour and to be with Charlie you needed a sense of humour yourself. Charlie does cartoons for me quite a lot; one took him over six hours to do. That's the sort of dedication he gives to those he likes. During my time with Charlie not once did he raise his hand to me or become aggressive and I felt proud to have such a man by my side. We still communicate even today and are still as close."

Tony Lambrianou
(Ex-Kray firm boss now an author and celebrity)

"I met Charlie inside prison, he is very infamous. No matter which nick he went to he would be followed by his antecedents, everyone is watching him and you have to react and Charlie reacts to that by lashing out. Charlie will feel the pressure; they do it to him to break him so he will end up in the block. I don't know anyone who has done as long as Charlie in solitary – 22 years is some time to be in the block. I don't know how he done it? They moved Charlie around a lot to get rid of him, let someone else have the problem for a while. Think about it, who would want Charlie in their prison with his background. He needs some humanity, but the screws won't give it to him. He only has his art and poetry to escape from solitary."

Lord Longford
(His Lordship has given over 40 years of his life to visiting prisoners, previously he has been an active member of the Government, now at 93 years of age is active in the House of Lords)

"Charlie's cousin, Loraine, asked me to visit, which I did. I met him a number of years ago, I didn't fear the man and I didn't ever receive any threats in the slightest from Charlie. We became friends and after first meeting him I did a press-up for him when I was in my late 80's, he found this amusing. I'm very fond of Charlie and he writes to me. I will always remain his friend. Charlie's art is wonderful, he's very talented and he has a gift for art. He's a charming man and I've always felt safe in Charlie's company."

Martin Oldham
(Legal representative and advocate)

"I met Charlie in '97 at Wakefield prison, Charlie had considerable respect for prison officers such as Governor Parry, Alfie Stockman and others at Woodhill prison. I visited Charlie at Hull, which he really liked and was told he was staying for five years, which turned out to be a lie, as it was soon to be closed. This I believe contributed, plus a death in the family and other pressure, to the latest siege. I don't believe Charlie is mad, but he has strange tendencies, he is not paranoid or schizophrenic. I have never had any indication that Charlie would harm me and I feel perfectly safe and content in his presence. Charlie is very entertaining and he has a good sense of humour."

Eira Peterson
(Mother)

"Charlie shaved his hair off for charity, for children, it was a really big thing to do back then. Charlie was always a very good boy and always shy. He had great respect for his father and myself. He was a very clean smart boy with all the women chasing him, which he used to hide from. He was very easily led and got in with the wrong crowd that had already been in prison. He hasn't murdered anyone as people and the papers have said, if they left Charlie somewhere to get on with his time then he would do it peacefully instead of being treat like an animal. My son has been beaten up in the prison by prison officers, put in straight jackets and urinated over and treat like an animal. So he's rebilling against the system, but they will never break his spirit. I do know that he's no angel. Charlie always sends me little gifts and cards, as he's a very sensitive and caring son. I was quoted in a national newspaper as having gave them an exclusive interview and some words were attributed to me that I never said, up to date I have only given one person an exclusive interview and that is going to be included in a documentary being made about Charlie."

Joe Pyle
(Ex-pro boxer now businessman, author, recording manager and film producer)

"I first met Charlie in Whitemoor prison on the wings. He's a lovely guy. He was infamous, as he wouldn't let the screws push him about, but he wouldn't create trouble, if he was left alone then he would do his bird like any other prisoner. I think that Charlie has gone along a street and as he goes down it, it gets dark and Charlie can't see a way out. Charlie is not insane; he's been proved to be sane, which means he has one up on the rest of us, as we haven't been proved sane. They don't want Charlie out of the prison; they want him in for life. He's no danger to screws or cons if he's left alone. I feel a lot for Charlie as he's been badly done to and he should be treat the way other cons are. They push him into things and make him do wrong. He can't handle those screws pushing him around. He wouldn't let them push him around, he would tell them where to go he's fine, he's no murderer or rapist. Charlie can be an asset to young kids and a guide to keep them out of trouble.

SOME OF CHARLIE'S PRISON MOVES

1974 – Risley Remand – normal wing

1974 – Walton – normal wing

1975 – Hull – block (dungeons)

1976 – Armley – block (dungeons)

1976 – Wakefield – block (dungeons)

1976 – Wandsworth – block (dungeons)

1976 - Parkhurst – special unit

1977 – Wandsworth – block (dungeons)

1977 – Walton – block (dungeons)

1977 – Wandsworth – block (dungeons)

1978 – Parkhurst – certified insane

1978 – Rampton – block (dungeons)

1979 – Broadmoor – block (dungeons)

1984 – Parklane – normal wing

1985 – Risley - remand wing

1985 – Walton – certified sane

1985 – Armley – block – (dungeons)

1985 – Walton – block (dungeons)

1985 – Albany – block (dungeons)

1985 – Wormwood Scrubs – block (dungeons)

1985 – Wandsworth – block (dungeons)

1986 – Parkhurst – special unit

1986 – Winchester – block (dungeons)

1986 – Wormwood Scrubs – block (dungeons)

1986 – Parkhurst – block (dungeons)

1986 – Wandsworth – block (dungeons)

1986 – Parkhurst – normal wing

1986 – Wandsworth – block (dungeons)

1986 – Albany – block (dungeons)

1986 – Winchester – block (dungeons)

1986 – Wandsworth – block (dungeons)

1987 – Gartree – block (dungeons)

1987 – Leicester – block (dungeons)

1987 – Gartree – block (dungeons)
Released October 30th from category 'A' from the block at Gartree

Arrested January 7th 1988 – Luton Police Station

1988 – Leicester – remand - block (dungeon)

1988 – Brixton – remand – cage (special unit) June 17th 1988 received 7 years imprisonment

1988 – Wandsworth – normal wing

1988 – Full Sutton – normal wing

1988 – Durham – cage (special unit)

1988 – Full Sutton – normal wing

1988 – Armley – block (dungeons)

1989 – Full Sutton – normal wing

1989 – Long Larten – normal wing

1989 – Bristol – block (dungeons)

1989 – Winson Green – block (dungeons)

1989 – Winchester – block (dungeons)

1989 – Wandsworth – block (dungeons)

1989 – Albany – block (dungeons)

1989 – Parkhurst – special unit

1989 – Albany – block (dungeons)

1989 – Gartree – normal wing

1990 – Durham – block (dungeons)

1990 – Parkhurst – block (dungeons)

1990 – Frankland – normal wing

1990 – Albany – block (dungeons)

1990 – Parkhurst – special unit

1990 – Wandsworth – block (dungeons)

1990 – Full Sutton – normal wing

1991 – Parkhurst – normal wing

1991 – Wandsworth – block (dungeons)

1991 – Albany – block (dungeons)

1991 – Leicester – block (dungeons) There for just one day!

1991 – Hull – block (dungeons)

1992 – Lincoln – special unit

Released in November 1992

Remanded for a short time in January 1993 and released a few weeks later.

February 1993 remanded for other offences.

1993 – Woodhill – remand

1993 – Winson Green

1993 – Belmarsh

1993 – Bristol

1993 – Wandsworth

1993 – Belmarsh

1993 – Bullingdon

1993 – Belmarsh

1993 – Bullingdon

1993 – Belmarsh

1993 – Wakefield – cage

1993 – Frankland

1993 – Hull – special unit

1994 – Leicester

1994 – Wakefield – cage

1994 – Bullingdon – block (dungeons)

1994 – Leicester – block (dungeons)

1994 – Wakefield – cage

1994 - Strangeways – block (dungeons)

1994 – Walton – block (dungeons)

1994 – Highdown – block (dungeons)

1994 – Belmarsh – special unit

1994 – Lincoln – block (dungeons)

1994 – Wormwood Scrubs – block (dungeons)

1994 – Wandsworth- block (dungeons)

1994 – Winson Green – block (dungeons)

1994 – Lincoln – block (dungeons)

1994 – Bullingdon – block (dungeons)

1994 – Wandsworth – block (dungeons)

1994 – Bullingdon – block (dungeons)

1994 – Full Sutton – block (dungeons)

1995 – Frankland – block (dungeons)

1995 – Armley – block (dungeons)

1995 – Frankland – block (dungeons)

1995 – Highdown – block (dungeons)

1995 – Winson Green – block (dungeons)

1995 – Lincoln – block (dungeons)

1995 – Frankland – block (dungeons)

1995 – Winson Green – block (dungeons)

1995 – Belmarsh – block (dungeons)

1996 – Full Sutton – block (dungeons)

1996 – Walton – block (dungeons)

1996 – Bullingdon – block (dungeons)

1996 – Belmarsh – block (dungeons)

1996 – Wakefield – cage

1996 – Bullingdon – block (dungeons)

1997 – Durham – block (dungeons)

1997 – Full Sutton – block (dungeons)

1997 – Belmarsh – block (dungeons)

1997 – Wakefield – cage

1997 – Belmarsh – block (dungeons)

1997 – Wakefield – cage

1997 – Belmarsh – block (dungeons)

1997 – Wakefield – cage

1998 – Woodhill – CSC (Close Supervision Centre)

1998 – Hull – special unit

1999 – Whitemoor – block (special CSC cell)

1999 – Woodhill – 'A' wing solitary no privileges.

1

I wasn't one of those kids that took pleasure in cutting up little pets or causing any animal harm for that matter. I've got to say it because those psychologist people are always on about the correlation between serial killers and people of violence having a sort of liking for starting out by causing pain to animals and then building up to bigger things, like people. The first bit of pain I caused anyone was to my dear old mum, Eira Peterson, and that was only because I was being born at the time. I'm a Luton lad born and bred. If I'd hung on a bit longer it would have been Christmas when I came into this mad world, but like anything else time waits for no one and I arrived on the sixth day of December 1952 at 56 Longcroft Road, Luton. My good old dad, John Gordon Peterson, (known as Joe) worked in a coach works as a coach painter way back then and he knocked out quality work; 'quality' then was something to stand by and be proud of. I always looked up to my old man and just like dad my middle name was Gordon, so there I am, Michael Gordon Peterson.

It seemed I didn't have much luck with schools because as far as I can recall I was kicked out of most of the schools I went to. Maybe if I told you that my nickname was 'Crusher' then it might give you an idea why I was expelled so much. I used to get a hold of the teachers and squeeze them in a friendly bear hug, but I don't think I really knew my own strength. I was always a physical person and didn't let anyone take liberties with me, although some tried. I remember my first taste of being on the wrong end of violence was when a teacher gave me something that was commonly called 'six of the best'. It left welts on my body did this six of the best; this didn't take long to arouse my anger. I gave him a bunch of fives in return and knocked him clean out, he deserved it for being a pervo and it's something that still comes to haunt me even to this day. Other kids would have forgotten the hidings they had taken at school and how some teachers would throw the blackboard duster smack bang straight into the middle of your head, simply because it was so long ago – not me though. For me, every time I get into a scrap with prison warders, it all comes rushing back. I admit that I do have a good memory and no matter what it takes I'll get my own back. I've waited for years just to get the last laugh, but not over silly things as if that was the case I just wouldn't get to have peace.

'Don't let the buggers get you down' was an inscription on some big knob's watch given to him by an MP pal. I should have had that tattooed into my forehead so I could see it whenever I get the rare opportunity to look into a mirror. Because every time 'they' get me down, they start to jump all over me, like what happened at the Scrubs (Wormwood Scrubs prison), more about that later though. It's during that type of one sided confrontation when they outnumber me by ten to one and all of them are tooled up that I recall that teacher laying into me with that leather strap. It's that what gives me the fight to go on, because they are all bullies and all bullies should be chinned good and proper, but bullies' minds don't work like normal people's, they know how to keep themselves out of harms way; 'cut and run' is their way.

Icknield High at Riddy Lane in Luton was the first school I got kicked out of and then Challney High School for Boys, it just went on and on, it wasn't that I wanted it to be that way, 'cos I was always one for searching out answers. My bedroom walls were covered in Dracula, Frankenstein and Rocky Marciano posters. No different to kids nowadays having posters of 'Pulp Fiction' or 'Reservoir Dogs' up on their walls along with the 'Spice Girls' and 'Mike Tyson'. My hobbies were very limited, there weren't such things as 'Nintendo' or 'Game Boy' computer games around then; it was either a skipping rope or a hoopla hoop, but them things weren't for the likes of me. I preferred collecting spiders and shoplifting, but not necessarily in that order and that made up a typical lad in them days. Every kid goes through some sort of psychological change and scares the hell out of their parents;

2

there's nobody I know what can say that their childhood was all strawberries and cream. Some kids shake off their tags, mine's just got that little bit bigger every time I'm in the news.

I was in the cubs and then progressed to the Boy Scouts, it was all the rage then and the fun of being by the campsite fire singing along with all the other boys made it seem as if though we were all special. Boys clubs were common and they led onto boxing clubs, where've they all gone, does anyone really care? You have the likes of these world champ boxers putting money into clubs to keep them going or opening a new one. These men know that if the kids aren't kept off the streets then they're likely to end up in trouble, because that's the only choice they had, not many go on to become world champs. Look at me, I'm a world chump, had I of taken the right steps then I'd have probably have made it big and be world famous for other reasons, although violence would still have been used to get me there 'cos that's all I knew.

I've an older brother who's married and lives in Australia and a younger brother who was in the Royal Navy, he served at the Falkland's War, a real brave fucker with all those missiles bombing overhead, he's one of my heroes. I remember I was scared of the dark as a kid and I had the occasional nightmare, like any kid. What I did suffer from though was something called 'Night Terrors'. I was described as having a bad temper as a kid, now what would make them believe that? I ran away from home when I was a kid, and what kid doesn't dream about this sort of thing, but it was written into a psychiatric report made in 1993 by Dr Anthony Maden, a consultant forensic psychiatrist at the Bethlem Royal Hospital in Kent. Dr Maden offered to accept me as a voluntary outpatient, when I'm free of course.

In that report he says a lot, but about my early years he states that earlier reports say I got into many fights because I felt other boys were looking at me. Well...isn't that how most fights start? 'Looking at me, pal!' 'Want a photograph!' I felt that was normal.

My mum described me as 'good looking' and I can't argue with that. After all, a boy's best friend is his mum. I know if that's the case then I get those looks from my dear departed dad. Sure, I'd have the ladies running after me and they'd be queuing up, but I always had other things on my mind. I remember working as a hod carrier and the lads voted me best hod carrier ever. I'd rather be carrying that hod then be stuck in the place I'm in right now,

3

but that's not for me, it's so that I could give my old mum some peace as I think she's had enough grief from things I've got up to, but like most mums she loves her kids no matter what. Everyone has a mother and his or her old lady might still love them even if they're the worst paedophile, who am I to argue with dear old ladies. I briefly worked in a supermarket and as a painter and decorator for three years.

I was pretty much under strict control when I was at home and it seemed that I'd grown out of my psychedelic period when I was to shock my mum when she spotted me getting out of a taxi. I'd just had all my hair shaved off my head for to help raise cash for a children's charity. Back then doing such a thing like shaving your head was classed as way out, now it's the in thing; even for women. Anyway I managed to get hold of a wig, a long wig at that. I sneaked it into my room and put it in the bed so that my old lady would think I had a woman in there. As I explained, way back then such things were classed as way out and this was classed as really taking the biscuit. Bringing a woman home was one thing but having her stay the night, well that was another thing.

My dad came running in telling me to get her out and he looked at the long locks of hair, lying next to me, with his eyes bulging. Here was me, his son, breaking the code of ethics by bringing a floozy back home for the night right under his nose. You can imagine the right laugh I had when he seen me pull the wig out from under the covers and throw it at him with my deep bellowing laughter chasing after it. Cor! He was right taken aback with it all and luckily for me he seen the funny side of it 'cos my old man could box for fun.

Dad boxed while he was serving in India as well as sparring with some big names; can · anyone remember a boxer called Turpin? Dad sparred with him, so you see I had a grounding in the fight game, real fighting that is. Professional boxers are athletes trained and honed to a fine point of fitness and deserve all the credit they get, but in the real fight game of the unlicensed boxing ring it's a world apart and all that fitness counts for nothing. Boxers like Frank Bruno just wouldn't have stood a chance against the likes of Roy Shaw, big Lenny McLean or me.

Respect is something I've always had for my parents and whatever they said was the law - I didn't see it any other way.

4

When I wasn't within earshot of them I was a law unto myself. One day I had an argument with my dad and I raised my fists to him, nothing happened I didn't' follow it through nor would I of, but the minute I did it I knew I had to leave home and I did. What caused it was my old man found me a job and I didn't turn up for it and he was right to tell me off for not turning up. It was only natural what happened because almost every kid looks up to his old man so who better to want to beat. I stayed friends with dad and he knew it was one of those growing up things, he was the tops when it came to forgiveness – what a guy. I moved in with my dear old gran in Cheshire. It's funny how grandmothers are usually the saviour of the day; my gran was a fantastic lady.

I wasn't a little tearaway doing things just for the sake of it, I wanted to get somewhere and whilst I seen other people going nowhere fast I wanted to get the fast train to riches and fortune. I did actually take in some of the culture from way back then. The first ever record I bought was by a man called P J Proby - 'Somewhere'. Proby later went on to star as Elvis in the musical and, a little like me, he failed at what he was doing and was dropped from the show. Here's a list of my top five tunes, starting with my favourite: 'Purple Rain'; it was playing during one of my arrests when I had a dozen guns in my face, 'When will I see you again'; (The Three Degrees) it was number one when I received my first prison sentence in 1974. It was relevant to me because I didn't ever see my wife again after that right up to this very day, 'Unchained Melody'; (Righteous Brothers) that was the last time I had sex and it still makes me feel in the mood when I hear it, 'I am sailing'; (Rod Stewart) I think it was 1976 and this was number one when I was on the ferry leaving the mainland for Parkhurst prison on the Isle of Wight and finally the earlier mentioned record by PJ Proby; 'Somewhere'.

In 1974 I was charged with my first serious lot of offences that even by today's standards are severe. I had hit the big time alright and along with it I seemed to have hit the brick wall of failure – there was no getting myself up and dusting myself down from this little lot of charges: Armed Robbery, Aggravated Burglary, GBH and carrying a firearm, it wasn't very clever of me! Along with me were three other guys; supposed mates. Some mates they turned out to be. The four of us were sent to Risley Remand Centre. By this time I was married to Irene and we had a little baby boy named after me. I had a house, a car, was a self-employed painter, so what the hell was I doing in prison, yeah what the hell, I kept asking myself that and have done for endless times. I was 2I years old, my son Michael was only two years old and he looked just like his old man! The wife, Irene, yeah...well, I loved her too, but we were young when we wed, maybe too young, but I sincerely loved her; she was a beautiful girl alright and I blew it, big style! Irene ended up divorcing me in 1976, who can blame her – I had my chance.

The Three Degrees had the number one hit that I mentioned earlier and it kept playing over and over at that time, 'When will I see you again...' It sure made me think while I was stretched out on my metal framed bed. The time really dragged – back and forwards to court, it's all the waiting and I had something to come out to so it made it even worse. The big trial was coming up and I had just had another bail knock back from the court, the other three got bail. I felt bad about that, as they sure didn't do me any favours especially when the big day came.

On my return to Risley I was waiting to be processed through reception with a few other guys, which is a job and a half itself as all the paperwork has to be sorted out, when this real evil bastard arrived! Typical nonce! (Sex Case) One guy was at the same court with him – and was brought back in the same van. We were told that the nonce was done for a small girl in a park, he'd heard the old bill (police) and the screws (prison officers) talking about it. Well I thought, yeah he's gotta get done, filthy nonce. I couldn't help thinking about that little girl as I looked at him with his head bowed and his eyes never stopped gazing at the floor. The screws locked him in a small cubicle, but my luck was in and they let him out to go to the can (toilet) and another guy and me got in quick, real quick. I gave the nonce a few cracks and got hold of a lighted fag from someone and stubbed it into his face, the smell of burning flesh had a sweet smell to it as I pictured that little girl all alone with this nonce.

That night I had me a good think as I looked out of the cell window, I remember it like it was yesterday; two fences, a wall, dogs and the ground all lit up with floodlights: 'You crazy fool, how am I going to get out of this one?', I said to myself. The things that flood your mind; I wonder how Irene's doing, wonder if the boy's alright, bet mum's upset, hope the old bill don't fit me up with no more. Time went on and I had a visit from the Wrexham police, they said they believed I had done a supermarket 'takings snatch' and they said it was best that I owned up or they would give me a gate arrest when I was released from whatever sentence I was looking at for the charges I already faced. No way do I own up to something I've not done, I never saw them again after that.

With the other three statements against me I knew I was going down, but for how long? The big day had arrived and it was held at Chester Crown Court, my sentences for each of the charges was as follows: seven years, seven years, seven years, four years, two years and a one year it totalled 28 years! Then the judge said, 'All are to run concurrently', which meant I was looking at a seven stretch; wasn't bad, I suppose. The other three put themselves away with their own statements, stupid gets. They ended up with small sentences though because of it.

Irene was in court with my son, also my mother and her sister Eileen; they came down to the holding cells to see me off. Irene was too upset to see me, mum told me she was heartbroken and that she had to get a taxi home, but she would come to see me very soon with Michael. I promised mum I would behave myself I remember the words I said: 'Don't worry mum, I'll be out before you know what, four years and eight months, maybe a bit of parole would make it even less, I won't do the seven, mum'. I grabbed her hand through the big iron gate, 'God bless you mum'. I asked Eileen to sort a few things out and I watched them walk away – heartbroken.

I was soon in the van off to Walton jail, if I knew then what really faced me in the months and years to come - well maybe just as well I never! The gates of Walton swallowed me up. I was in and in to stay. That night was the longest of my whole life and I had this feeling within myself that it was going to be a long time before I was ever to walk free. Irene brought Michael on a visit and as I held him I could feel life flowing back into me, hope started to surge through my veins, did I miss them both.

· The weeks passed and I was doing okay then one day they made a mistake. I was on the long-term allocation wing separated from my co-accused due to them having small sentences when they let my wing out on exercise with another wing and who did I bump into – one of my co-accused who had grassed me up! I followed him into the toilets and steamed right into him. All the built up frustration, tension, all came out on him. Luckily for him I wasn't tooled up. A few of the boys covered me; he was seen a few days later in the hospital – caught him some belters I did. Soon after that a copper doing three years got done with a chair leg in the bath house, just one of those things, I was there although I didn't take any part in it. Then we had a sit-in in the workshop so it wasn't long before I was on my way to a top security jail – Hull. I was new to all of this sort of thing and it seemed pretty normal to me, but I was to find out that all of the eventual moves to different prisons were meant to destabilise me even further.

I noticed the cameras all along the top of the wall and this was my first taste of such a high security lockup. Razor wire, dogs, cameras and even a large camera that faced a door that was at the end of 'A'-wing – those cameras moved about and watched everything. Behind that door, I soon found out, was the punishment block, they called this the 'Seg Unit'. I met a few of the lads, some staunch guys; Wally Lee, Harry Johnson, Stan Thompson, Ernie Page and Johnny Woods, yeah some great guys – they had that wing sewn up; nice and peaceful on there it was. Snooker, TV, table tennis and a cooker, it had the works. If only the screws had of kept me on that wing, but no good iffing and butting.

They ended up moving me to B-wing, what a poxy wing that was, I felt mugged off. They put me into a workshop I didn't want to go in to, sitting behind a sewing machine like a wet melon. I didn't like any of it and to make things worse the cell I was in was one of the new kind, not big enough to swing a cat around. I told them I wanted moving to another wing and how I felt about the job; it wasn't for me. Did they listen, no? I sat in that shop for a week and done nothing. Then they moved me into another one with only eight guys in it, none of us did anything, we just played cards and scrabble. Then this screw said to us all: 'Next week some mailbags are coming in. You've all got to sew them up, it don't matter if it's only one a day, but you must do them!' I never said a lot – all I said was 'Stick 'em up your arse'. The others all said very much the same, one guy said: 'We don't do mail bags in a long-term jail'. Well, that was good enough for me I thought and none of us would be doing them.

Over the weekend I knew that there would be some lumber over this, but I made my mind up and no way was I doing mailbags. If we all stick as one we can't lose - so I thought. So Monday morning arrived and the screws looked tense, then more of them were brought in. One come up to me and asked if I was refusing to work, I told him I wasn't refusing but I wasn't doing mail bags. He said: 'You're nicked!' Then he asked every other con in the place the same and they all said 'yes' they would do them, fucking hells bells I was the only one got nicked, can you believe it? I was taken to the seg unit and put on what's known as 'governor's report'. Seven days solitary! Right you bastards, and that was the start.

I done all seven days nice and peaceful, the seg wasn't too bad, but I didn't like the cameras watching my every move, being watched by them screws, even the exercise yard had cameras. You wash and shit – all on camera. I was banged up for 23 hours a day, one hour per day exercise. My bedding was taken off me during the day and returned at night, I was brooding and I had to fight back or be mugged right off.

When I got back on B-wing I went straight into the assistant governor's office and told him I wanted a wing move plus another job – no joy! 'Right', I thought. The next morning I went into the shop and waited for all to settle, and then I started. I picked up a table and smashed all the windows out; all the screws ran out as I threw the table at them - the other cons just sat there. The alarm bells were going, twenty screws or more were running towards the shop plus the ones that had run out were there as well. I noticed several holding their truncheons; 'Well this is it', I thought. I grabbed a brush and they came charging in at me although I had no intentions of hurting anyone, but they kept coming closer and closer. The one in front of all of them told me to put the brush down before he rams it up my arse, well I thought why not.

It turns out he was a works screw called Bootsy Clarke. I smashed it right across his neck, crack! It broke clean in half. Just as I was going to give him another go the others mobbed me and I was down and well out of it. I couldn't see a lot, as there were bodies all over me, but I could hear the other cons shouting, 'LEAVE HIM ALONE'. I was soon carried out of the shop double fast and taken into the prison building, dragged down a corridor, then it started. The bastards started working me over, even while I was half dragged and carried the boots were flying in at me from all directions. One of them was even doing a Vinnie Jones on me -

squeezing my balls! I know what Gazza went through now, remember that photo that appeared in most national newspapers? Poor fucker!

The bastard that had me around the throat was squeezing my airway closed and cutting my air supply off, I felt myself going into darkness but I also felt pain shooting throughout my body from where one had been squeezing my privates - what an animal! When we got to A-wing I cooled off and they just carried me through and straight through the seg door, which was already open waiting for me. Then we changed direction and went into a big door to my right and it started again, the punching and the kicking. One was already hysterical he kept shouting: 'He's done Nobby, he's done Nobby with a brush'. I knew him later to be called 'Bootsy' although they called him 'Nobby'.

Then I was stripped off, held down and strapped into a body belt as well as that my ankles were strapped. I was helpless, I couldn't defend myself no matter what, I was lying naked on the cold floor when one brave bastard put the boot in then a screw, a stern faced screw, in a white shirt told them to give me the works. Way back then it was the senior and principle officers what wore white shirts and ordinary screws wore blue shirts. Now they all wear white shirts.

I felt heavy, I felt humiliated. This belt was about six inches wide, it was locked at the back and on each hip was a handcuff where each of my wrists was locked. My ankles were bound together; such a thing like this was alien to me, 'What's this?' I thought. How can they use such a thing, it was 1975 and I was treated like that! I could move my fingers, I could see my whole body, but I couldn't even move my arms or legs, never in my life had I been through such a terrible thing as this. Of course now such a thing wouldn't cause me any concern as I've been through it that many times before.

The hiding was expected, yes, but what followed was brutal I was aching all over, my mouth was bleeding I could taste the blood, my head was pounding, my legs felt like they didn't belong to me and my eyes felt heavy. These were all feelings that I would experience many more times in the forthcoming years and, although, it gets no less it becomes tolerable and expected. What more can they do to me? I've been to hell and back – the devil looks after his own, but that very day I had been to hell and back.

I was in a square cell with nothing other than a chamber pot for company, oh...there was also a concrete mound with wooden boards embedded inside with a straw mattress and two blankets, that was it. No windows, nothing! A peephole was built integrally into the wall, never have I known a cell quite like it. The door was bigger than normal cell doors; it was strong - reinforced. King Kong couldn't have budged it, there were no water facilities, my clothes were left outside the cell door on the floor: jeans, T-shirt, socks and underpants. (My shoes were missing.) I managed to get on top of the mattress, which was very difficult; I just lay there like a trussed up chicken ready for the pot.

I passed out and woke up to the sound of the door being opened there were plenty of screws with the doctor. He came over and asked me if there were any injuries, I told him to 'FUCK OFF'. And I spat at him with what little strength I had left and they left. I'll never forget this, never – trussed up like a wild animal! To beat a man is one thing but to demoralise him is something else, sure I was wrong to lash out with the brush, but two wrongs don't make a right. Am I wrong, not on your life I'm not, these bastards are wrong. I lay there for god knows how long, I could have done with some water and felt the urge to be set free, my survival instinct kicked in.

I know I've taken lots of people hostage over the years, but none of my victims have suffered anywhere near this sort of legalised thuggery. I've done real solitary, some people consider those from the public civilian sector that've been taken hostage to have suffered...well maybe they did and I don't question that but my solitary has been done on my own. I've had no cracks in the wall to speak to other prisoners through.

Terry Waite, a good Christian man, suffered as a consequence of his over zealousness to help those in need – he paid a price for that; he was taken hostage for a number of years. I take my hat off to the man, did you see how gaunt he looked after such an ordeal and how he nearly lost it, well I've done 22 years of solitary and, hell, I'm still here, strong and willing to go on until I'm as old as my friend Lord Longford (Frank), he's 93 years young.

My door opened, the screws put down a plastic plate with food on as well as a plastic mug of tea. A screw in a white shirt, a senior officer, asked me if I was going to behave and said that he would undo one of my hands so that I could eat? I didn't make a reply so he left me cuffed up and left me lying there as I was with the food and drink on the floor. I could have drunk the tea but no way was I going to drink like a dog – I'd sooner die. They came back later, one bent down and picked them up: 'Not hungry are we Peterson or is it a hunger strike?' They shot off, but I also heard another door bang up. Then it hit me; this is the strong box! It has two doors to get inside, always well away from the ordinary cells, you can guess why? This was my first ever time in the box, but not the last. There's always a first time for everything, but this wasn't one of the most enjoyable things.

It was quiet, too quiet, unreal, unnatural. The box was soundproof and the only time I heard anything was when the first door opened, which meant they were on their way in. There was nothing to see, I couldn't move and was still naked how could they get away with this? Sure I'd heard of nut houses with straight jackets, but I'm not mad, I'm no danger to myself, 'How can I be a danger to anyone in here?', I thought to myself? I'm a prisoner and being treat like a fucking animal!

Somehow I got my ankles right up to my back and turned onto my side, it really hurt my arm, I then got a hold of the strap across my ankles with my right hand. I felt winded in this position I felt for a few seconds hoping to catch hold of the buckle, just a little further and there it was. I got a hold of it and managed to undo it somehow. What relief to move my legs, but no way was I going to get my hands free from the belt as by now my arms were feeling dead. I then got to my feet and moved about a bit, I felt bloody awful but most of all I felt humiliated. I felt pure hate for them leaving me in such a state in a medieval contraption. What about if I needed to use the toilet, surely they weren't allowed to do that?

Time seemed endless, if there's such a saying it existed for me. I needed water so I got down on the cold stone floor and started banging the door with my bare feet for them to get me out of this belt. I banged for a good five minutes then they come, I heard the first steel door open and then a bolt and jingling of keys on chains and the door opened slowly. But when I saw them I couldn't speak I felt only resentment.

The screw in the white shirt told one of the dozen screws to bring some tea then he warned me that if I started then I would 'get it'. He took out a key and with it opened the lock and freed my arm from the body belt, wow! Did it feel numb; 'Right you can eat, drink and use the pot then I'll have to lock your arm up again.' I then felt my mouth, my lips were swollen and with cuts on the inside, on the back of my head were two lumps. My jaw ached, my ribs were sore and there were many bruises on my legs - AND THE DOCTOR ASKED 'ANY INJUIRES?' A screw put a plate of food on the floor, there was no fork to eat with or spoon - nothing! 'Right, we'll be back in a while Peterson'. Before I did anything I slipped into my underpants and jeans I used my free arm while I could then I drank the luke warm tea, I never touched the food and then I thought I had better relieve myself in the pot, which I did. I emptied my bladder, yeah, I felt better, but why did I have to have my arm done up again? Surely if anything they should have undone the other arm, I wasn't any danger.

They came in team handed, 'Okay, Peterson, let's be having you'. 'NO! I don't need to be in this belt!' 'Grab him, men.' I never did nothing, Christ; I never had time they were on me like lightening. I was soon back securely, except for my ankles, as they knew it was no use since I could free them. As they left me a couple of them trod on me, they seemed to love it, big brave bastards. There was no need for this sort of treatment being dished out to a first time long-termer like me. I was left like that 'til breakfast, all throughout the night the red bulb was the only company I had and I couldn't really sleep with the restraints on. It was the most uncomfortable night I've ever spent, that was my first time; my virginity had been robbed from me. I can't sleep too good on my back, I'm a side sleeper.

That night I made a vow to myself, never to forget. I learned something out of that! I learned just what really does go on. I felt it. I breathed it. I was full of hate. I felt so hateful. I could feel the adrenaline pumping around my body from what they'd done. I learned something else too and from now on it was violence with violence. No matter how ruthless one becomes the penal system will become more ruthless.

I lay awake that night thinking all sorts of things, but the thing that kept coming back and bombarding my mind over and over again was 'MICHAEL - IRENE, MICHAEL - IRENE'. What were they doing, how were they? I also thought of mum and dad and my brothers and all the rest of my family. I wondered what they would think if they knew what was happening. My family are all good honest people none of them have ever been in trouble. Sure I went wrong somewhere, but I never done nothing wrong, evil or bad. The way I see it is that as long as women or children don't get hurt what's a blag (robbery) or two. Of course it's wrong! Course it's wrong to steal, use violence or even to kill, but life's strange. A man steals for a reason either to live or for greed or he's just a nut. We're all different and that's the one thing everyone has in common apart from that one thing we can't all be the same, can we? And if a guy robs a bank or nicks the 'Mona Lisa' and nobody gets hurt then good luck to him. Take the 'Great Train Robbery', that was magic. Ask the average person what they thought about the prison sentences dished out to them that took part in the robbery. Bruce Reynolds, one of the robbers, got 25 years - disgusting! Ask the same people though what they think a child molester or a rapist should get!!!

That night everything went on inside my head. It was so quiet I was totally alone, emptiness surrounded me, loneliness. Somewhere within my deepest thoughts I was searching for myself, maybe my soul. Yeah, that night I felt pretty low alright. Luckily throughout the night I didn't need to empty my bladder or body waste. The embarrassment and degradation that would have caused me would have suited them right down to the ground. Now that I had my underwear and jeans on there was no way I could have unzipped them from the position my hands were in. This makes my blood boil even now, all these years past, just writing about it.

The same lot came into me with breakfast and the same screw undid my wrist. I had to ask about the other one, 'Behave and we'll see, you'll be on adjudication later on this morning so we'll have to see what the governor and the doctor decide.' Still no spoon or fork, I ate the porridge with my hand I was that hungry. I was, as bad as it sounds, no better than a monkey, but it was what the system had done to me. They enjoy seeing someone like me suffer in such a way and behind closed doors. I've been on hunger strike a few times since this incident and I always get the feeling that they would love to see me waste away, but for that moment I needed food.

It's a very vicious circle and once caught up inside of it it's so damn hard to get out of it. Then I had to empty my bowels into the pot this is a thing I despise having to do, but what can one do? I thought about slinging it all over them when they came in, but I decided against it. That decision wasn't because I feared them or feared another kicking, the reason I decided against it was 'cos I needed out of the body belt.

My left arm was practically numb, my right one was just getting used to being undone when they came back. 'Right, Peterson, wash.' I walked out of the door and there in the left hand corner was a toilet and a basin. I asked for my left hand to be freed but I was refused this most basic of requests so I washed with one hand. There was no mirror and I emptied the pot down the can, there was no means of flushing it from where I stood. I was starting to feel a little better when a dozen screws surrounded me and I was told what to expect if I ever attacked another screw, my life was threatened! My free arm was locked up and I was led back to the box.

Not long after that the doctor came in and I again told him to 'FUCK OFF'. Later on that day I was marched into the adjudication hearing whilst still secured in the belt. I still had on my jeans, but no top, no shoes, nothing. The governor read out the charges: 'Gross violence towards a prison officer, damaging Government property', and with that he remanded me for a visiting court. For those of you not familiar with what I'm on about it was called a VC. A governor was limited in how much time he could add on so it was down to the VC to up the sentence. I was led back to the box and for the rest of the day I was kept in that belt. I never had no dinner and when they came in with tea the governor was with them, I could see it was tea and not dinner so I said: 'I've had no dinner!' The screw with the white shirt said I'd refused it and I called him a 'fucking liar'.

The governor asked if I would behave if the restraint was removed, I nodded. I was then taken out of the belt and never have I felt so relieved, I loosened up a bit to get the blood circulating. I was then asked if there was anything I needed, 'Yeah a water container and a bit of piece'. They left me; I ate my food and gulped my tea down, which tasted sweet. Had I of had any experience then I would have known that you don't get 'sweet' prison tea, but I know now what it was they had put in it – drugs to sedate me. I should have realised something was up, they came back with a container full of water and took the plate and mug away, my head felt strange, weird. I'd never felt like that before this although I've felt like that and worse since with the drugs I was on in Broadmoor, but more of that later. My legs felt like lead and my mouth quickly dried out, my vision went blurry and I could feel the nerves twitching in my face. The bastards had spiked my tea! Drugs, yeah, there's no other explanation.

I fell to the mattress just watching the ceiling spinning around and around, I can't remember much more. I awoke looking at the red light bulb so I knew it was night or early morning, I felt terrible – really ill like I've never experienced until then. I got to my feet and my legs were very weak, I just had no life in me, I felt wobbly all over so I drank the water all in one go. What this drug was - I don't know? Why they done it I don't know, all I can say is it was sweet. This was my first experience with the liquid cosh, but it was nothing to what faced me, shear hell faced me, all that had happened in this short time was nothing compared to what lay ahead!

I spent the next few weeks in that box, but things got better. Sometimes they left the first door open so I could use the toilet and wash in my own time plus they'd let me have a book. That time in the box taught me many things, one of those things was I discovered the meaning of the word 'isolation', I'm the master of that and nothing can compare to the sound of silence. I knew what it was like to be completely isolated from the world outside, and inside. I never spoke to anybody.

The governor and doctor visited me everyday, but I ignored them, I would turn my head and stare at the wall. They started giving me one hour a day exercise, which I ran away. I just jogged around; the two cameras were on me constantly out there. The yard was about fifty feet long by sixty feet wide with a twenty-foot high fence all around and it was topped off with razor wire, not barbed wire. Razor wire is exactly that, imagine putting razor blades into wire, imagine gripping that and trying to pull yourself over! Most of my time in the box I passed away by exercising, but no way can I fully explain that feeling of loneliness, man wasn't put on earth to stare at four walls for as long as I have – no way!

Some of my personal belongings were given to me; I treasured all of my photographs. I looked at them endless times, sometimes I got so cut up I pushed the mattress up against the wall and kept punching it 'til my knuckles bled and I had no more left in me. I found this really took a lot of frustration out of me; it helped relax me and keep me cool.

hell broke loose, shouts, bells, they were on to me, punching me, pulling me, screaming at me. White had actually gone through the death rattle – he was to all intents and purposes - dead. As I was being dragged away I could hear shouts of 'Get the oxygen.'

I was beaten so badly that I couldn't stand, but I can remember laughing insanely, I'd killed the monster, the nonce, the pervert, the paedophile call him what you like but to me I'd killed him and he was 'dead'. I'd never felt so free of all the shackles of life in my life. A weight had been lifted from my shoulders, I was now a killer, or so I thought. Would you believe it though – the screws had revived him, the filthy monster. After all my hard work, all my sleepless nights to kill him they bring him back to life, like. I faced years of isolation; my future was grim the pain had just begun.

I was a rebel fighting the system and my violence had got out of control and now I was paying for it. But here I was out of my depth and a new type of person became obvious. Bovver boys on the street were like kindergarten children compared to this lot. Guys attacking guys over voices in their heads telling them to and other guys smashing their heads off walls. I've seen it all and more. I've also been as bad, tearing up TV sets, billiard tables, roofs, cells, sinks and offices. When I look back there isn't much I haven't tore up, but madness overcomes us all. I was in such a rut that I felt like a brick in the cell. The solitary I was spending was starting to get to me. I started imagining that my family were spies, obviously I fought it, as I love my family, but I kept thinking it was all one big game at my expense.

I finally flipped! I believe the drugs were the cause of it. The whole fucking world was against me. I ran out of my cell, when the door was open and jumped onto a civilian cleaner and began to choke him with my bare hands. All seventeen fucking stones of him. I couldn't have picked a bigger victim. I was pulled off and injected. Again the usual happened to me but by now I was starting to become immune to the violence used against me.

Rampton for me was a nightmare as I was treat differently, I was the high-risk loony, the one who could cause problems if given half the chance so I was treated very differently, and screws were forever with me. They watched me so fucking closely they knew me as well as I knew myself. Can you believe that I wasn't even allowed to shave myself – they shaved me. I despised this.

Rampton at this period was regularly slammed by pressure groups and investigative reporters for the violence of staff on inmates. I was declared by a Rampton psychiatrist to be untreatable. I've many fond memories of Rampton, for instance the liquid cosh, the cold needles that filled my body full of liquid death and the wonderful team of 'experts' so interested in my welfare.

While I was at Rampton I was made to beat up fellow patients with wet towels. The screws would pull me to one side and offered me a choice of either carrying out their demands or being put on heavier dosages! What could I do in such a position? The bathing area was watched over by the screws and when a particular nasty was using this area I would be pointed in the direction and given a towel. I knew what to do with it, by time I'd finished they were as red as a lobster and it worked off a lot of the drugs in me, these weren't ordinary cons, they were beasts of the first order.

Okay, now you're starting to feel sorry for them, well just imagine they've raped your child or killed a few children or were using children in their paedophile games, does that change your opinion? These fucking nonces get right up my nose, they've got flats inside of Nottingham prison, their own key to the door and get a police escort whenever they go into town? Here's me, I wouldn't hurt a woman or a child or anyone not wishing me harm and all what I get is a syringe full of liquid cosh for my troubles. Don't for one minute sympathise with them, don't for one minute feel sorry for them 'cos if you do then that makes you one of them.

My old pal, Lord Longford, sympathised with Myra Hyndley, the Moors Murderer, and gave her a lot of time. That's what made me fall out with him a while back, but after I'd sent her a pack of cigarettes telling her to smoke herself to death I didn't feel so bad. So Frank, Lord Longford to you, and me are back on track as being pals. He's 93 years old and still going strong and working away for the good of others, how can I knock him when he still speaks up for me in TV documentaries and visits me as well as attending court on my behalf. He ranks as one of my living legends and as he gets older he becomes more energetic, he even composed a poem about his walking stick, more of that later.

Yep, this sure was a Five Star nuthouse in the Egon Bronson guide to good mental hospitals, recommend it to anyone! It was time for me to move on to pastures new.

2

Broadmoor asylum is the nuthouse of all nuthouses and I say that in a way you might not be able to understand because what goes on there is mad. Okay some of the people in it are 100% certifiably mad, but when you consider that quite a lot of people who've been there are in your midst walking about on the streets doesn't it make you think that you can't be mad one minute when it suits the authorities then sane the next? My stay there began in 1979, so little is written about this place – doesn't that seem strange? This is the top secure hospital for the criminally insane, little is really known about what goes on inside, until now that is!

I tore the roof off there on three occasions causing over £1million worth of damage, ('81, '83 and '84 – my hat trick.) but this book will really blow the roof off - sky high! I was Broadmoor's most unpredictable inmate and certainly the most destructive man ever to enter. If I wasn't insane when I arrived then I certainly was when I left. November of 1979 Broadmoor admission ward – Somerset Ward One. No words can describe how I felt arriving at Broadmoor, I've been everywhere, but nothing topped the atmosphere this place had, it's built on top of a hill at Crowthorne Village, Berkshire it's stood there for over 100-years and it hides behind a twenty foot wall that emits fear into the air, just stand outside and smell the air!

It's the madhouse for Britain's danger men and women, mass killers, rapists, poisoners, arsonists, people with paranoid delusions, schizophrenics, psychopaths and psychotics. This was the end of the road or so it looked, how much higher in the penal chain could I go there was no other place for me to go, this was to be my home indefinitely. There's people in this place that've never seen the light of day for over forty years.

As the Rampton van drove through the gates I turned my head to watch the massive gates bang up, clangggggggg! The echo of that noise reverberated around the inside of my head as if though the gates were speaking to me, trying to tell me something, some sort of subliminal message. With the closing of the doors my belly went weak within, not a weakness that would make me go to the toilet, but a weakness that told me there was something unusual about this place – a strange emptiness came over me. The van turned right and drove through another set of gates and pulled up outside of Somerset Ward.

Six attendants wearing white coats came to greet the new lunatic. I was led onto Somerset Ward One where I was taken into an office where a doctor and some nursing officers were waiting for me. They all seemed very relaxed and there wasn't the usual intimidation waiting for me as had happened at every other penal establishment I'd visited. I was cordially given a plastic mug of tea and some sandwiches, they started asking me questions: 'Name, date of birth, colour of eyes, hair, skin, scars'. I noticed their eyes on me, they never left me, searching me, observing me, weighing me up, analysing me, 'Fuck this', I said. I watched them all tense up, but their eyes never once strayed from mine as if though they were dogs trying to 'domineer' me with their stares, but there were too many eyes for me to win this battle of staring! 'FUCK ALL THESE QUESTIONS, YOU ALL KNOW WHO I AM AND WHAT I AM, READ IT THERE'S A FILE AS BIG AS A TEACHEST!'

They told me to calm down, one said to me: 'You can do it how ever you want here, easy or hard, as we tame lions here, you wont get no trouble from us and we don't want none from you.' I was given a bath, clean pyjamas and locked up in a cell. The cell was twelve foot long and six foot wide the only bit of furniture was a cast iron bed, which was bolted securely to the floor, a plastic piss pot and a plastic mug filled with water. The window had a locked steel shutter with a vent built into it I peered through the slits and could see the outer bars on the window. As for heating that was non-existent, nothing to read and nothing to do but climb into bed and dive under the blankets.

I lay there in the silence, thinking. It was a tall cell; about ten feet high the walls were dirty, old and damp. I thought about how many lunatics must have slept in this cell before me – there must have been thousands! I thought about my past and my present, but there was no future tense, as far as I could see – past, present. All I felt was a big hole engulfing me in its emptiness. There was no light it seemed like a big black bottomless pit. This was a labyrinth of horror for me and as though my existence had come to a halt. Everyone's heard of Broadmoor and more jokes have been cracked about this place than any other asylum, here I was – it was no joke!

I counted the bricks, I would stop and re-count time and time again, but it was never the same number? I tried to picture everything I saw as I arrived, walls, gates, doors, faces, windows, drain pipes. I thought of escapes, I thought of a way to beat them, I didn't like the place or the stigma that goes with it. Mad dogs are shot, mad men are caged - it just doesn't seem right. 'We tame lions here', kept going through my mind, like when someone says something to you and it isn't until later that you start to wonder what they meant by it so you re-run it by the conscious part of your mind to decipher it. What sort of a metaphor was this? Why did they say it, why should I accept I'm mad I thought? If they write down that I'm mad it don't mean I'm mad does it?

As everything was rushing through my mind I heard a loudspeaker echoing out load and clear: 'Ronnie Kray to the office.' I knew Ronnie had came to Broadmoor from Parkhurst only a short time ago, but obviously I never knew he was to be on my ward. This put a smile on my face as I truly love and respect the Kray twins. I first met Ron and Reg in Parkhurst 'C-unit' in 1976 and in my eyes they are absolute men of honour, I respect everything they stand up for, their morals, their beliefs and their staunchness.

About half an hour later the loudspeaker blasted out: 'Colin Robinson, to the office.' Robbo, I've known since 1974 when he got lifed up, then received another life sentence for an attempted murder up in Wakefield jail on a sex case. Robbo was sent to Broadmoor for his unusual ways, cutting himself, cutting others and swallowing objects such as razor blades, bed springs, tobacco tins, nails and screws. He's legendary for his unpredictability, I' was close to the guy and love him as a brother so I had a double smile on my face over hearing about him and Ronnie being on my ward. The last year has been hell, a lost year, soulfully ripped, tortured, beaten, drugged, isolated and there I was with my two pals, Ron and Robbo.

The staff came to have a chat, they told me that both Ron and Robbo were doing well and were soon about to be allocated to their new wards. The staff told me they never wanted me in Broadmoor, they told it to me straight that they don't like accepting inmates like me. I assured them that I'd behave and I felt relieved to know that I had two friends on the ward, but they explained that both Ron and Robbo were soon to be moved on and went on to explain what Somerset Ward was all about and how it worked and what was expected of me – it all sounded okay to me.

I was on an assessment ward that held 25 patients and all of us were to be observed, monitored, given psychological tests and psychiatrists had to see us. The average stay on this ward was six months and then it would be decided where within Broadmoor I would be moved to next – so we were to be guinea pigs.

Nothing more nothing less, guinea pigs, I can't describe it in any other way. Each of us were experiments, to be prescribed drugs and then to see how it affected our nervous system and see what side effects they would cause. Some got convulsive electric shock therapy, which basically means a lot of volts are pumped through your head. Some got group therapy, some got occupational therapy, but for me it was and always will be bollocks, I'm nobody's guinea pig!

After our little chat they measured me up for clothes, they told me that the following day I would be allowed out and I would be able to see Ron and Robbo. As the door banged up and I heard the bolts go on I felt great. I was all excited for my first morning inside of Britain's notorious madhouse, amazing isn't it? Only a short while before I felt gutted and demoralised, but after knowing Ron and Robbo would be there for me to speak to the following morning I felt at ease.

I had to face the facts that I was labelled 'Criminally insane' and in their eyes I am the 'mad dog'. In my eyes I was a very desperate young man of 26-years old. I'd been caged for the last five years and had lost everything and truly felt that I couldn't lose anymore, maybe I was really mad, maybe I deserved to be in a cage, but there was no way I would go along with their mental games. I knew from day one I would be the 'lion' and they knew they would have to tame me and that was what they meant when they said this, know I knew where I stood with them, encore! It was going to be a battle, a battle that I could never win. Whoever listens to the insane, who even cares? I'm just another forgotten face inside of a forgotten world. A world that the public fear, fear of the unknown, I knew it was going to be some battle.

Yeah, that first night's sleep sure was a strange one, I awoke several times and on one occasion I could hear screams, some poor sod having a nightmare, screaming out in panic. I woke again when the night warden turned my light on, 'FUCK OFF!' I shouted. It was a restless night with very deep thoughts; I was like a youngster waiting for Christmas day to arrive.

The first morning they opened me up I was given a mug of tea, a bowl of porridge and a bacon sarnie. I was told that I'd be slopping out (emptying of chamber pots from the cell into a communal sluice called a recess) later after all the others, which wasn't a very nice thought as the stench from this was worse than a slaughter house in the summer.

The reason for this wait was that my clothes had to be collected from the stores, I was exacted, I told them not to keep me waiting as I wanted to see Ron and Robbo, plus I wanted to slop my pot out as it had a turd in it. I hate having to crap on a pot, well really a grown man having to stoop to such low measures to relieve himself is babyfying, aint it! That's how it had been for the previous five years and still was.

I told them to hurry it up and to stop teasing me, they knew I was all excited. After breakfast I paced up and down my cell like an animal, like a lion, up and down, up and down, three paces up turn and three paces back and turn and so on. I soon got fed up so I lay on the cold floor on my back and began to kick the door with my bare feet, kicking a steel door with bare feet is no fun, but it makes a lovely noise. They soon arrived with my clothes, they led me into the recess where I was allowed to empty my pot, and I was given a clean towel, soap, a toothbrush and tooth powder and a lock safety razor!

I shaved myself for the first time in a year. Previously the Rampton rats shaved me everyday as I wasn't allowed to shave myself there after the strangling incident on White! Bloody hell! It really felt great to be trusted with a razor. The staff even commented on it and asked me how it felt to be trusted: 'How does it feel to shave yourself, Mickey?' I told them the truth: 'GREAT'. I used to despise being shaved, it humiliated me, it made me feel bitter, useless, old and infirm, I hated the Rampton Rats – they hated me. After my wash and shave I put on my new clothes, new shoes, new shirt, new everything, it felt good, human – I felt human.

The time had arrived, I was led into the day room and there facing me were twenty five sets of eyes, but it only took me a split second to find the two sets I wanted to see. Ronnie, the Colonel as he was called, came straight over, like the gentleman that he was, and gave me one of his firm handshakes and a friendly hug, Robbo done the same, I felt great.

Ron had lost some weight, he'd gone through a bad spell at Parkhurst it was no secret that he was a paranoid schizophrenic and he used to turn violent with a vicious temper on him. Parkhurst never helped Ron it tortured him for nine years. I knew about Ron's final few months in Parkhurst before they certified him mad, he suffered, he was in the back cell, the silent box, the concrete coffin, the same evil room that drove me mad. I was slung in there for a violent attack on a screw; Taffy Jones, a big-mouthed screw and I cut the bastard. Ronnie was slung in there because of his violence so we both went mad in the same room; we both ended up in Broadmoor. That room at Parkhurst is a hell on earth.

Robbo looked his usual self, mad eyes, he had recently recovered from his latest swallowing bout and they both sorted me out with tea bags, chocolates and biscuits. Ron's locker was ram packed with tins of salmon and tuna, Ron knew how to live and even inside none of the glamour had deserted him. When Ron ate then his pals ate, that's the way he was he looked after his own, see, a good-hearted man. We sat down, we had lots to talk over, I hadn't taken a lot of notice of the other patients as I was too engrossed in our conversation; I was too excited.

Until you've lived amongst the insane you'll never understand it, I've lived it, I've seen it, I've done it, I can smell madness. All of the people I was amongst in that room had problems, as otherwise we wouldn't have been there, but I can put my hand on my heart and say that three quarters of these guys were so mad it was impossible for me to relate to them. They were the craziest fuckers I ever did meet, double dangerous, unpredictable, unstable, volatile and completely fearless just like the drunk you bump into on a Saturday night! Until you've witnessed a mad psychotic loose control then you've seen nothing! There was all sorts in this here room, wife killers, baby killers, mother killers, sex beasts, killers of strangers, robbers, arsonists the list is endless. This room was full of dangerously disturbed men and for me to be saying that you can be assured it must be true!

Most had just recently been sent from courts or prisons. All of us were under observation, but all treat the same – cautiously. To go to the toilet was a big event, we could never go into the toilet until one came out, we were watched and monitored. Doctor McGrath was in charge of Somerset Ward he was also the superintendent of Broadmoor, he was a very clever man, a professor of psychiatry, a leading forensic psychiatrist, a man not to be taken lightly and I considered him to be a dangerous man with a lot of power. Dr McGrath had been at Broadmoor for over thirty years, I personably respected the man and we had several discussions, his nanny goat beard and specs added to the title of professor, I found him to be an interesting subject. He'd seen everything and dealt with the worst.

Violent prisoners have been coming to Broadmoor since the beginning of time, here are a few names: Frank Mithcell, Frank Fraser, Winnie MGee, Timmy Noonan, Marty Frape, Fred 'The Head' Mills, Stevie Lanagan, Jock Smith, Roy Shaw, Steve Booth, Steve Shoane, George Heath and a host of other infamous people. Frank Mithcell escaped as most of you will know who follow such things and that's how he got his name 'The Mad Axeman'.

Dr McGrath saw them all come and go, all but Jock Smith as he had done as long as Dr McGrath. He pumped a lot with drugs including me – 'drug control' as it was called. McGrath put me on an injection called 'Modecate', other drugs I had to take orally or be injected forcibly, which some of them were to my knowledge: Stelazine, chloral hydrate and largactil. I hated the drugs, I despised having to take them, but these times we had no choice – if a doctor prescribed it then we had to take it, or else! 99% of us were on prescribed drugs. Later on I'll explain what these drugs are designed to do to you.

My diagnosis was complex and confusing, three psychiatrists that had certified me: Dr Cooper of Parkhurst, Dr Falk of the

Home Office and Dr Tidmarsh of Broadmoor gave conflicting reports – none of them were the same! One diagnosed me as being a psychopath, another was more for having me down as a psychotic schizoid and another couldn't decide between psychopath or paranoia. To me it had become a big joke – a label, a tag. The prison authorities just wanted me out of their jails, but to say I was suffering with so many mental disorders at the same time was so pathetic.

Firstly, 'psychopathic disorder' isn't a mental illness, psychopaths are untreatable. The only psychopaths that are in hospitals are the ones that accept they have a serious personality problem or as has become more commonly called a 'Personality Disorder'. If a psychopath does not accept the problem or come to terms with it no doctor, no drugs and no hospital can help.

While I'm on with this subject I might as well raise a matter that's come up at the present time of me writing this. The current Home Secretary, Jack Straw, wants to bring in a law that will see anyone with a 'Personality Disorder' being jailed!!!!!!!!!!!!!!!!!!!!!!!!!!!!! I know I might be knocking my chances here but this man's got to be fucking kidding here, hasn't he?

Whilst I've been in prison a lot of people have written to these big mental health charities on my behalf asking them to campaign for me – not one of them has helped me; now you'll see them all jump on the publicity bandwagon. Don't fall for it, they're only after your money in the name of mental health. Tell them to 'FUCK OFF', if they really wanted to help then they should've stepped in when I needed help not some poor fucker like Spike Milligan. Spike's an ex-member of the 'Goons' and a few years ago he shot an intruder with an air rifle only problem was the intruder was only a boy in his garden, yet I can't see Spike being locked up with me, can you. Spike's got a certificate to say he's sane – so have I. I believe that law, if applied, will be dished out in a funny old way, believe me!

Secondly, schizophrenia and paranoia are both considered being a mental illness. Both can be treated or controlled by psychotropic drugs, there are untold sufferers of mental illness such as schizophrenics or paranoid deluded people, but they're not all in asylums, maybe you're a one or your next door neighbour is!

If I was asked what I thought my problem to be, as obviously I had a serious problem, I would say that I was suffering from anxiety and stress caused by years of mental and physical abuse, beatings, mind games, isolation and a lack of humanity. I truly believe that I was a very messed up young man and very dangerously disturbed, as I never feared the consequences. I'd lost my wife, my son, my family and my freedom! I may have been a psychopath I honestly don't know, nobody knew, but I did know one thing and that was I should not have been on those drugs because I firmly believe they've caused other syndromes to develop within me that I wouldn't have otherwise suffered from. I also knew something else and that was once Ron and Robbo moved on I would flip my lid. They were my only connection to my sane past and I could see a connection to my sanity being severed when I lost touch with them.

After only weeks both Ron and Robbo move forward, Ron went to Somerset Ward three and Robbo went to Cornwall House and I went to fucking pieces, my mind began to wander. Gordon Robinson arrived, a black guy, from the start we never hit it off. He was just a big mouth - we had words! I managed to slip into the toilet unseen whilst he was in there, I hit him so hard with a right hook that I thought he was a goner, it was a perfect punch and that's all I needed. I never needed to follow up but I did, I left the lunatic in a pile on the floor and I knew our paths would cross again – instinct told me so!

I was eventually allocated Gloucester House, some said a good move; I got trough admission in three months whereas most others took six months. I was told from Dr McGrath that he thought I was becoming unsettled in Somerset ward so he was accelerating my move since I had responded so well. I'd never heard so much bollocks! I was being moved for one reason – and one reason only. They were afraid my head was going, it was, as I was now sick of Broadmoor - sick to my teeth of it!

Gloucester House for me held no friendliness and from the moment I went in to the place I knew our relationship would never last. The whole structure and atmosphere hit me smack in the face like a pickaxe handle, but most of all what really tensed me up was the lunatics' eyes! Old men who'd been inside Broadmoor since World War two. Some of these old guys had 30, 35 even 45-years behind them; they were Zombies. They had dead eyes, staring at nothing, bulging, dreaming, lost, empty and painful. They truly were pathetic men - lost souls. My heart felt heavy for them...I truly felt a sense of doom – 'Fuck ending up like that!' That sight convinced me that I would never accept being labelled a 'lunatic'.

Dr Tidmarsh was the resident psychiatrist in Gloucester House, the same doctor that came to Parkhurst to help certify me! It was this man that started increasing the dosage of my medication, which I told him I wasn't happy about, but he still increased it. After all I was supposed to be the patient, surely I knew what was working and what wasn't and those increased doses weren't working. I personally believe it was a power thing for him and his way of domineering me, as I had serious words with this man and after all he's only human. Can you imagine me shouting at you telling you to decrease my dosage; wouldn't you have the urge to play around with my medication? It's only natural and when it's someone pushed into a corner then they'll come out fighting.

I was put in a dormitory, me in a dormitory? There was a dozen of us, some had been in there for years and they loved it, it wasn't my cup of tea; I fucking hated it. A strange bit of fate occurred the first night in the dorm, although I don't want you thinking I'm colour prejudiced when I tell you this, as I'm not.

A Paki was snoring, he was keeping me awake, I was getting restless, I took it for as long as I could – then I snapped! He was four beds away from me so I jumped out and went to his bed, I picked it up at one end and lifted it up like a slide and then dropped it, lifted it up, dropped it and then I punched him in the mouth. I went back to my own bed; he never snored again after that. I'd cured him, but the crazy thing is my friend, Neil Adamson, who was sentenced to two life terms back in 1970 for murdering a copper and a warehouse man up in Leeds, was in Broadmoor a couple of years before I arrived...well he was in the same dorm on his first night and he chinned the Paki, but he didn't cure him like I did! If this isn't fate then what is, I often smile over it.

I survived less than a week! The inevitable had to happen, it was a week of shear madness for me. I saw things that even disgusted me, I heard things that shocked me and I was sick to the teeth. The second night in the dorm I got up to go for a piss only to walk into a lovers session. One loon was sucking at the bell end of the other loon's cock; they never even stopped when I walked in on them. That's what upset me more, that they carried on.

'FUCK OFF you dirty bastards!', I said. I kicked one up the arse as he ran out, I was fuming, don't get me wrong I've got friends who are homosexual, but they don't act like these pair of scumbags. I don't give a toss what anybody does but when it's this sort of activity in front of me it's different; there's a time and place for everything. It was what I would consider to be a sign of disrespect; the pair stayed well clear of me after that. Days later I caught another pair during the daytime, bang at it, literally, in the recess. One was right up the other one's arse going at it like Woody Woodpecker, this blew my head completely, I actually attacked these two as my head went.

I lay in bed that night 'brooding', I felt the danger signs coming on, signs that I've warned people about in the past and they've not taken a blind bit of notice about it, to their peril! I had morbid thoughts and violent urges; madness came over me. I looked at the other loons in their beds, some just lay there awake. I thought to myself if they could read my mind they would all be screaming to get out of my face. I thought of attacking them and I had to fight the urges within me and looking back I was one dangerous mother fucker, but it wasn't my fault it was the drugs!

Next day I pulled David Francis. He put himself about as 'one of the chaps'; tattoos, ex-Dartmoor con and he gave the impression he was tough. He worked in the kitchen, I done a deal with him and he was gonna do me a favour in return. My plan was about to take shape. Dave was gonna get me a knife, snap the handle off and bury the blade in a large potato so that when they searched for it they wouldn't find it. Then as soon as the search was over smuggle the blade to me. NOBODY knew about it, only Dave and me. Not even Dave knew why I wanted the blade, ONLY I KNEW and ONLY I STILL KNOW!! The day after, we got it together and he agreed to get it for me. That was the day six big 'white coats' came for me and put me in what's called a 'seclusion cell' I was stripped bollock naked and left; there were no words spoken. Soon after they returned with Dr Tidmarsh and he asked me what I wanted with a 'knife'. I couldn't believe it, obviously I denied any knowledge. I'm not saying I was an angel, but even a saint would've cracked up in such an environment as this.

I was given pyjamas, slippers, dressing gown and escorted out of Gloucester House by the six attendants and I was taken to the 'Refactory Unit'. It was called 'Norfolk Intensive Care Unit' of which I'd heard all about and most inmates feared this place as it was the dungeons of the asylum. There's no such word as punishment in Broadmoor as we're all classed as patients and are in an area designated as a hospital and we're not accepted as prisoners nor is it acknowledged that there's a punishment block, how can they?

What you are about to read proves that there's a hell inside of Broadmoor and the next time it's on the news or you hear about it then remember what I've written here, which is THE TRUTH. This comes from me, Charlie Bronson, a man that has spent his time in top security prisons and dungeons all over England; I'm an embarrassment to them! So I'm saying that Broadmoor is worse than any seg block in any prison in England, as it's run by drug control.

The security door opened in Norfolk intensive care unit, the red light went on, we went through, the door locked, the red light went off, the next door opened and there facing me was a good dozen psychiatric nurses in brilliant white coats. I could smell the tension; they were ready and alert like a boxer waiting for the bell. I was led to a double door cell and no words were spoken.

They locked me in, first one door then the second, the bed was a plastic one and the cell stunk of stale piss, the piss pot was filthy, the walls and ceiling had tea stains and bits of food sticking to them which made me feel itchy and dirty.

Within five minutes the nurses had returned and I was told to take two tablets that were passed to me and a medicine top full of red syrupy liquid, 'What for?,' I asked. 'Dr Lucas has prescribed you them, if you don't take them orally then we'll inject them into you, either way suits us!' I had all this bollocks in Rampton and I knew they meant what they said and either way they would see that I took them, yes it's a liberty. At this time we had no choice and if a drug was prescribed for us we had to take it. Lunatics can't be responsible to decide, the doctor's the brain, lunatics don't have brains. That's how it was, 'The doctor knows best.' My argument was and still is how could this Dr Lucas prescribe drugs to me when he hadn't even met me? I was being, in my opinion, given these drugs illegally for one reason and one reason only – control.

I apprehensively took the drugs handed to me as I only had a split second to run through my head what I've just explained.

Would you've taken them? My hell had started; the red syrup tranquilliser is called Taractarine, which is a psychotropic drug used for psychotic illness. It was a nerve killer of which I can tell you the side effects.

My whole nervous system broke down and I had muscle spasm attacks so badly that I collapsed in a heap on the floor. You've heard of those date rape drugs that are slipped into people's drinks and it makes them into cabbages so as anyone can have their evil way with them, well these are ten times worse.

My first attack occurred in the double door cell. Only half an hour after swallowing it my head spun so much that I thought it was going to spin off, my tongue seemed double its normal size, my saliva dried up, my vision was blurry, my body trembled and the pain in my neck, shoulders, spine and arm was agony. My spine felt bent and twisted up; I couldn't stand or sit. I was in a confused state and I lay on the cell floor a beaten man. A beating a man can take, but this was beyond any pain I've ever known. It actually terrified me as I was bent up, contorted and twisted like some sort of spastic and that is not meant as disrespect to those that suffer from this infliction merely to show how I was.

My only conclusion is that it's a form of Parkinson's disease the drug affects the nervous system and lasts a good hour. My next attack happened to me when I was on the exercise yard the pain got so bad that I had to lay on my back on the concrete ground. It was a sunny day, not a cloud in sight and I lay there in a twisted agony crying, yes, Charlie Bronson lay there crying! Something more powerful than any pain another human could inflict on me was happening. I couldn't fight it, it was a torture I'd never experienced, I'd been injected many times in Rampton and prisons for my acts of violence and I was injected with Largactil, Paroudide (apologies if incorrect spelling for this one), Valium and Modecate. Side effects I had suffered before but never on this scale, I cried in revulsion. Anyone connected to the prison service reading this might just take a different view of me because you just aren't ever going to match up to what these drugs did to me and are still doing to me.

The 'Gulf War Syndrome' has become a phrase that attracts sympathy when attributed to ex-squaddies that fought in the Gulf War. Saddam Hussain was going to let off chemicals so the squaddies had to be hurriedly injected with an antidote in case he carried out his threat, which turned out to be a bluff. Years later these antidotes were blamed for creating behavioural changes within some of those squaddies, changes such as depression and outbursts of uncontrollable anger were blamed on the drug. What about me then, don't I get some sympathy????????????????????????? What I've had done to me over the years they wouldn't do to laboratory rats as there'd be a human outcry and some of those people from the animal liberation front would go berserk and start threatening nasty things. People in this country don't value human life, you can't do or it's a case that you've no sense of shame, which is it? People throwing paint over models wearing fur coats, people sabotaging fox hunts, stupid fuckers - get yourselves outside of these mental institutions you daft bastards.

I couldn't do to a maggot what's been done to me over the years, and there, at Broadmoor it was inhuman. Beat, me, cage me, throw the key away, but why this, why me? What had I done to deserve this, no human being should have to endure such torture. The humiliation was to be carried on, this was the final kick in my balls and it hurt me so bad I felt bitter and hateful. I knew in my heart I would get my own back and in time I would get my own back, I knew, I felt it and I sensed it.

It's strange how a drug can become part of your life. Anyone who comes into my life and gets to know me will tell you how I feel on drugs, I wont even take an aspirin, I believe in the power of the mind and that it can overcome 90% of illnesses. Obviously there are times when drugs are necessary such as an epidural needed when a woman gives birth, etc. That's only an example, out there we are bound to get a psychiatrist picking up on this saying it's my way of being reborn by giving that childbirth example, I say to that: 'BOLLOCKS!' It's because I wouldn't see women or children in pain and I'd give my right arm to help them.

There I was swallowing all sorts of shit just because some shrink said I had to! Some of these drugs I am sure were only in the experimental stage at the time they were enforced into me. So who really knows of the permanent side effects, has anyone conducted a study? My whole life turned upside down, my sleep altered I awoke in a confused state, I suffered constipation and my body weight ballooned up. I'd always been a super fit man, strong, energetic and my weight had always remained around the twelve stone mark (168 pounds) yet here I was soon up to seventeen stones in weight and that was without me trying to increase my weight through training! There I was a fat, tired, weak, breathless and soul destroyed young man.

Dr Lucas, this psychiatrist I hated more than any man on earth all five foot nothing of him he was a Greek Cypriot, which I only say to help you picture him, as I have no quarrel with Greeks or Cypriots. I personally believed him to be an evil man, from the word 'go' we clashed and I wanted to mess this little man's unit up, as he ran it like a Nazi concentration camp. Some of the patients claimed Lucas abused them beyond belief and I firmly believe that he was taking liberties with them giving them electric shock treatment. 90% of all shrinks are against these electric shock treatments as it's inhumane and barbaric, but it's still used today.

Just look at the comedian Freddie Star. Freddie was reported in a national newspaper to have been given this sort of treatment on a voluntary basis to put him back onto his feet after a few setbacks. Okay it worked for Freddie, fair enough but one success out of hundreds of thousands over the years isn't exactly a good percentage in the success stakes, is it?

During this sort of treatment guys have bitten their tongues off, shit themselves, pissed themselves and even had fits whilst given these shocks. It's obvious to any rational normal person that it can't be rational to have these sorts of shots of electricity passed through your brain! As these shots are sent through your brain from the ECT (Electro Convulsive Therapy) machine your whole body goes into spasm, convulsions occur, you lose control of your bowels and your bladder, it's a fucking torture! Charlie Richardson received 25-years for using a similar torture on his victims yet here we have people like Dr Lucas making a decent wage packet out of it!

Before the shock is done the patient is given a muscular relaxant and a sedative, but it's still torture as the same pre-treatments are applied to those fried by 'Old Sparky' the electric chair in the USA when undergoing the death penalty! Dr Lucas has even given the shocks raw, meaning without giving the patient a muscular relaxant or a sedative. Either way it's a torture and nothing will ever change my mind. I've witnessed the trolleys with the patients being pushed into the surgery room and I've seen the same patients being pushed out, I've seen blood on the pillow and shit on the sheets and I've seen the same patients hours after. They're confused; loss of memory and some are still shaking. One had bit his tongue off, if this is humane treatment then I'm the Mayor of London! Speaking of which, I put in my bid for the campaign but I was told that my criminal record debarred me from going in for the running in the year 2000. You'll just have to put up with the nominees in question since we've lost my pal 'Screaming Lord Sutch'. Lord Archer suggested that Scotland should have their clock turned back two hours further than here in England so they could get their crops harvested in?

The shocks from the ECT are supposed to be for chronic depressives, I know for a fact that most of the guys weren't depressed, but they bloody well were after it was all over. I've heard some screams going on whilst in there and when they come out, we were always locked up, but through a hatch in the walls in our cells we could see clearly and I saw it all. I never had it, but Lucas threatened me with it. I just said to him: 'You tell my family, not me and see what they'll do.' Lucas was in a meeting that was held to look at my progress and my dear old mum was in attendance when an argument broke out and Dr Lucas lunged across the table with his eyes bulging and he said to my mother: 'You're the mad one, it's you he gets it from'. My mum's never forgotten that, neither have I!

It's a sad fact of life but most inmates in these sorts of asylums are forgotten people, I don't say this in a bad sense, it's just a fact. A lot have never had a normal life or a stable relationship; some have been forgotten owing to their crimes. Killing mummy or daddy, shooting cousin Beryl or Auntie Mary and cutting sister's head off. These crimes are unacceptable so the family or friends would sooner forget them; it's just a fact of life, ain't it? Lots of them are going to die in an asylum; they'll never be released so they're really the ideal guinea pigs, even if they complained who would listen, who gives a fuck.

Life inside Norfolk was depressing, you start off on ward one and then work towards ward two 'til you make it to ward three, if you make it to ward three. On ward one is seclusion, cells, there you are just allowed pyjamas and slippers. Some of the Norfolk inmates had spent untold years in this unit, many of them forgotten people. Violence was an everyday occurrence; some of these guys were the most dangerous men I've ever known. Voices in their heads told them to kill, madness fascinates me, mad people are truly unique it's the unpredictability that excites me, the unknown of what will happen. Isn't this what attracts women to the likes of me?

My life became a part of this madness, the screams in the night, the banging of the door, the violent outburst, the epileptic fits, the slashing of wrists, the swallowing of objects, the heads banging on walls, the suicides and even the murders. The whole days were insane from morning 'til night; it all scarred my brain. Bob Mawdsley and John Cheeseman killed a man called Alan Francis before I arrived; they were both sentenced to life.

The staff were forever watching me - my every move. They knew everything about me, my moods, my personality, my dislikes and even which hand I wiped my arse with. Every single day reports were written on us all. Fuck knows what they found to write about unless they just made it up. If you got one bad report this could result in the shrink increasing the dosage of medication and one good report could see the dosage decreased. We had to be good or we wouldn't get any sweeties this was the sort of shit they played on us. I had other plans – escaping was constantly in my mind. In this unit though it would be near impossible.

I made it up to ward two where there were fifteen of us on this ward and I found it difficult to keep my cool, as it was total lunacy at its best. Here there was double observation more than before as we were all up out of seclusion and dressed sitting in a room. We couldn't leave our seats unless we asked and this was supposed to a hospital! Some of the guys were so dangerous they made me look like Little Red Riding Hood – it was so unreal! I witnessed incidents that even I still can't believe.

One guy stabbed himself in his own eye with a needle, his own fucking eye! Another guy stabbed himself in the stomach with a biro pen, one cut his own throat, one stabbed another guy in the eye with a plastic knife, one used to piss and shit himself in his own chair, one heard voices telling him that he'd killed his whole family, one guy attacked me believing that I was the reincarnation of Adolf Hitler, one guy used to jump on the staff regular just for the fun and one guy believed he was the pope! Maybe now you can understand why I had to get out of that place – my life was going nowhere fast! These guys you don't give an inch to or they take a mile, all danger men – completely unpredictable.

I fear nothing, but even I had to be on my toes with this lot and when I was drugged up it made me feel even more paranoid about them. My survival instinct told me to be prepared as mad men have no fear, size and strength meant nothing to them, Mike Tyson, even, wouldn't have stood a chance with any of them! An eight-stone psychotic is more lethal than an 18-stone muscle man as the psychotic is insanely fearless. I gave a few right hooks into a couple of jaws that upset me, but I always watched my back afterwards.

This was insanity at its best and no amount of muscle would frighten anyone off, that's why these guys were in here – one minute calm as a cucumber then the next all hell would break lose. The nurses, if you could call them that, were huge bastards and looking back I can understand why it took at least half a dozen of them to be able to overpower just one of the loonies when the kicked off!

I then progressed to ward three and maybe you can understand my willingness to conform after reading what I've just explained. And now there were twelve of us up there – the 'Dirty Dozen'. This is how it works, one comes over to Norfolk, one from ward one goes up to ward two, one from ward two goes up to ward three, one from ward three goes to another location – it's like a bloody conveyor belt. Some were never likely to leave Norfolk as they were too disturbed to mix with the stable lunatics. Since most of the lunatics in Broadmoor are stabilised on medication it means that 90% never have to touch Norfolk and it's this 90% that never see the real badness. A man can spend thirty years caged up in the place and never see and experience the evilness so even Broadmoor inmates could be shocked with the reality of my story.

I see it my duty to open the closet for all to see as most of the poor sods in Norfolk couldn't write a letter let alone a book and I'm not belittling them at all, in fact I sympathise with them, I feel for them. I'm no nutty professor or intellectual brain bumpkin, my spelling is bollocks, my education is average but I'm trying. I'm trying to get the truth out for all lunatics in every asylum in the world just to enlighten what does go on or what can go on. Lunatics should have rights.

I finally made it out of Norfolk and went to 'Kent Ward'. This ward was to be my last chance; Dr Hamilton was in charge of Kent. It was spotlessly clean and there were plenty of sane guys that I could relate to. Aubrey Cunningham and Stevie Shoan, both ex-jailbirds and two good guys, they helped me in lots of ways, but they were settled and boxing it clever, I wanted out my own way.

Dr Hamilton was a Scottish man, a pretty fair guy and he practically took me off all my drugs. I began training, it was all hard work, but I fought it and it was hard. I had ballooned in weight and was carrying in excess of twenty stones in body weight and the road was a long one.

I now had a slight problem, I was back in a dormitory and Gordon Robinson was in the very next bed. He was bugging me! I knew that when I hit the fucking idiot on Somerset ward that our paths would meet again and here he was as arrogant as ever in the next bed to me, but I swallowed it for the time being as I had something to do – escape!

My whole time was looking, searching, plotting and hoping that I'd see something. This wasn't like planning an escape from jail, this was double the trouble as there were grasses everywhere, if these loons heard a bar being cut then they'd run to sir. If they so much as even thought that I was escaping then it would be sir, sir sir; really pathetic. I had one or two ideas, one of which looked half decent, but the problem was it was all speculation, a terrible gamble, but all the time I was plagued with fucking lunatics.

I was gradually loosing my cool; one fucking lunatic completely messed my head. I was watching 'Top of the Pops', Madness were number one with their hit 'Driving in my car' when this loon sat by me starring at me and at the TV, he made me feel very tense and agitated, just starring at me, why me? 'Look, pal, what's your problem', I said. His reply fucked up my whole thoughts when he asked me to hit him, yeah hit him! No man has asked me such a stupid question, how the fuck can I hit a guy just because he asks me to, he kept going on and on and on at me so in the end I gave him what he asked for.

He loved being hit; I'm talking punches to the face and in the ribs, the harder the better. This guy was the first sexual masochist I ever met in Broadmoor, but I'm told that there were loads. The more I punched the shit out of this guy the more he loved it. He would buy me chocolates and sweets and he would tell me I was the best puncher he ever had! My head just couldn't take a lot more of this; I was confused. Being complimented for punching another guy was beyond my understanding.

I've suffered terrible violence in my years inside, I've even been whipped with wet towels whilst at Rampton, but to enjoy having a man punch you up is just too much for me to absorb. Another loon attempted to hit me with a saucepan, fortunately I spotted it in time, I still don't know why he done it, but he certainly knew why he shouldn't fucking have done it afterwards! I hit him so hard I almost snapped my wrist on his crazy head.

There were incidents so insane I couldn't possibly describe them. I remember the time poor old Doug Hamil was being interviewed by the doctor; Doug grabbed the doctor's gold pen and swallowed it. Old boys were dying there some of them had served 40+ years! It used to depress me to know one had died, I had some lovely chats with some of these old timers, some of whom were certainly no angels but they were certainly characters. They told stories that made my life seem a bed of roses, these men were the true gladiators and true survivors.

Broadmoor caged them 'til death and just to show you what I mean you might want to know of a man named Willian Giles. William was the longest incarcerated person ever to serve time in Broadmoor; he served 72-years in Broadmoor from the age of twelve he was locked up inside the belly of the beast 'til he died at the age of 84! Can you believe that, it's really terrifying to know that boy of twelve spent 72-years caged up in that hell hole, maybe that guy slept in my very cell?

At times Broadmoor could stretch a hand out to try and grasp reality by holding a disco. There are both male and female inmates at Broadmoor and once a month they party, if you can call it that. I went to one disco in all my stay there, it was enough for me, total false, total madness, the girls strolled in and the loons began buying chocolate for them, oh yeah, it all sounds great – disco, girls, party. Let's look at it sensibly, we're humans, we're caged up and deprived of sex and here we are dancing with women! The loons thinking to themselves that they want sex, not a soppy dance.

The staff were very much in force, watching every move, bear in mind some of these mad men were sex killers, women haters and so on! Some of the women were no angels either. I knew of a few cases which are as follows: one woman put her own baby in the oven and cooked it another bit a man's cock off and I mean right off! Another strangled a man with her bare hands and then there were all the hard cases that Holloway women's prison couldn't control – tattooed tomboy street fighters; fearless. I respected them. These girls were a mixture of sadness varying from tragic cases to pure psychopathic maniacs.

I watched it all from a table, I watched some of the madmen approach the girls with chocolates, their eyes said it all, it was madness at it's best. One girl got over excited on the dance floor and began kicking her legs in the air like a show girl, she soon got taken away, it was probably the disco lights that caused her to take a fit. It was really amusing and I took it all in

I even had a dance, a slow one, with a big black girl; she grabbed me close and grinded herself into me. I hadn't had sex for over seven years, I was rock hard and she obviously knew. I ain't ever had sex with a black girl, but seven years is a long time; too long. When a woman is grinding herself into a man it makes it all the more difficult to control those urges, but she was a mad girl her arms were closing tight, around my neck, I swear I could hardly get free from her grasp, but I eventually managed to push myself away.

This was to be my first and last dance; I needed a good long fuck with a sane girl not a soppy dance with a lunatic being watched by dozens of eyes. For me it was a complete wind up, frustrating, but I'm told by some of the guys that they've had a wank under the table from the loon women and even felt them up, so they say. I've no reason to disbelieve them, but it wasn't for me as I respect a woman a bit more than a wank under a table. If it's your wife or girlfriend and she does because she wants to then that's different, but these women loons weren't in Broadmoor for nicking milk off your doorstep! What if you touched them up and they went mad, what if they were giving you a blowjob and wanted to bite it off then one way or another you're bang in trouble, no that wasn't for me. The madmen couldn't wait to get back to their wards to pull their cocks, that's the ones that hadn't already shot their load. It's really very sad, it's a lonely existence being insane.

After only weeks of being on Kent ward all my hard work come to an end, all my dreams were wiped out and all my escape routes blocked. I had fell off the edge and if I never was insane then I was now. This Gordon Robinson had pushed me over the edge and it was time to show everybody who I was! My mother and father had just been up to see me and I was happy, their loyalty towards me was beyond anyone's. After the visit I went back to my ward and found Robinson with his key in my locker trying it out. His locker was on another level so it was impossible for him to have mixed mine up with his own. The toe rag was trying to open up my locker – a locker thief! What little you accrue over your time inside becomes your gold, what might be rubbish to someone else is your gold.

One of the number one prison rules amongst cons is that you don't steal from other fellow cons and this cunt was after stealing from me. I pushed the scum away, he started his verbal abuse, I then chinned him, but that wasn't enough for me, I was going to kill the mother fucker and my sanity had now gone, he was gonna to die. I told one guy, a trusted friend, who I've known for years and he said that it was a bit extreme, but a man's gotta do what a man believes in. Words of wisdom and my time had arrived.

Subconsciously I may have been killing myself, burying myself deeper as I'd become a very desperate man, I saw no future so what the hell. I got a silk tie; my old man had given it to me some years ago, my favourite tie. I locked myself in the toilet and tested it's strength on the toilet cistern it actually held my weight; it would do the job! I was to strangle him that very night, I was very excited, it was the same buzz you got from an armed robbery when waiting to attack, I can't describe my feelings, but I was on an all time high. It was like running the four minute mile when no one had ever done it or doing a hundred meter sprint in only nine seconds!

The time had arrived! I walked into the dormitory, wearing my pyjamas, with my tie around my waist out of sight, I climbed into bed and waited. Robinson's left eye was almost closed from where I'd punched him earlier on, his other eye was alert; I smiled my best smile. There were a dozen of us in this dorm, in the couple of weeks I survived Kent ward I saw it all in this dorm. One loon masturbated every night so much and so bloody noisy that his bed rocked, blankets flying up and down it was so over the top. Another farted like no fart I've ever heard. I'm sure he had a gas cylinder up his arse, one sleep walked another shouted in his sleep, but one tonight was about to never wake up!

The guy opposite my bed was a big fat useless piece of dog shit, a known sex case on kids, I actually warned him never to look my way, before I arrived a friend of mine, who'll remain nameless, stuck a spoon in the fat fucker's ear almost killing him; the right side of his body was still semi-paralysed because of this. I thought this was a classic - we learn something every day.

These dormitories were well observed throughout the night. A red night-light was on all night, the night patrol nurse looked in every half-hour through the observation slit, he could see us all. Obviously I had clocked his times before, some were on the dot, some were very lax. Still I only needed a couple of minutes, fuck the night watchy.

There was no saving the thief! I lay there still, in deep thought, the tie wrapped around my hands, under the blankets, just waiting like a spider waits for the fly the time was plentiful. I had all night long, this was my night and this was my fly! Some will read this and think me a callous bastard and maybe a heartless animal, I'm not going to justify my actions and I knew it was over the top, but I'm a very over the top man and don't claim to be something I'm not. I'm me, and mad or bad it's me, take me or leave me.

I was buzzing, twelve O'clock, one O'clock, I waited patiently, watching every bed, watching the night nurse then it happened. It was as if I sent the thief a telepathic message! He moved, he sat up, he bent over to put his slippers on and he was probably going to go for a piss. I leapt out of bed in a second, the tie was wrapped round his ugly neck, I was strangling this guy, it felt like magic, it felt right surprisingly there was very little noise. A sigh and a groan at first then nothing, I pulled tighter, I leaned over to watch, his eyes bulged, his face was going grey, his tongue protruded, dribble ran out of his mouth, I could smell shit and he had pissed himself.

He was on his way out of planet earth then it happened! The fucking tie snapped! I was in shock! I had half the tie in one hand and half of it in the other, he began making noises, loud animal grunts, deep chesty moans the others woke up and I was in trouble. I had to act fast, I quickly hit him and straddled him over his bed and I told the loons he was having a nightmare. I was now strangling him with my hands, unknown to me a loon had rang the emergency bell and the nurses came charging in. Gordon Robinson survived, but the welt around his neck tells the story.

I hit Norfolk unit so fast that my feet never touched the ground, my next four years were to be spent in Broadmoor's hellhole! I would never get the opportunity to strangle again when the double door cell cut me off from the madness. I covered myself under the blanket and cried in frustration at what I'd just attempted, I went through a bout of anxiety, a loss of sanity and no hope, I tore up my photos and I destroyed my letters. I was more alone and empty than I ever had been in my life it felt as if I was back in my mother's womb; helpless and lost – blackness came over me.

I was 'insane' and I now knew it, my true battle had now begun - a fight against myself. To lose would mean old age and to die a lonely death in Broadmoor.

Norfolk Intensive Care Unit (NICU) was now my home within the boundaries of Broadmoor. My depression lasted some months and I was in a state of panic and fear. My cell was becoming a concrete coffin and my life was being sucked out of me, there was no life it was only an existence. I knew I had to do something to fight back so I had to behave again. My plan was simple! It took three months to work my way up to ward three – it was now time to fuck Lucas and his band of merry men off.

Protests are a way of attracting attention to a plight; I was up to my neck in plight and needed to put on a show. It was pissing it down on canteen day, which was a big day for us loons. Sweeties, chocies, ice lollies and goody goody gum drops. I was gonna fuck it for the whole asylum, three months I had planned this escapade, three months biting my lips, three months swallowing this shit. I even let a loony get away with jumping on my back, I just restrained the nutcase even the staff commented on my lack of violence – even us mad men can be crafty.

Twelve of us were being escorted to the canteen and this day was the highlight of the week, we all marched along in a line, but this day was going to be 'my day'. I'd prayed for this moment. The rain was literary chucking it down, which made my intended mission double hard – doubt entered my mind? Maybe it would be too slippery, maybe somebody might grab me, fuck it I was off like a rocket!! My decision to go for it had been made and that little reflection on the 'will it or wont it work' was quickly dispensed with, that's how I do it and once the move is made it must be followed through.

I ran a good twenty metres, I never looked back, I heard a whistle blowing, I heard shouts, my heart was pounding, I leapt on to a metal beam and it was slippery! Somehow I managed to pull myself up, but some cunt had a hold of my right foot, I lashed out with my left and caught a staff on the head, I then pulled myself up. I had to balance myself and then dived towards a cell window, could I make it with everything being so wet and slippery?

I mustered all of my strength and managed to reach towards a drainpipe, which my finger ends just managed to touch, just another half an inch, come on stretch! Yes, my hand was now around the pipe and I could safely let go of the cell window with my other hand and pull myself up hand over hand up the drainpipe.

My knuckles were hitting the wall behind the pipe as I pulled myself up, I couldn't let go as I'd crash to the ground and that would mean failure. My feet were running in mid air trying to get a grip on the wall so as to relieve my aching muscles in my arms and shoulders. Had I of been an eight or ten stone person then the effort needed to get me up wouldn't have been so great, but I was pulling over 200 pounds of body weight up. Up, up I went, I was on top of the world the rain pissed it down, but it felt magic.

A friend of mine, Jimmy Boyle, wrote a book it was called 'A sense of freedom', well…this was my freedom. I met Jimmy in jail although I must point out that he wasn't serving a prison sentence as he'd popped in to do a talk show about prisoners. The show was a prison forum and we both appeared on the show together although no one seems to be able to help me trace a copy of that debate even the Prison Reform Trust couldn't trace it? I've lots of respect for Jimmy, but he escaped being sent to the asylums and he never had the psychological crap I've had. Now here was my sense of freedom and I was the King loony on top of the loony bin. Fuck Lucas, fuck the dungeons, fuck the whole asylum.

Doctor McGrath came to the top floor cell window, he asked me to come down and talk, I ripped a slate free and threw it down at him: 'FUCK OFF', I shouted. I had begun my mission – a mission of destruction, a mission of madness. Slates flew through cell and office windows in the opposite building. I aimed the slates at workshop windows, I aimed them at anyone within distance and I tore out electrical wires, TV aerials, copper pipes, water tanks and structures of timber. Below me was Kent ward three, which they evacuated, they turned off the water and electrical supply.

Hour after hour I emptied myself of years of pain, all the hatred oozed from me, my hands bled, my head was cut, my body soaked in rain, sweat, blood, grime and dust, my eyes were full of dirt, my muscles ached and my back was sore, but I loved it.

I was fucking the system good style where it hurt most, financially. Every slate I slung off was a day of my life caged up, it felt good and it felt smashing. I was shouting, singing, screaming and laughing. I lost all senses, madness overcame me, I was making history. The filthy hypocrites won't forget me; real men live on in the memory. Obviously I blew myself out, but it took 'til nightfall. I managed to find a place out of the way of the searchlights they had on the roof to pick me up, it was like a war blitz. I lay there tired, fatigued, hungry and cold. I wrapped up in some polythene I found.

This was the first night I spent looking up at the stars for over eight years; eight fucked up years. My son was eleven years old then and I'd not seen him since he was three years old - life had passed us by. Irene was last seen seven years previous at Hull prison when she walked out of the visiting room. Her words came back to haunt me: 'You'll end up in the mad house, Mickey, the way you're going!' Funny isn't it the thoughts that rattle around inside your canister when these sorts of situations arise, you've no control over what pops up - how right Irene was that day. I was now fulfilling the prophecy Irene made all those years ago.

This was my freedom; maybe my son would see his old man up there and maybe the country thought I was mad. The fact of life was that I was the gov'nor, yeah, that sky, those stars, that beautiful breeze was heaven. The Berkshire countryside was lovely to see. The lights shone for endless miles, streetlights, car lights, house lights and pub lights; I saw it all. Crowthorne Villagers were over the wall they'd been watching for most of the day. Kids were shouting throughout the day 'Jump, jump, jump.' This upset me; it was now peaceful and time to reflect on life. I was on top of the world.

The media fear Broadmoor as nothing but bad news is attached to the place. Back in the 1950's John Straffen was sent to Broadmoor for strangling two little kids. He was found to be subnormally insane, but within five years of being in Broadmoor he escaped and this caused the biggest fear amongst people nearby. Within 24 hours a little girl's body was found a mile from Broadmoor – she had been strangled! Straffen was again lifed off, over thirty-five years later he was still walking around the place -

a walking death. Broadmor was put into the shadows of hell by Straffen's escape and the death of the little girl.

People living in Crowthorne fear the place, every Monday morning a testing siren would blare away and for miles around it could be heard. The villagers must have dreaded those Monday morning calls and if they still occur now will still send shivers down the spines of those that remember Straffen the beast of Broadmoor. So me up on the roof would not get a lot of support from the media. I was just another madman and that's how it is.

I thought of my mum and dad, my brothers and family and the closest person alive at this period in my life – my lovely cousin Loraine. She's the most perfect human being that I know and her friendship is second to none. Loraine has been a tower of strength to me, one smile from her and my pain disappears, one word from her and it's poetry, but there I was alone and on top of the world.

I was lost in a world that left me behind; I actually felt the sadness that had overcome me, death thoughts, morbid sensations and no future. I was going nowhere. To stay up would be to die, to jump off would to die and to climb down would be to die. I had no life to look ahead to except a double door cell, emptiness, solitary, drugs, boredom, no sweet smells and no company, no nothing just everyday the same. I thought about it all, deep thoughts, I thought about Ron Kray and Colin Robinson how come they've settled why can't I settle? I knew I never could, escape must now be my goal.

To escape I had to stay strong, train and be prepared so I decided to climb down later. I would take the treatment to come; double doors and drugs, I'll beat it all and as for Lucas, Lucas wouldn't ever beat me, ever. 'He's only a psychiatrist, I'm the madman', I thought to myself. He would have been on the dole if it wasn't for us loonies, but he was too thick to realise this.

I climbed down the same way I got up, but it was double dangerous as my fingers were so cut and splintered plus I couldn't bend them. They asked me to climb down the skylight but I told them I would come down the way I wanted to. Once down I was surrounded by white coats, one grabbed my arm: 'Fuck off and get off', I shouted. Big charge nurse Roger Russell told them to leave me alone. Roger was 6'-7" tall and weighed 16 ½ stones, he was a good footballer in his day, he loved me and respected me and was always decent to me.

I was led into Norfolk and allowed a bath, Roger got all my splinters out, patched me up and cleaned my eyes. The doctor gave me some medicine then I was led through the double doors and I climbed into the plastic bed. I can't remember any more. I never felt anything, just heaven, but in my subconscious mind I knew hell awaited my awakening.

I slept all that day and most of the night, fuck knows what that doctor gave me, but it knocked me out. I awoke stiff, aching, in pain, in agony and every time I inhaled I was in agony. A doctor examined me to find I had pleurisy from the rain, the damp and the cold. They'd got into my lungs and kidneys and it felt like Mike Tyson had worked out on my body for fifteen rounds. Just to breathe was an effort and to move was even worse. When Dr Lucas came in later to see me I swear he had a smirk on his face. He told me I would never ever get an opportunity to smash roofs up, I told him to fuck off! As he left it was me smirking as I knew our battle had just begun. I knew in my heart that I would never bow down to Lucas – he knew too.

Jonathan Silver, every institution has one – a legend. Whether it be in an asylum or a prison anyplace where people are crammed together someone will always stick out as a special person whether for good or bad this guy, all 6'-10 ½" of him, was the most talked about loony in Broadmoor. A giant with size 14 shoes and hands like shovels, but sadly I blanked him for the first two years in Norfolk in fact I despised the fucker, but my hate for him turned to compassion.

Back in 1969 Jonathan Silver killed his three children, attempted to kill his wife and then attempted to kill himself, it was a horror story. I first heard about this case from Ron and Reg Kray back in the mid 70's as he was in Brixton jail on remand the same time as the Kray firm. Obviously someone that kills children is a hated person by cons, screws and everyone it's unacceptable and goes against humanity.

Silver was found too unfit to stand trial and sent to Broadmoor indefinitely a man who's life was military outside of Buckingham Palace. Then he wakes up in the Queen's asylum this has to be some shock obviously the man was mad, he had to be. Since his arrival in Broadmoor 90% of it had been in seclusion as he was forever punching the staff up in the air, he'd hit more staff in a year than any loony had hit in thirty years. He was famous for his right hooks; he'd even chinned Dr McGrath the superintendent of Broadmoor. So for all the 1970's he practically rotted in hell with nothing and I mean fuck all. Good enough for a child killer three times over, we lived in the next cell to each other for almost two years. No words were ever spoken between us, I heard him get beat up and I heard his screams as the hypodermic needle pierced his skin the same as he'd heard my bad times. It's just not nice to hear another man in pain at times I had to stop myself from banging on his wall just to see if he was okay. Often I wondered why he'd killed his kids, what makes a man snap, obviously he had snapped, but why and how? My code of conduct stopped me from getting close to him although our miseries entertained each other through our adjoining wall.

Then it happened, one quiet evening I was miles away just looking up at the ceiling thinking when my wall knocked; he was knocking me on our wall. 'Mickey', he shouted, 'come to your hatch Mickey.' There's a hatch in the wall by the door for passing food in or tots of medicine when all's peaceful the staff leave it open, it's big enough to put a hand out. I got up out of bed, 'Yeah?' I said. 'Mickey, you got a plastic bag?' 'No', I said. 'What about a razor blade?' 'Nope', I said. It never took Einstein to work out his drift - suicide. This thing within him had drove him to kill himself; no man alive can keep bouncing off walls. I said to him: 'Slow down mate and take it easy.'

This evening was the beginning of a long friendship, I felt a lot for Jonathan; bearing in mind we were together in hell. If it wasn't for it being in hell then our paths wouldn't have ever crossed, but this was a bizarre set of circumstances for both of us. He killed his kids because he believed the world was evil, he tried to escape from the world with them and their mother. I saw photos of him pushing the kids on swings and them sitting on his shoulders, you could see it was a lovely happy family and he just snapped. Who the fuck am I to torture him anymore than he's survived.

The guy arrived at Broadmoor 18 ½ stone, ten years later he was only 13 stone in weight! They had brutalised him, 6'-10 ½" and only 13 stone? It's a fucking nazi concentration camp not a Broadmoor! I'm not justifying what he done, that was inhuman, but I felt this man's agony. His misery was my life and my misery was his. The whole of Norfolk was a fucking hell on earth with loony devils. I can understand somebody saying, 'Why talk to him?' My only answer to this is I witnessed the real guy and I felt the man's sorrow. Even today, years later, I'm confused as to why or how. It's senseless and unreal, but everything and everyone in an asylum is a sandwich short of a picnic including me. Some can't face up to dying so how can they face up to living, Broadmoor is not living. Maybe the place is a living hell and if that's hell then I've already had taste of it in readiness if that's where I end up.

Lucas despised Jonathan Silver as much as he hated me, as we would always be a pain in the fucker's head. Untreatable, incurable and unpredictable so fuck Lucas.

George Shipley - I'm never wrong about guys, he followed me on from a ward we shared. He hit Norfolk and ended up a long-term inmate over in the hell house. George had a bad day, he picked up some scissors and stabbed another loony filling him with more holes than a watering can, how the guy survived was beyond everyone – the surgeon must have been Jesus Christ. When I finally got to see George he was heavily drugged, his eyes were heavy and his speech was slurry. I felt so sad for the guy as basically he was a good lad; just a little head strong and quick tempered. He'd told Lucas that he'd stabbed the loony so as to brighten the day up! Like I said, George is a case, I told him off, as the poor sod he plugged was not a sex case. George just seen him and plugged him for no reason, but George would pay for it with more years of his life in the Lucas dungeon, a sad, sad case.

Dr McGrath retired weeks after my demolition job I carried out on his precious roof. I was told that it broke his heart, as no superintendent wants a farewell party with the roof gone. It's a shock to the system, an embarrassment and very costly. Questions were asked, like how the fuck can a loony get on the roof when he's in the secure unit. Yes, he left Broadmoor a very sad man and I guess I'm still in his bad books. If he's still alive and he gets to read this: Dr McGarth was one of the best psychiatrists I ever did meet, a fair man. Basically most psychiatrists are clowns and it's all just guesswork, I mean how the fuck can they see into our minds? Dr McGrath said to me on Somerset ward one in 1979: 'We only take the best in Broadmoor and you're the best, Mickey.' I don't know to this day if it was an insult or a compliment? But for all it's worth I did respect the old git.

Jesus! Was I in trouble, pain turned to agony. Sadly mental people are not always believed as mad people imagine things in illness terms it's called hypochondria and as much as I told the fuckers I was in pain the more I got blanked, no cunt believed me, obviously this made it worse. I ended up attacking a Paki doctor and losing my control, pain will finally drive a man insane, but violence will never ever win, it brings more pain and more misery. I ended up in a bigger mess, as now nobody trusted me, so the pain turned to agony.

This staff charge nurse, Stewart Elliott, was a genuine man and I had the utmost respect for him. Many times he had helped me over bad spells and this time he actually believed me. Anyone with half a brain could see I was ill as I was punching walls, banging my head, shouting and going berserk. This was toothache, earache, constipation, appendicitis and lumbago all at one hit! It started in my right ear, spread to my face. The right side of my face was twisted with pain, I couldn't eat, I lost weight and I looked and was a sick man. Again I went berserk and again I was injected, but I only woke up to more pain.

Stewart Elliott made sure that I got painkillers, but none helped. It finally burst and I got treatment immediately, the proof was on my pillowcase. It had happened in my cell at night. The pain became so much that I bashed my face and head so hard I caused concussion. As I drowsed off into a black hell a loud explosion went of inside my head, I remember no more until I awoke the next day weak and sick. My pillowcase was saturated in brownish pus. I'm no doctor but I knew it was bad as my ear was caked in blood. There were no call bells in the cells at Broadmoor unlike prison cells. I always thought this to be a liberty as if a loony was to become ill then there was no means of him alerting anyone to that fact. New cells being built had the facility of these call buttons – so I hear!

I got on the floor and started kicking my door for a good half-hour before anyone came, what a fucking liberty. When they did arrive to see what all the noise was it just took one look at the blood and pus to tell them I 'REALLY' was ill.

An ear specialist was brought in who examined me properly and it turned out I'd had a giant abscess behind my mastoid (projection of bone behind the ear) in my right ear, which was a tumour that had burst open! Fortunately it burst as I lay I on my right side so the poison was able to run out of my ear. If it were to have burst as I lay on my left side or on my back the poison, pus and blood would have ran straight into my brain.

I spat straight into the face of our doctor as he'd said all of the time there was nothing wrong with me and that it was all in my head, yes he was right, it was all in my head alright! I almost fucking died – some hypochondriac I am. Can't you understand now why I hate the sight of a fucking prison doctor? I'm a firm believer, to some extent, that you can heal yourself, up to a point that is!

Little George Heath arrived, a breath of fresh air, all nine stone 5' -2" of him – fearless. He only lasted days on Somerset ward and ended up over on Norfolk with me. George got life for stabbing some arsehole in London then he got another life sentence for a stabbing in prison. George admits he's not big enough for a punch up so he stabs his way out of trouble, he'd a few ups and downs in Norfolk ward before they sent him back to jail. He wasn't mad, he was just too much for them and he was just living by his code; kill or be killed. George was still plodding on years later in Parkhurst.

There wasn't too many prison guys arriving that you would call disruptive elements, subversive, troublesome, problematic or dangerous. The only ones I met that passed through Norfolk were: Phil Hall, Mickey May, Charlie Smith and Michael Smithers.

In 1981 there was two lovely escapes: Alan Reeve and James Lang. Alan, a personal friend of mine, is a smashing guy, he was sent to Broadmoor at the age of sixteen after he'd killed his friend. Whilst in Broadmoor he was found guilty and convicted of murdering another inmate. Twenty years on and no hope of release he then escaped from Essex House, Essex is the trusted house. Most of the guys there are the trusted loons some have served thirty to forty years! All had long gone accepted Broadmoor as their home, I named this house the house of doom..

Obviously Alan made it work for himself purposely to escape, it was a classic, he used a TV aerial and over the wall, a car waiting he hit Dover and over on the ferry then he was free. Three months later over in Holland he walked out of an off-licence, a copper approached him and Alan ran off and he was shot in the back, but he spun around and shot the copper dead! He got fifteen years for this and was eventually freed although what has happened to him since then I don't know?

James Lang's escape was similar, but his was not to last – simply because he was a fucking sex killer. Laing got sent to Broadmoor in the early 70's for rape and murder on a sixteen-year-old girl. He made it over the wall, breaking his ankle in the process; he limped to a field and gave himself up hours later, obviously realising that no one would harbour a sex monster. He was later sent to Ashworth hospital and released in 1985 only to rape and torture two women – once a monster always a monster.

The thing is it was always these sex beasts that were let out on parole and do you want to know why? I'll tell you why and anyone worth his or her salt from the parole board or Home Office will tell you. The reason was that it was considered that sex beasts would have less likely chance of re-offending!!

Pull the other one, come on, do you honestly believe that people like Myra Hyndley, Rose West, Ian Brady, Peter Sutcliffe and the likes wouldn't re-offend. It's only because they've been given enormous press coverage that they will not ever be released otherwise some of them would have been or be making tracks in the right direction and be working towards release – I've seen it with my own eyes, you've got it first hand. I know of people that have done terrible things and they've been released back into the community, probably living right next door to you now! Who would you rather have as a neighbour, Myra Hyndley or me?

My escape was still flowing through my mind, it was being planned, but unfortunately it was double the effort for me, as I had no trust, Lucas had me hemmed in. This was going to be a battle of wits and I just had to win it.

Although Broadmoor was already a mad place there were accepted levels of madness and mad, mad things. I remember mad Dickie Langnell jumped on my back trying to bite my neck out, Dickie's only little and was in his late 50's but he was a terrible violent psychotic. A voice says to him 'Attack' and Dickie attacks, I happened to be his victim twice.

I once dived on a male civvy (civilian) domestic cleaner and strangled him with my bare hands, most of which I don't remember only what I was told about it. Mad; mad moments, but legendary and mythical and absolute insanity at its best. I've seen it, done it, had it and lived it. I fucking love it, madness rubbed off on me; it's like gold dust. Ronnie Kray told me that 'Madness is a gift of life – as long as you control it', how true he was.

Mad Gouff killed his old mum, I never could get on with this toe rag and I remember the time he attacked me. He slung a punch at me with a six-inch nail in his fist – aimed at my eye, very naughty! I managed to block it and get the nail and restrain him with nobody seeing the nail. I gave the mug a few slaps, obviously staff saw a scuffle, but that cunt was lucky that day, so lucky! I was being so nice as I had my escape plan coming up otherwise he would have got the same as what his poor old mum got from him - decapitated!

A lot of these guys I soon found out, were only ever brave when staff were nearby to jump in; not as mad as they made out – eh! I'm an observer, see, I weigh it all up carefully. I soon found out the real mad ones from the actors. Mad people smell mad, it's a fact. I can actually smell madness; it's a real smell. Like throwing off an aura it's a presence, a sensation of wariness. Guys like Spencer Thorn, Barry Quigley, John Ince, Dickie Lagnell, Malcolm Morgan and Dennis Smith were the maddest loons I ever met. No disrespect to any of them, on the contrary I fucking loved the guys, they were exciting and dangerous to be with, all long term Norfolk inmates. Malcolm Morgan spent eighteen years in solitary alone with nothing, all over his mad ways.

The maddest event ever in my time at Broadmoor was a loon tearing out one of his testicles, yeah, his own ball bag! He tore it open with a razor and ripped out his testicle. He cut the skin open and reached in with his hand and pulled out his testicle complete with an attached mess of gore. I felt sick just to think about it, it's just too insane to imagine, but life in the asylum is completely unpredictable, nothing's impossible.

I again worked my way up to Norfolk ward three, a bloody hard time, but I made it there in one piece. I got a hold of an angel wire, which is a tungsten roller; it can cut through bars – prison bars. I got a car key, money and a screwdriver; I was now ready to go. We were not allowed anything in our cells, no clothes, no shoes and no radios. We had to strip off outside of our cell, hang the clothes up in a cupboard and go in naked. I managed to smuggle in all my equipment, clothes and shoes. This was a great achievement on its own. I had to first work on the shutter against the window; this would be difficult because of the noise alone.

The first night I worked hard on it, I done it in half-hour shifts then I jumped in bed and waited for the night staff to spy through the Judas hole, every hour on the dot. I worked on it I held a blanket with my head against the shutter to deaden the noise, fuck me! It made a noise, but I kept at it. I had no watch on, but I could hear the chimes of the gate lodge clock. I made it by 5.00 a.m., the shutter was left hanging by a silly little piece of metal that I could snap easily, that left me with only two hours to do a bar – impossible! So I decided to clean up and climb into bed and I would play sick when the staff arrived to open us up. I'd stay in bed all day, preserving my strength, I'd go that night; I was buzzing! I made sure the shutter was safe and got into bed, 7.30 a.m. my door unlocked, 'Come on, Mickey, up you get.' 'I'm sick guv', I said. 'Come on get up for a shower', one of them said. 'I don't feel well guv, flu. I'll stay in bed.' 'You get up for a shower and then we'll see about you staying in bed', one said. I didn't want a row or to get them suspicious, 'Alright, guv, I'll have a quick shower and get straight back to bed.' 'Good lad, Mickey', one said.

Whilst I was showering they went in and found the loose shutter so I landed back on ward one. Obviously they found everything and because of that my visits were all stopped. Lucas said I would never get another visit until he knew where I got the equipment. 'Go fuck yourself', I said, 'What are you going to do, stop me seeing my family for the next thirty years?' This guy was a real pain in my arse with the shit he came out with. Obviously he had power, but to stop my visits could only be temporary, which it was only weeks.

My true belief is I was grassed up, I have my idea who it was, but I never got the chance to take his eye out. Depression now set in; I needed to put something together, but what? I got so depressed I went through a spell of suicidal thoughts, which obviously I kept it to myself. I kept thinking of hanging myself, would it painful, how would it be and what would it be like and how long will it take? Fuck me, I was getting low!

Ronnie Kray had obviously heard I was on rock bottom, but I never got to see him all the time I was in Norfolk House as we were totally segregated, but Ron was a special friend and still holds a special place in my heart. I had the pleasure of meeting Ron's dear old mum when I was at Parkhurst. She would visit with Charlie, Ron's brother. Ron always arranged something special for me and his dear old mum left them at the gate for me;

meat pies, fruit and sweets. All of this I respected. All of his support, his letters and Reggie's letters; they never forgot me.

This day I received a letter off Ron telling me to expect a 'special visit'. Who was it that come to see, ex-middleweight world champ, Terry Downes – one of my boxing heroes! What a boost it was for me, what a visit, what a lovely man coming to see someone like me. As I always say and always will: The twins are special men, may God rest the soul of Ronnie. Reg has done over 30 years, he's never ever moaned about it not even privately, he's plodded on, a man of steel just like Ron – solid.

Roof job number two at Broadmoor, June 1993! This is the reason you're reading this, isn't it, so as to read about all them rooftop sieges I carried out and the entire hostage taking situation, here goes. It was a glorious hot summer's day; the sun was kind to everyone, too lovely of a day to be caged up in a mad house. This day was to become one of the greatest days of my life as I had fucked Lucas and his merry men like no other lunatic had ever done in the 100-year history of Broadmoor. This was 'V' day, the most costly, most embarrassing, most troublesome three days in the history of Crowthorne Village!

It begun at 10.00 a.m. from the exercise yard. Young George Shipley was with me and he wanted to do it with me, but I had to say 'no'. George was on a lot of medication, too much to make a climb. This was no ordinary climb – my way up was suicidal. It was to be one of the greatest climbs of my life. Fuck Everest and all of those silly climbs that are kids stuff. I was about to go up a 100-year-old building, an untested and untried mass. Okay I take my hat off to Hillary and his team for attempting Everest, but they didn't make it! I was going to make this one that was for sure otherwise, like Hillary, I would die trying!

Unlike my last climb at Broadmoor this was not like that last roof, the pipes, guttering and masonry were falling to bits. This was a different location in Broadmoor grounds; Norfolk and Essex Houses were adjoined together. If I made it then two roofs were mine! But even I had my doubts and it's why I knocked George back, he was gutted, I was gutted to knock him back, but this is showbiz you've got to take life on the jaw and George would get over it.

There were ten of us out on the yard. Dave Wright – Dave was a 24 year-old resident. I respected him – as he kept his self-respect, but he was a psychopath. He wasn't insane, just a danger man, a double killer! Peter Griffin – Pete was a great chess player, he played like a grand master! He killed a man for winning at chess (not many played him, only by letter.). George Heath was out with us. I gave him the nod, he knew I was making one. The others were too far-gone in the head to give a fuck if the moon dropped out of the sky.

The staff were at their observation points. The time was now. I ran past a warden so fast that he must have shit it. In seconds I got on top of the toilet ledge. I heard the bells go off, shouts and boots running. In a split second I pulled myself up onto a cell bar and swung over to another cell. I just got my fingers on a sill! Dangling ten foot up I pulled myself up. The risk was now the drainpipe! Could I reach it, would it hold my weight? I was about 220 pounds in weight at this time.

I looked down at the mob of staff who had formed below. The other loons were being led back inside and I actually saw a pair of eyes looking at me – Lucas! He must have been inside Norfolk as the alarm went off. To see him gave me that extra boost of confidence that I needed at this stage. I made it over to the pipe and without even testing it up I went! All the way to the top, but as I thought, it was a difficult climb. My knees were cut, my fingers could barely get a grip on the pipe, as it was so tight up against the wall.

Then it happened, feet from the top! The fucking pipe started coming away from the brickwork. To say my heart stopped would be like saying I don't like Guinness. I truly believed this was my lot, my time had come and it was to end like an old 'Keystone Cops' movie! I had a choice of either going with it or making an incredible dive that would stand the test of time in never being bettered by anyone. I dived for the guttering, again my heart stopped as this too started come away, I looked down briefly and could still fell Lucas' eyes on me, willing me to fall off and that made me even more determined to stay alive or at the very least keep me from serious injury.

God only knows how I got up that day 'cos I don't? A 100-year-old building is not a good climb, but I was King of the Castle and Lucas was the Dirty Rascal. The beautiful sensation that passed though me at this particular second was equal to any sensation I've previously put down as the best. It was electrifying beyond explanation. I shouted down at them: 'THIS IS THE FUCKER. Anybody comes up here I'll sling you off, I'll die up here!' I meant it; I truly meant it and believed it! I was the gov'nor of Broadmoor once again.

Dr McGrath's post was filled at this time by Dr Hamilton (my old doctor at Kent House), but he was out of the country while this was going on. No soppy superintendent could or would get me off this roof. Almost ten years I'd served, no sex, no love, no tenderness, nothing! My ten years had been a war and I felt what I had become – a desperate dangerous man who never gave a shit about life.

I swear this is a time in my life I look back on with disbelief. As even I can't understand why I was so crazy. I started my demolition act. I begun by smashing all the windows out in the workshops with slates, causing inmates and staff alike to run for it. Then I slung slates through Kent House cell windows, then I begun slinging slates over the wall hitting parked cars, then I tore out water pipes and cables and this went on for three days. I tore out and destroyed Kent and Essex roofs. Untold thousands of pounds it cost the taxpayer and the more the better as far as I was concerned.

The TV cameras and the press were out. I shouted down! But unfortunately they write and say things that they want, bollocks and a lot of lies. Anything to sell a paper, no one was listening to the real me. Unknown to me they called me a 'Killer on the roof'. 'Madman tears off roof'. The more dramatic the headlines the more newspapers they sell. Very few newspapers have told the truth about my life over the years, but there are some I respect.

Unknown to me at that time my dear old mum suffered terrible anxiety over the media lies. My name was given as 'Reggie Peterson' and I was put down as a convicted killer! People were approaching my mum and asking her whom it was that I had killed? I'm an armed robber; I've never killed anyone, well...not fully! Remember the silk tie? Oh, and a loon in Rampton who was clinically dead – for a short while. Staff gave him the kiss of life and started him again, I was never charged with anything, as I was too insane. I've never been charged with murder or manslaughter.

Broadmoor inmates are all classified as mad and who gives a fuck whether I was a convicted murderer or a bank robber, I was classed as a loon no matter what. Who gives a shit? My second day up there my dad arrived. They'd phoned my old man up and begged him! They used him to get me down. 'Dad', I shouted down, 'leave me, I can't come down tell mum I love her – go, dad!' I watched my old man go.

From my perch up on the rafters I watched him walk out, his head hung down heavy. I saw him go to his car and drive off. I swear I even saw the old bugger wipe his eyes. 'Cry'. I cried my bloody heart out and I've no shame in admitting it – big deal I cried. I'm human, aren't I? I cried for the pain I brought to my folks, good honest people, god how it hurt me to go through all of this. All I ever did was hurt them! Dad had shouted up to me that mum was ill with worry, but he never told me about the 'killer' story going about in the newspapers.

I got so eaten away inside of myself that I actually tore out twelve foot joists weighing god knows what. This was pure hate coming out of my body and I would have killed any man coming after me at that time.

Late at night I could see the female wards. York House and Lancaster House – their lights shining. I saw their silhouettes; shapes, sizes and I heard their shouts. 'Show us your cock, Mickey', 'Look at my tits' and 'Come down you lunatic' were some of the things shouted by them, I had to laugh and maybe it lightened me up a little, I don't know? They were as fucked up as I was; we were all crazy lost souls.

Our lives are ruled for us, take this, do this, don't do that! 'Show us your tits', I shouted. 'Yipeeeeeeee!' Obviously I couldn't see much (too far), but my imagination was good. 'Only if you show us your cock?' I dropped my trousers, 'Yawoooooooo!' Laugh, they loved it! 'Yoo hoo, yoo hoo! Show us your bum, Mickey', they shouted. 'Bollocks, show me yours.' Bums were up at the windows, legs dangling out. Tits. Bloody hells bells, what a laugh.

Late in the night though, as it goes silent, reality hits me like a hammer over the head. I ate some raw pigeon eggs and some moss out of the gutter; I was starving. I'm a born survivor, see! The loons below were just completely institutionalised. Essex loons were actually shouting up to me: 'Come down you idiot, stop causing all this trouble. We can't watch telly nor have visits.' In a proper jail cons would be throwing up food and blankets for me –

praising me. Here though, in the asylum, they were slagging me off! Anything you done was for yourself and here every man was on his own.

Old boys were upset over it. This was their home, their life, all they knew and all they had. It just fucked up my head to even think about how it was. Bats are plentiful around Broadmoor; I wondered what they tasted like? The only problem was catching one of them as well as the fact that they worried me. They were in the rafters making squeaking noises looking at me as I could see their eyes glint in the summer moonlight. Some whizzed past me, rats with wings! I saw an owl, a beautiful owl, a real beauty.

Those nights were all treasured memories. The destruction was heaven, but the peace at night was like paradise to me. A true feeling of being free, air tasted like food. How could I ever make myself heard? How could I tell any young tearaway to throw down his weapons and never take the road to destruction that I've taken? I can't tell anybody as nobody listens to a mad man. Up on that roof was the answer to every part of my life. I knew I was disturbed, but I had to live with it. Dr Frankenstein or Dr Lucas, it made no difference to me as no head shrink could cure me. I was the ultimate challenge to the system and I was actually winning, so fuck them!

The third day my old dad came back, but this time he had my brother Mark with him. Mark's in the Royal Navy he worked for the Queen and I was staying in her boarding house. Mark and I have had our differences, as most brothers do, he don't agree with the way I take on the world, but he loves me and I love him. We shouted to each other, our hearts were heavy, emotions flooded us. Even from where we both stood we could see each other's eyes well up with tears. Mum was the sole conversation, then I decided: 'FUCK IT! Enough is enough, alright, I'm coming down.' I was aching, cut up, splintered and dirty. No way could I climb down, even a loony wouldn't attempt it so they opened up the attic shaft and I came down a ladder. My dad hugged me, my brother hugged me and I phoned my mum.

Later on after treatment and a clean up the double doors banged up on me. Depression overcome me like never before and I now felt like I'd buried myself. Why did I come down, why couldn't I have jumped? My mind was tortured, there were only four walls in my vision and I could see no future, a very depressing thought!

It took me weeks to come to terms with my life after this. Lucas had said his party piece yet again: 'Never again will you do that!' 'FUCK OFF', I told him. It was at this period my poetry begun, I wrote some beautiful poems. I wrote one called 'Life', John Turner a charge nurse, a good man, got it typed up for me. We got some copies done; he took a copy and encouraged me to do more. I wrote thirty more and compiled them into a book.

After the embarrassment of a third rooftop protest I was shipped out to Park Lane. The only ones sorry to see me leave was the roofing contractors. The screws had Union Jacks in the windows to cheer me on my way. I missed out on a rooftop siege in 1982 as they had me on so many psychotropic drugs I guess it took me all my time to climb out of bed let alone climb a roof. I was labelled the £1m lunatic, but the satisfaction I got over destroying Broadmoor was worth any label to me. I'm the only man to have caused so many problems for them at Broadmoor.

I've no regrets over what I did here, but they have, they lost more than I ever could. I've been asked may times after I left Broadmoor why I did it? Well the truth is this – until a man's lived in a hole and been jumped on, he can't ever understand the meaning of emptiness. I demolished Broadmoor for my own sanity. If I hadn't of done it then I would never have survived it. I had to reach inside myself and find extra power to fight the unknown, that's why I done it. My beautiful hat trick was my reward and I survived it! Ron Kray used to cheer me on from his window when I did the roofs.

I was given dosages of drugs in my food and I know screws on their own initiative put them there. I know it can happen because a psychiatric nurse was reported in a national newspaper to have injected milk with a drug he got from work as a prank on some of his pals. He was taken to County Court and lost his job, which proves those that are not supposed to administer them can obtain drugs. I know that I was abused in such a way, proving it is another matter, but I stand by what I say and really it should be the screws from Broadmoor that should stand in the dock, not me.

A final tribute to a man I met at Broadmoor was an old boy called Ron Greedy. Ron looked on me as the son of madness and I took that as a compliment since he'd done 25 years at Broadmoor and then 15 years at Ashworth. There aren't many loons around like him, what a guy!

Chloral hydrate is a water-soluble sedative and hypnotic and very fast acting. Particularly good for inducing sleep in children or the elderly although the drug must be administered in a very mild solution otherwise gastric irritation can occur. It can be administered orally or alternatively rectal. Overdose results in toxic effects! Prolonged use can lead to addiction.

Side effects: Speed of thought, concentration and movement are affected, drowsiness, dizziness and dry mouth. Sensitivity reactions are common and include rashes. Some patients may experience excitement or confusion.

Administration considerations: Should not be given to those with sever heart disease, inflammation of the stomach, impaired function of the liver or kidneys. Should be given with caution to those with lung disease and respiratory depression and contact with skin or mucous membrane should be avoided.

Largactil is a proprietary preparation of the drug called Phenothiazine used to treat patients suffering or undergoing behavioural changes or who are psychotic and that particularly means schizophrenics. It is also used to treat severe anxiety or as a pre-surgery drug. It is produced as a tablet in three strengths or as a syrup as a suspension. Anal suppositories are also available, believe it or not and also available in ampoule form for injection use.

Side effects: Speed of thought and movement are affected. Dry mouth and blocked nose, constipation, difficulty urinating, blurred vision, impotence, weight gain, sensitivity reactions, cold, depression, poor sleep patterns, low blood pressure, irregular heartbeat, prolonged high dosage may cause opacity in the cornea and lens of the eyes, skin may turn purple.

Administration considerations: Not if suffering from glaucoma, poor blood cell formation, already on other drugs that depress certain parts of the brain and spinal cord, lung disease, cardiovascular disease, epilepsy, Parkinsonism, abnormal secretion of the adrenaline glands, impaired liver or kidney function, under secretion of thyroid hormones, enlargement of the prostrate gland.

Prolonged use warning: Regular checks on eye function and skin pigmentation, withdrawal should be gradual. Withdrawal of treatment should be gradual.

Modecate is a proprietary anti-psychotic drug, available on prescription. Used for long term maintenance of tranquillisation for a person suffering from psychoses one of which is schizophrenia. Comes in ampoule form for injectionable use and comes in two strengths, the stronger being called Modecate Concentrate. Modecate is a preparation of fluphenazine decanoate.

Side effects: Drowsiness, pallor and hyperthermia, insomnia, depression, restlessness and nightmares! Jaundice and rashes can occur, dry mouth, constipation and difficulty in urinating, blurred vision and raised or lowered heart rate.

Administration considerations: Should be given only with extreme caution to patients who suffer from heart or vascular disease, from kidney or liver disease, from parkinsonism, or from depression.

Stelazine is another proprietary form of an anti-psychotic drug – Trifluoperazine. This is only available on prescription and is used to treat and tranquillise psychoses such as schizophrenia including the control of behavioural disturbances. It can also be used to control anxiety in the short term. Stelazine is produced in the form of tablets in two strengths, as a sustained release capsule (spansules) in three strengths, as a sugar-free syrup for dilution (the potency of the syrup once dilute is retained for 14 days), as a liquid (cosh) concentrate for dilution (the potency of the syrup once dilute is retained for a period dependent on the diluent), and in ampoule form for injection.

Side effects: Concentration, movement and speed of thought are affected, restlessness, insomnia and nightmares! Rashes, jaundice, dry mouth and gastrointestinal disturbances may occur, blurred vision and muscle weakness.

Administration considerations: Should not be administered to patients who suffer from reduction in the bone marrow's capacity to produce blood cells or from certain types of glaucoma. Caution should be exercised if the patient suffers from heart or vascular disease, kidney or liver disease or parkinsonism.

That little lot is not half nor quarter of the concoctions pumped into me! I'm expected to be normal after that little lot, I fought it all the way and I knew all along that I didn't need any of them, but it was designed to liquidise me – it worked.

3

I was out of prison some fourteen years after I'd been sentenced to that seven-year stretch I received way back in 1974. It was October 30th, 1987 and I was finally on my way home sitting in the back of my old man's car, looking out of the window at sky, grass, cars and people as we drove down the motorway. Fourteen years and in all that time it seemed that I'd only seen daylight when I was being ghosted from one nick (prison) to the other. Fourteen years of punishment blocks and segregation units from Walton to Wakefield to Wandsworth to Winchester to Wormwood Scrubs and they're the only ones that begin with the letter 'W'. There were plenty more from Durham to the Isle of Wight then there were the special hospitals, the nut houses: Rampton, Broadmoor and Park Lane. I'd gone through all of these as well, but now I was on my way home.

I felt good, really good, but it wasn't to last. A couple of hours down the motorway and dad pulled up in a service area. Dad was tinkering with car while mum went into the café and ordered the tea so I dashed into the toilet for piss. As I'm standing there I suddenly clock (see) five guys looking at me. Some of them were having a piss themselves, some of them were just standing about. This strange feeling came over me, I couldn't do anything about it and started sweating and I felt ill. These guys were part of a plot, waiting for me, waiting, knowing that I'd be going for a piss.

I wasted no time, I attacked first, I tore the air blower (hand drier) off the wall and made it clear I'd kill the first one that came near me. They all backed up against the back wall while I waived the machine about keeping them at bay.

Something must have told my old man that there was something wrong because the next thing he shouts and defused the whole situation. I dropped the air blower machine and left the five geezers against the wall and we went out. We got mum out of the café and shot off a bit lively and never told her what had happened, but she knew something was wrong as we travelled in silence all the way home.

Sitting in the back of the car I could see dad's eyes in the mirror as he kept glancing at me. He was worried and he had good reason to be. Only recently they'd retired from running a club in Aberystwyth and now lived in a little flat with a spare bed for me.

In prison I would dream of living at home with my parents making up for all the long lost time. I'd dream that I was there with them and we could all be happy, but it could never be in reality. I should know mum is a very strict person and she would worry herself silly if I wasn't home by a certain time. I sat there in the car thinking about all of this knowing that I couldn't put it on them. I'm a proud man and I had to get on my feet alone, my way. They would have kept me for a s long as it would have took, but how could I sponge off my parents or sign on the dole. I needed to be free and independent. I knew deep down that there was nothing for me in Wales.

It was a lonely old journey for me, I love me mum and dad but there would be no choice I would have to leave and make my own way. For now it could wait though. It felt lovely to sit in the back and sip a beer without being surrounded by screws and cuffed up like a mad dog.

Yeah I felt fresh, clean and excited. I thought back to the business in the toilets as we drove on leaving it far behind. I knew I was well in the wrong and it made me afraid that I'd lose control again. I'd try to convince myself it was a one off, a shock, but I truly believed I was mad. The people in there had caused it; it was a paranoid attack because I wasn't used to being with strangers. Nothing had prepared me for this as I was released straight from the block as a cat 'A' prisoner back into the wild.

I wondered what my dad was thinking; we'd have to talk later. In the other lane I spotted a cat 'A' van pass by and I wondered if there was anybody I knew in it? Who was it and where were they coming from or going to? Prison kept moving back into my mind. I thought about the pals I'd left behind. My mum said: 'You're quiet, Michael, are you okay?' ' Yes, mum, smashing', I replied. They were both smoking away, I said: 'Why don't you pack it in for your health sake?'

Before we hit Aberystwyth I asked dad to stop the car in a lay-by. I'd seen this field and took my jacket and shirt off and had a jog around the field. It did the trick it released some energy and made me feel fresh. It was cold but bloody lovely and I enjoyed it. I could sense that mum and dad were more relaxed as I got back in the car.

Aberystwyth was my parents' home having moved there back in 1979 to run a club, which they loved, but I felt strange. It wasn't my home and it didn't feel like my home. I was a Luton man, I was English not welsh, it didn't feel right although I have the utmost respect for our Welsh cousins having heard some of the things the people have been through from my dear old mum so in a way I still hold Wales close to my heart. My distant relation was the late Richard Burton, Liz Taylor's ex-husband. In fact my Auntie Eileen, whose 100% welsh, often joked about writing to Liz Taylor asking if she had any spare diamonds from her rings. That's as far as it went and joking to one side they took that part of the family seriously and wouldn't have accepted the diamonds.

Even their flat wasn't home for me, my bedroom seemed cold and isolated, it felt like a cell and I was closed in. Don't get me wrong it was a beautifully decorated room with a nice soft bed, it just didn't seem right!

After we'd had a meal dad and I went for a stroll along the sea front and that felt terrific and I was amazed at how many people my dad knew. He introduced me to them as we walked along and then he asked me about the business back at the café toilet on the way here. I told him the truth about how I felt, we both knew it was serious. I told him I'd only be staying for a day or two and then I'd be off. Dad was gutted and so would mum be, but he understood the reason, my dad was from a good school, solid.

My Uncle Jack was an old aged pensioner and I loved the old git. He lived on the twelfth floor of a block of flats in Luton. When he died in 1991 I was devastated! He loved a drop of scotch, but he could handle it. I remember as a kid I was always close to Jack now I needed somewhere to go so I rang him. The old rascal was over the moon to hear that I was out, he loved me like I was his son. He said: 'Get your arse down here', I said I would be seeing him soon.

I then phoned Paul Edmunds in east London and he said the same. I phoned Wendy Boss a friend who had visited me a few times. She wasn't my girlfriend or anything like that she was just a friend. Then I phoned Kelly Anne Cook.

A couple of months before my release I had this letter off Kelly Anne, her letter and the ones that followed really touched me. She lived in the same block of flat as my Uncle Jack and she was six months pregnant by a guy called ' the bear'. This toe-rag had treated her bad, he'd beaten her and abused her, he was a drunkard and somehow Kelly Anne had become involved with him.

Her life was a history of disaster, but I had a lot of compassion for her. Maybe I could see a bit of myself in her, I don't know? I'd seen a couple of photos of her and I could see that she was no beauty queen but then I didn't think I was too attractive either, although my mum says differently, god bless her. She had a lovely smile though and a lovely pair of eyes. In prison I thought about her and thought about serving up this bear guy. I dreamed of seeing him down a dark alley and I knew that one day we would meet.

Kelly Anne was delighted to hear me on the phone, she was excited that I was out and all what she could say was: 'Come down, now!' She had such a lovely voice and it had been so long since I'd felt a body next to me, how could I resist? This girl loved me for what I was, but did I love her, could I love her, time could only tell?

For three days I stayed in Aberystwyth, three days of heaven and I'd have loved it to be three years. If I'd had money and no mental problems then I have no doubt I would've stayed. In those three days we ate out and we went to pubs, we let our hair down. Just once in a pub I went strange, but my dad got a grip on me before I could start on a table of Welsh lads. I was having problems counting up my change and addressing the bar staff. The money had changed from the old pennies and shillings to new decimal money during my time away. I did feel strange and weird, but I held on to my sanity for my parents' sake. Without them I would not have got through the first three days of freedom.

It was a difficult time for me, I felt so different, I was a different man to the one who'd been locked up some fourteen years earlier. I hadn't met normal ordinary people for so long and the world had changed so much while I'd been a way. All that time I'd gone without sex, now I needed a woman. Dad introduced me to some girls that worked at his club, but it was no good. I was too tense to relax. Ah well, I'd get my loving as soon as I felt better.

My best memory of Aberystwyth is having a jog along the sea front on the first morning I awoke a free man. It was lovely; I got up bright and early at 6.00 a.m. buzzing on adrenaline...pumping excitement...oozing all sorts of energy. I put my head into a sink full of cold water, brushed my teeth and got rigged up in some training gear. I put on my army boots and set off running. I found the sea front about quarter of a mile away from my parents flat. The spray splashed in my face and I could taste the Welsh salt in my mouth. My eyes stung, but it was terrific! There was hardly anyone about as I ran along, past the hotels, the college, the pubs, the snooker hall, the small pier; this was freedom.

For years I'd dreamed of being able to do this simple thing. Ever since my parents moved here and told me about the place. My dreams were fulfilled; maybe Wales wasn't such a bad a place after all and it might have been a case that I needed time to settle. It was just so lovely. I truly wished I could live here like a normal person. Settle....maybe get a job – who knows. But I wasn't normal and it would soon be time to leave Aberystwyth.

Mum and dad saw me to Aberystwyth station for the 7.00 a.m. London bound train...I was bound for Euston. I could see the sadness in their faces the same sadness that would one day come back to haunt me when my little Michael had grown, but more of that later. I assured them that I was doing the right thing. I had about £200 and two suitcases. Armed with this I was ready to face the big wide world like a little child starting school, but for me it was déjà vu. They made me promise I would return if I didn't make it. As the train drew away I watched them grow smaller and finally disappear as the train pulled out. Yeah, I felt gutted. Who wouldn't, was I doing the wrong thing? Too late now, I was on my way.

The journey began with just myself and a young girl sitting in the compartment, she was aged about 19 or 20. She was sitting across from me reading a magazine, immaculately dressed, short skirt, lovely legs...why couldn't she put that silly mag down and notice me? Or was I an ugly bastard, an old dirty pervert? That's how I felt at that moment I'll admit. Sod her I thought read your fucking mag. Just then our eyes met and I swear she gave me the eye – was I going off my flippin' nut or what? She spoke: 'Going to London then, are we?' I very nearly had to look over my shoulder to make sure it was me she was talking to. I stuttered my way through the conversation, which touched on the weather and other boring details when really all I wanted to do was talk about her.

I've been brought up strict and it wasn't in my nature to start chatting up young women on trains, no sir, I was no sex pervert. So I didn't want to say or do anything that could be construed as being lewd or too forward when bugger me if she didn't sit there in front of me with her legs uncrossed and her skirt was starting to ride up her legs, what little of the skirt there was.

I averted my eyes from that area and talked as normal as I could! Her name was Debbie and she'd been to visit some college friends for a few days and now she was returning home. Debbie commented on what a quiet time she'd had in Aberystwyth and that she could do with some livening up and with that she gave me a sultry look that said more than a thousand words could ever say.

Other people were starting to get on the train and for a moment I lost myself in our conversation that turned to her lack of a good time during her stay. I told her that if I'd had someone like her I'd have given her the time of her life, which she wouldn't have forgotten, ever! I meant a good time in the sense of wining and dining her, but Debbie had taken it the wrong way and a double entendre was made of it. Here's me going on about a good time thinking of something totally different. It didn't take Debbie long to make it clear what she wanted from me and I asked her if she would like to get some air and take a stroll.

We walked past the toilet cubicle, which was open, and before I knew it Debbie dragged me in with an unknown force that shocked me. She pushed the door shut and said: 'You're that Mickey Peterson fella, aren't you?' 'How do you know that!' I replied with a sense of shock, which betrayed my astonishment. 'I was in one of the clubs when I overheard this woman saying she'd been introduced to you, but you didn't really pay her any interest and you were that Mickey Peterson fella who'd just got out of nick. She thought you were gay, as you didn't show any interest in her.'

'I'll show you who's gay!' I said and with that we started undressing each other. It'd been some time since I'd done this sort of thing, but it was like riding a bike – once you know how, you never forget. Debbie wasn't wearing any underwear and that made the job easier. I stroked her inner thigh until I reached her mound, but Debbie was more interested in getting my tool in her mouth. I pushed her head away as I could feel myself starting to climax and she grabbed the base of my manhood and squeezed it, which stopped me coming. Boy, Debbie knew more about sex than I ever did and that twenty minutes gave me more pleasure than any Ferris wheel or big dipper on a fairground could ever do. This chick knew a trick or two, thankfully.

I left the cubicle and returned to my seat, which was taken up by an old boy with a little goatee beard, Debbie soon followed. I sat next to a woman of about forty and a young girl of about seventeen sitting opposite her. I started chatting to the old pop; I said 'Where are you off to then'. He was going to London to see his son who he hadn't seen in ages. We talked about boxing, soccer and the weather. He was a smashing old boy, good company.

The journey was going well. I got talking to the woman next to me; she was accompanying her daughter to London for a job interview. I got chatting to them all, it was going really well and I felt good, especially after that jaunt with Debbie. When the trolley came around I got them all teas and coffees then I fucked it all up! I do love a joke, but some people are so serious and I was sitting with the serious lot.

The girl asked me where I'm going? Now bear in mind I'm dressed completely in black, black shoes, black suit and black shirt plus I'm wearing shades 'cos I love wearing shades even though it was November. And I've got a shaven skull to top it all off. This girl asks me where I'm going? 'I'm going to London to kill the Queen', I replied. There was silence all round. The only sound I could hear was the train clattering across the sleepers. Nobody said a word they didn't have to, their faces showed the shock, their amazement and their fear!

I felt terrible! As soon as I said it I knew I'd made a mistake. They sat their in their seats looking absolutely terrified so I smiled and started to say I was only joking, but it was too embarrassing for us all. I don't suppose it helped, me being dressed all in black and with a shaven skull.

I excused myself and returned to the toilet that Debbie and I had been in. I stayed there for a while and splashed cold water on my face and told myself that I'd have to be more careful about what I said to people even in fun. As soon as the train hit Euston I shoot off a bit lively, grabbed my luggage and off down the platform just in case they told the police I was going to waste the Queen. I had no time to look for Debbie, I stuck my case in a left luggage department, took a few bits and pieces in a holdall, got a ticket and bolted sharpish. I was racing, buzzing; my brain was travelling at 200 mph.

There's been a few people got sectioned off for just wanting to see the Queen, remember that guy who got into the Palace and sat at the end of the Queen's bed? He just walked straight into her bedroom after entering the place at night, but the funny thing about it was that she was sleeping in a single bed, ain't she married to Phillip? So my joke was a bit inappropriate!

On the corner by the station there's a pub. I dived in but as soon as I got in through the door I felt the bad vibes. It was packed with people - crammed solid. I was in a sea of people, I felt lost, I needed to escape the street but this was no better, I needed help, I needed somebody to help me before I lost control. That's what I was scared of, blowing it in here amongst all theses strangers, not a soul who I knew.

I made my way to the bar and picked up an empty fag packet. On a clear bit of cardboard I wrote: *A pint of Guinness and one packet of peanuts.* The barman gave me one strange look as he read it, pulled me a pint and put a packet of peanuts beside it on the bar. Then he took the cardboard and underneath my words he wrote £2.10. I then wrote underneath: *Bollocks,* without a sip of the pint or a peanut. I couldn't stay in there I knew I had to find help, but where? Wendy Boss, she would know what to do! Wendy was a good friend so I made my way over to south London.

What a dump. I couldn't believe what I saw. Most of the flats were boarded up and only the odd one seemed to be occupied. As I got into the lift it stank of stale piss the walls were painted in graffiti and everywhere I looked was rubbish piled up high. This place made Wandsworth jail look like a five star hotel.

The door of Wendy's flat had boards where glass should've been. I was in two minds whether to knock or walk away. No! She'd come to see me when I was in prison; I had to go through with it. I knocked and there she was in front of me, she'd put on a lot of weight since I last seen her.

I've got to be honest, her flat was a mess, it smelled stale and there were dirty pans and clothes slung everywhere. The place was dirty and when I walked in I felt dirty just being there. Looking at Wendy didn't help; she had greasy hair and old clothes on. She's got a good heart but she's a bit eccentric.

We shared a couple of bottles of wine and had a good chat long into the night. Then she went to bed and I slept on the settee. I never fancied Wendy in prison and I never fancied Wendy on the out. The final straw came as she broke wind as she bent down to turn an LP over! That did it, by the early morning I was gone, never to return. I respected Wendy's guts, but it was just as a woman she lacked femininity and no, I never went back.

Back on the streets I wandered around trying to work out my next move. Then as I happened to glance in a shop window I happened to see a toy gun, it was just a toy, but it looked real. I went in and bought it, when I got out of the shop I pulled the green nozzle out of the end and it really looked the bizz. So much so that I wanted to try it out.

My brain was racing away like an express train and I couldn't think straight at all. A strong urge came upon me to hit the nearest bank or post office. The urge was so strong I knew it wouldn't go away and that somehow I would have to release it.

I ended up in a car park, pulling the gun out on a geezer, in a striped suit, as he was about to get into a Mercedes. I stuck it into his belly and told him to get in and open the passenger door. He didn't argue - his eyes told the whole story as he saw it.

In the car I told him I was in trouble and he was to do exactly as I said or he'd be in trouble. His trouble would be, I told him, I'd shoot him. The guy was terrified but he did as he was told; though his hands did seem to tremble a bit on the steering wheel. I told him to head for the M1 and to do nothing that might attract attention, or we'd both die! I've got to say I felt fucking great. This was the true excitement I'd longed for. I looked through the geezer's tapes and told him to put U2 on.

So there we were driving through London, with 'In the Name of Love' blaring out. The guy was shaking now so I thought I'd better calm him by telling him I'd no intention of harming him and he would be okay just as long as he did what I told him. After all, there was no need for me to take this man's dignity away from him just 'cos I needed a lift.

We got on the motorway and I told him to stay on it 'til I spotted the Luton turn-off and said to take it. At this he panicked and started mumbling that I was going to kill him and take the car. He took some convincing that I didn't want to kill him, then as he pulled off the motorway I lost my bearings. It had all changed in the fourteen years that I'd been away!

Once I worked out where we were I told him to stop. The guy was shaking as I told him I'd let him go if he'd promise to forget all about it. If he didn't I'd hunt him down or my firm (gang) would. I got out of the car and I hadn't even shut the door as I felt the car lurch away and off in the distance at a very fast speed. I never saw or heard of the geezer again after that. Looking back at that it was a very irresponsible thing to do and my mind was out of tune, but what other choice did I have, okay I should have thumbed a lift – point taken. It was only a water pistol though!

As I walked down the landing towards my Uncle Jack's flat I thought of prison. Cells, rows of doors and the people behind them. It's not an easy thing to shake off, ask anybody that's done real time behind the door. I rang Jack's bell and as he opened up his little eyes lit up. Well...one of his eyes shone – the other one was glass on account of him losing it in the Second World War.

'Come on in son, come in Mickey my boy'. He grabbed me and pulled me in. We had a few cans of Special Brew and a good old natter. I'd always felt good in Jack's company, even as a little kid. 'How did you get here, son?' he asked. Cor, if only I'd told him I'd hijacked a car he'd have fallen off his chair so I left that part of my journey out. He showed me my bedroom and told me it was mine for as long as I wanted it. I had a bath and a shave and got down to settling in and getting to know all the visitors dropping in to see him, especially his female friends.

Alison Hughes was the prettiest girl I'd seen in a long time, she was the daughter of Beryl who used to call round to Jack's a couple of times a week. Alison was only 18 years old, but she was mature and her personality bubbled with excitement. Just what the doctor ordered – a godsend! I was in heaven with a jellybaby, as I called her and every minute with her was a treasured memory. Nothing remains forever but at this time, undoubtedly, I was in love.

Life felt good at last. Alison cheered me up no end and I'd got other women friends – Sara. Again who I'd met through Jack. Kelly Anne – who'd written to me in the nick and one or two others, they were just friends, not like Alison, she was something else. I know what psychologists are going to say here, that people mixed up in crime usually tend not to be monogamous (don't have just one sexual partner) well...if that's the case what can we say about MP's sexual lives. Does it mean they're criminals too?

I spent a good bit of time at Jack's local, the Moaks Inn. The landlord, Jimmy Brookes, is a great friend of mine; he helped me in a lot of ways. He'd done a lot of boxing in his day and I'd go to the pub, have a few pints of Guinness and keep an eye on any potential troublemakers. There's always some mug about who doesn't know when to stop. Even though Jimmy could handle himself another pair of mits (hands) never came in wrong.

Look at what happened to John L Gardner, ex-heavyweight champ, he ran a pub up north and some junkie jumped over the counter to rob the till, John tried to stop him and got cut severely for it. You should see the scar on his gut from the surgery to keep him alive. John's now frightened to go out on his own, could you imagine a man his size being frightened in this way? Such a man should be able to walk freely in this country without such fear, me I'd fucking gas the lot of them junkies!

A pal took me to Dunstable to meet Cliffy Fields, a well-known fighter. Cliffy fought Lenny McLean and Roy Shaw, both unlicensed against two of the hardest fighters in the game. Unfortunately Cliffy had recently lost an eye through some bastard hitting him with a bottle. It was sad to see a man of his quality like that. Life can be cruel.

On Sundays I went round to another friend's for dinner. I'd met Hilary in Jimmy's pub and I got on well with her kids and her mother. It was nice to have a laugh there and they wanted me to stay, but I begun to realise that I needed a place of my own, somewhere I could retreat to and shut off when I felt people were crowding me.

One thing on my mind was the other guy that Alison (Jellybaby) had on her books. She was messing up my mind, as she couldn't decide between the two of us. The problem seemed to be that he was twenty and had a big motorbike and I was thirty-six and had fuck all! It occurred to me to go around and break his legs, but I reckoned I'd only make matters worse and drive Alison into his arms – so I swallowed it. Jellybaby was just too sweet to hurt – it hurt!

Kelly Anne's bloke was a different kettle of fish. He needed serving up for the liberties he'd taken with Kelly. She was six months pregnant when I got out of prison and her life was in a bad, sad state. One day she came round to Jack's and told me the bailiffs were on their way to empty her flat. I dashed round there fast and emptied it and hid the stuff before they got there, then I put everything back once they'd been and gone. Then one way and another we sorted her bills out. All along she'd been getting grief from this geezer who she'd been having this relationship with and I found out he'd been knocking her about.

One night our paths collided in the Moaks Inn. He was a big lump, about forty, loved a drink. We had a chat and he came across as a nice bloke, well mannered, no problem sober. The only problem was that he wasn't always sober, and that's when he picked on Kelly Anne – beating the shit out of her as I'd heard. I made it very clear to him that if he so much as touched one hair on her head I'd blow his legs clean off. I also told him that if she'd been my girl before, I'd now have killed him. This was the guy known as 'The Bear', a big man. He got the message did 'The Bear' – he never went near Kelly Anne again.

The strange thing was, he was going out with a barmaid in the pub and I found out he treated her very well. She said he was a gentleman! So why did he take liberties with Kelly? I didn't know, but I did know that if he did it again I'd have to serve him up good style, because I was starting to feel close to Kelly Anne in a weird kind of way, not sexually but spiritually.

By now I was more settled, but I needed some real cash, some security. The giro from the social was okay, plus a bit of door work along with some ducking and diving here and there all helped. I needed to earn some real cash though so I called up Paul Edmunds in London and asked him if he would fix me up a fight. He was putting a bill together for late November at the Bow Royal Theatre and he fixed me up with one. I was to fight the Mystery Man, fuck knows who he was?

I was in great shape and at 36 years of age I felt 26. My body was firm and muscular, I weighed in at fourteen stones and my stamina was second to none. I had bundles of energy and a good punch-up would get me some steam out of my head. I told Paul that I wouldn't let him down and I immediately went into training at the Marsh Farm Centre in Luton. The mystery man was supposed to be a bit lively and an ex-pro, but he was going to have to be very good to put me away. I would be looking at him through eyes of hate. I'd imagine him to be the worst screw I could picture!

Training was severe. I'd get up at 6.30 a.m., swallow six eggs with milk and honey, have a cup of black coffee and take a five mile run around the housing estate. I'd follow that up with breakfast and a bath and that would be followed by Jellybaby – if she was about. I'd have her massaging my neck and shoulders and my bishop if I'd let her. I told her that I needed to preserve my energy and that I'd have to cut out all of the hanky panky, but she still got her wicked way most times.

At ten o'clock I'd run the half-mile to the gym for weight training and a swim at the Marsh Farm Centre, a lovely place run by good people. They liked me being there because I showed the boys a few moves. I'd sing as I skipped and that would make everybody happy. This was a great time for me; I was full of happiness. I was sparring with a handy amateur, a black lad, 21 years old and very fast. I can't say his name as it could get him into trouble with the amateur boxing people. He was six foot four inches tall and a good mover. Lovely footwork, nice jab – he helped put me through my paces a good few times a week. As long as I was doing something like this I was out of mischief's way.

This guy was so quick! He'd jab and move...jab...jab...then he'd spin out of a corner and make me look silly. A lot of my punches hit thin air, 99% of his hit my brain! In the end I had to wear a head guard, as he punished me with speedy combinations. But when I did connect he buckled up. We had a god time and he helped me a lot.

At 36 years of age I had to admit I was passed it as a pro boxer. What manager would give me a break? How could the Board of Boxing Control give me, an ex-lunatic, a boxing licence? But fuck their rules I was a back hall fighter known and respected. I didn't need them and they didn't need me.

What I did need though was a name. A stage name, a gimmick. I fancied the name Jack Palance. Palance was and still is as far as I know a damn good actor, I really fancied that name, but I was given the name 'Charles Bronson' instead, I was named after him because of a film he starred in, I think it was called 'Street Fighter'. There's been so much bollocks said about me taking the name in honour of Bronson and how my favourite film was 'Death Wish' in which Bronson starred, that just wasn't so. Michael Winner directed that film, I've got a lot of respect for Michael as he originally wrote some bad things about me in his *News of The World* column, but he was put straight on a few points and very cheerfully corrected the wrong. Not many men have given me that honour; Michael's a winner for sure, thanks.

I was now doing street fighting for real, 'Bronson' was my name and fighting was my game. The name Bronson has stuck to me like shit to a blanket. Most names are irrelevant to a lot of people, but the name 'Charles Bronson' would stick out and be lucky for me – so I thought!

I got a few quid together and went down to Aberystwyth for the weekend. It'd been three weeks since I'd left mum and dad and when they saw me again they both said how much more relaxed I seemed. We all went out for a night out on the town and had a good time. I had a chat with dad over a calming game of snooker the following day. He cheered me up a lot. I didn't tell him I was about to become known as Charles Bronson – I wanted to see how things went first. Maybe I'd get my head knocked off and mug myself off on the first fight. If so then my family would never know, but if I turned out a winner then I'd be proud to tell them.

The day before I left for Luton I took a walk down by the seafront, alone. I wanted to think and what better place to do it in than Aberystwyth by the sea, yeah, I could see myself settling down here one day. This thinking took me in a sad way. I'd had three great days and here I was leaving again. Christmas wasn't too far away and it would be my first one out as a free man for fourteen years. All those Christmases in prison and now I was out, free. I felt strange, like I never belonged anywhere anymore? I was so unsure in everything that I truly felt lost in the world as it went round me. Prison had fucked my head up, no doubt about that at all. I no longer felt human, or thought human or thought ordinary thoughts.

The train ride back to Luton was depressing; it was a gloomy journey with no Debbie this time. As we passed Dudley Station I thought of my friends the Anslow brothers, lovely guys. I thought of other friends in prisons all over the country. I was out and they were still there – I felt lost! Something must have jogged my mind because suddenly I felt a lot better. Fuck it! The fight was all that mattered right now. It was time to get back and prepare for the Bow Royal Theatre. Yes, fuck it – I'd knock this Mystery Man's had clean off and send it to Dartmoor! Why Dartmoor? I don't know it seemed like a good idea at the time!

Back in Luton I got back into training and everything was looking good for the big night. The old bill was tagging me so crime was out, but I'd got enough to think about with my training and my nightly sessions with Jellybaby. Most nights she drained me but on one occasion, not long before the fight, she messed my head up completely and I was so upset that I went out on my own for a drink. I ended up in a fight with three young yobs.

What happened was this – they were coming towards me in a very aggressive manner and I felt intimidated. My heart pumped fire and I decided on surprise tactics. I rushed into them lashing out and landed some heavy blows, biting and kicking at the same time. This was fighting birdy (prison) style. One coward ran off and the second hit the deck while the third was on my back. A quick twist and he joined his mate on the floor, it was all over and done with in a few seconds and I'd won. These pricks are only any good for mugging old ladies and bullying weaker people. They came unstuck with me.

I have to admit I enjoyed the rough and tumble of it, but I was in a bit of a mess. My jacket was torn, I'd bruised a few ribs and blood was pouring from an eye wound. A pro boxer would be fucked with these sorts of injuries just before a fight, but I was unlicensed and I'd still fight. Nothing could stop me boxing on Paul Edmunds show – nothing and nobody.

All the plans were set. Jimmy Brookes, the landlord of the pub was to drive Uncle Jack and his mates down, but I was leaving two days ahead of them to stay with Mrs Edmunds, Paul's mum, in Canning Town, east London. Mrs Edmunds spoilt me rotten, she's a lovely lady, a true angel. She treated me like her own son, as did all the Edmunds family.

The night before the fight I ended up working on a pub door 'til 3.00 a.m.! Although I did get £50 in my sky rocket (pocket). I couldn't help thinking that this might not be the way Angelo Dundee prepared Ali for his fights. In the end I got a few hours kip and still managed to get some roadwork in.

Before I come down to London I decided to give a pal of mine some publicity at the fight, so I had the words 'FREE ALAN BYRNE' written, in big letters, on my back in lipstick and lacquered over. Alan was serving life with a judge's recommendation that he serve at least twenty years and this was for a murder Alan says he didn't do. So I thought to put that on my back would give him some support as there would be a good crowd at the fight and I knew there were some people there filming me.

Before we set off for the theatre Paul arrived at his mother's house and took me over to his flat. He gave me a suit to wear and told me to choose a shirt and a tie from a rack of twenty or more. I picked a shirt out and Paul said: 'You've picked my favourite!' I said I'd pick another but he wasn't having any of it and wouldn't hear of it. I asked him what was so special about the shirt I'd just picked? 'Alan Byrne gave it to me in Brixton, years ago', Paul said. I stripped off my shirt and showed him the handiwork on my back – 'FREE ALAN BYRNE'. Fuck me if we didn't both have to sit down and have a drink to get over the shock!

I was ready, as I would ever be, all fired up for it. I hoped this Mystery Man was strong, because if he wasn't I'd put him in a body bag. There were six fights lined up, which were to show off boxing skills, as this was a charity show. My bout, though, was to have been for real and was earmarked for the last fight on the card. The show was in aid of someone dying of cancer, but my purse of £500 wasn't coming out of the night's takings. I was being looked after by the local mob. They all knew I was on my arse as far as cash went and that I'd hit rock bottom, but they knew I was good value and a draw. (An attraction.) I got £500 and backed myself at 2 to 1 for the lot!

As I warmed up in the dressing room Paul kept coming in saying the Mystery Man had not yet arrived. I was a bit concerned about this, as the fights went on I knew something was seriously wrong. In between fights they would auction off paintings donated by various serving prisoners, still no sign of the Mystery man as time went on. The geezer should've been here ages ago. I was here – where was he? I was gutted when Paul came in and I could see by the look on his face that the fight was off. This was too much. I told Paul straight 'Fuck it, Paul, I've got to fight somebody. I'm so psyched up – either I fight or I explode!'

Paul got up on stage and announced the bad news. There were some groans because I was top of the bill, but if the crowd were disappointed they weren't as half as gutted as me. I'd worked and waited for this night for too long for it to be taken away from me by my opponent not turning up. Paul put out a challenge to the audience, and to great applause, a black guy took it up. He looked fit and young and it turned out he was a bit handy. He was good looking, of Hispanic appearance, good teeth and alive eyes. It seemed a pity that I had to disfigure him, but I needed this fight so bad I was aching. As fights go this was to be a scrappy one with the length of rounds having no specific time, watch the fight.

As I climbed into the ring I felt terrific. Fourteen years pent-up fury and frustration within me - the moment had arrived where I could unleash it. When the crowd saw my back – 'FREE ALAN BYRNE' - a great cheer went up. They appreciated that. It was the moment I'd been waiting for and the moment the crowd had been waiting for – the main fight on the bill.

I spotted Uncle Jack in the front row, sitting with his mate from Luton. Jimmy Brookes, the landlord of the Moakes Inn, was nowhere to be seen? It turned out he arrived five minutes after my fight was over. He was gutted!

The bell went and we both came out of our corners...I followed him...lining him up. The guy was fast on his feet, but the way I felt he couldn't hurt me even if he had a lump hammer in each hand – I was invincible. I caught him with a quick right, a peach of a punch and I followed it up with a left hook. Down he went. I should've stood back at that but I was so excited I dived on top of him and carried on punching. Had this of been a licensed fight I'd have been banned for life for that, but it wasn't so about ten geezers jumped in the ring and pulled me off him. One or two of them must have been mates of his because they laid into me as they dragged me up.

These geezers obviously didn't have a clue about unlicensed fights - this was tame compared to some. Usually before the bell has even gone to start the round the nut goes in and when anyone goes down it's usually a stamp to the head, as they lay, if they're that daft enough to lay there waiting for it. This guy was lucky I wasn't using him as a doormat and if I'd been on the fight scene with an entourage of followers all hell would have broken out the minute anyone of them had laid a hand on me.

The second round: I came out blazing magnum shots, admittedly he was quick and some of my shots missed and made me look clumsy, but I was a little ring rusty. He slung a few nice punches himself, but they had about as much effect as a fly landing on me. I could not be hurt! I was so keyed up, so ready to go all the way...to die if necessary. On this night I could have beaten Mike Tyson.

Again he went down...and again I went down with him, to punch his fucking pretty face in. I didn't see him as a boxer, a guy who'd come out for a night out and accepted Paul Edmunds' challenge when the Mystery Man failed to show. I saw him as a screw who'd kicked my balls in, I saw him as a screw who'd stuck a needle in my arse, I saw him beat me up with a wet towel, I saw him slam a door into my face, I saw him sling my food over me as I lay tied up in a body belt – defenceless. I wanted to hurt this mother fucker. Black, white or yellow – colour had nothing to do with it. He was my enemy!

Once more I was jumped on as I tried to hit him on the deck. They dragged me off the poor blighter and Paul warned me to slow up before I caused a riot. He told me if I didn't then I'd be disqualified, which accounted for the short rounds!

Third round, it was toe to toe slogging, but all his efforts were a waste of time. He was brave, very brave, but that only made me stronger! I hit him even harder and he went down like a sack of shit. I was right over him kicking him in the guts when I heard them announce I'd been disqualified and the mob dived in once more to drag me off him for the last time.

I'd been disqualified in an unlicensed fight? Who were they kidding, this was kids stuff to what could've went on and they knew it, but since it was for charity their bottles must've gone. As the crowd dived in something fell out of one of the guy's jacket pockets, a gun! This gun was left lying on the floor of the ring as we all scuffled and someone noticed it lying there and picked it up!

Back in the dressing room I was still buzzing. Paul came in and I asked if I could fight someone else if he'd put out another challenge? I couldn't have been thinking straight as no one in their right mind would've taken me on after that display, but I was so psyched up it was all I could think of!

Just out of interest – this fight can be seen in its entirety in a documentary being made about me, as this is being written. The thing is going to be about three hours long and I believe it is being marketed commercially in bookshops and at my good friend Andy Jones' crime museum called 'Crime Through Time' in Newent Gloucester. Everything I've described about this fight can be seen in that documentary called *'Charles Bronson, Sincerely Yours'*. I'll tell you more about that documentary later on though.

At the end of the fight Paul asked if anyone wanted to challenge me for a fight to take place at a later date as this venue had women and children present. He said that a fight would be arranged for a few weeks time when women and children wouldn't be there.

Needless to say Paul didn't even consider the idea of asking for another challenger after my dressing room request so I'd got nothing more to do than get dressed and have a drink. He never had to pay me as I'd been disqualified, but Paul's a brother to me and it was arranged I'd fight again in three weeks time. This would be in a pub on Boxing nigh after the Christmas. And I decided there and then I'd back myself to win. If I won I'd walk away with a grand – that thought made me happy – something to look forward to.

My only concern was Christmas. I'd planned my first Christmas out to be at Aberystwyth with mum and dad, but that was out now. Instead I'd be fighting for my turkey. But I'd make it up to them soon enough; right now the main thing was the money to help support me.

The week before boxing night I got a phone call from Mrs Edmunds. Paul had been arrested for promoting unlicensed fights, the pub had been raided and the ring taken away. What did the police think the ring was going to do, get up and chin someone? Funny fuckers! The fight was now off 'til at least sometime in the New Year. Bad news, it was disaster. I was skint and already in debt to the tune of a monkey (£500). I was in trouble and I knew it. The only good news was that Paul didn't get charged and that really pleased me no ends.

I had two other fights, won them. It got to the point where nobody would fight me. Although there was one fight arranged that became legendary, the only fight I ever had that I felt sick over. I only don it 'cos the fighter I was supposed to fight bottled it at the last moment. Someone came up with the idea of me fighting a Rottweiler!

Here I was at the fight site, the opposition hadn't turned up and someone else's on the spot idea pushed me into a corner. The money and the deal were put to me. I had to survive; a man's gotta eat. I only had two choices, either take the dog or go back on the pavement, I chose the dog, but I knew I'd have to kill it 'cos you can't play about with a killer dog. This dog was reckoned to be a killer and had savaged men before. I've been asked by many my feelings on it. I've even been approached by mags and papers to give the full story, was I scared?

Well they say a dog can sense fear in a man, but I believe he was feared. I was weary and anxious to get it all over with fast. It did pass my mind that it could rip into me at lightning speed and could rip me apart before I could get my lightening plan into action. My plan was to attack it like a mad man, get in so fast I would terrify it. My only doubt was I may lose an arm if it got me, but to say I was scared would be a lie, I was just tense and unsure of the outcome. I accepted that I'd probably get hurt big time, but death never entered my mind. The dog would be the one dying, not me.

The battle took place in a warehouse, sawdust floor with a rope ring. The atmosphere was electric, many faces I knew, a lot of them from inside (prison) and there was also a lot of them I never knew, but they all knew me. They wanted to see me hurt, this was their big chance to see history, to say to their grand kids 'I saw Bronson ripped apart', 'I heard him scream', 'I heard his last words, he said...' But these guys were gonna lose their bets!

The dog was in a caged crate, it looked awesome and weighed in at 195 pounds and I was only 215 pounds. At that time I was super fit and fast and at my most dangerous, I'm nearly six foot in height, but at that time I might as well of been seven foot tall – that's how I felt! I wished the world could've seen it. I felt just like a Roman gladiator, this was a 'death wish for real'. Maybe subconsciously I'd like to be torn apart in front of a crowd, what a way to go, but my time wasn't now.

I done my stretching and limbering up, I was ready. I'd never sensed such madness, it was mad, every fucker there was mad. Fortunately my main promoter wasn't involved. He said he wanted 'fuck all to do with it'. In fact he respected me too much to lower myself and looking back at it, it was low. But, was I lower than the crowd who had paid for it and were baying like wolves for it to start. I make no excuses for my life; I am what I am. Some men will bend over and take a length for money and others will beg for money, isn't that low life? I was at least fighting to live, but I don't feel proud of my behaviour. This crowd was mercenary and without feeling, I'd teach the fuckers real pain!

The dog, as it was led towards me, looked massive, its head neck and shoulders were humungus and with its tongue hanging out it looked more evil than the anything I'd seen for a while. I can still see those teeth, the crowd had frozen and this was now reality! Did they really want it? I looked hard at the dog, was it maybe as lost as I was? Its collar was black leather, studded, a huge collar. The owner had it on a chain; he was smiling, but nervously. All of them had heard about me, so it was time to act, I began to growl and jump up and down like a madman. I was pumping myself up for the charge. It was at that time I felt a rush of adrenaline; my memories of hell were now in front of me.

This fucking dog was everything bad that had ever stepped on my face and it was time to explode my hate. I believe I lost it at this point. I was shouting obscenities at a crazy bewildered dog. It was I foaming at the mouth; I had the rabies.

I don't think the dog knew what it or where it was, I just broke into a run as it went past the ropes. I heard it growl and I heard it no more, I had it all to do! It's really hard to describe the rest as it happened so fast, although it felt like hours. I remember hitting it full on the nose and somehow I got on top and wrapped my legs around its midsection and I squeezed hard. I got its neck and held on tight, its legs were kicking out at me, its head was moving and teeth snapping and snarling coming from its mouth.

I nutted it a few times, but it was like nuttting a wall. I had to get a go at its eyes or mouth, it's never easy to decide in a split second to decide what's to be. I couldn't stay in this position and to let it go would be in its favour.

I kept one arm on its neck and jabbed into its eye, my finger went right in, I kept stabbing its eye with my fingers, two of them stiff. The noise it made sickened me, I then punched into its mouth and kept pushing my fist down its throat, it was at this point that I knew I'd won. It took ages to end its agony, but it was inevitable, I had pulled out a lot of filth, blood and gore from inside of its body. I was covered in filth, stinking filth, slime and blood and bits of all sorts. I hardly had a mark on me, but mentally I was wrecked. I felt a terrible sadness in what I'd done, not so much for the dog, but in how low I'd dropped. The dog, you see, had been bred for this job, the humans around the ring were the ones who were really the animals in this part of my life. As I looked around I may as well have been back in the asylum – they all looked mad. Each one of them had features that were exaggerated by my heightened awareness.

I'm a man of strong morals and didn't like what I'd done nor did I like any of the mugs that had come to watch it, we were all animals – worse than the dog. It was all on video. I've never seen the video nor do I ever wish to see it. It's a part of my journey I'm not happy with and I've always tried to make amends. I believe the dog froze, another time or place he would've taken me to bits. You may ask, would I do it again, could I do it again? Some would say it's not in me, but I say again, that if I needed to eat, if I were on the floor it would be a choice of crime or that. I may have to take it on, although I love animals and it makes me a hypocrite, but I'll not beg or take another man's length and that's how life is.

The dog's name was Satan, it was said maybe the dog was doped, so if it was then it was news to me. The rumours will go on for years to come, but all of those that were there will remember it for all time as it was exciting, it was a challenge, it was pure madness and it was part of my journey and my mission is madness all the way. Maybe now you can understand how why I didn't get that many fights, not many turned up. I was no 'Ali' but I fought with my heart. But the fact is I loved it, unless my light was blown out how could I lose as pain has no effect on me. Obviously now I'm older I'm slower and life creeps up on us all plus I still face more years, many more years inside, but I can still see more fights up ahead of me when I'm 50+. Even to lose is no shame as long as you give it your best shot. Again I stress I needed to eat and I love to train and eat, but you can't do it on fresh air.

I was asked if I'd fight a lion? I gave it some thought and said 'Yes if I can have an axe', so if any guy wants to promote it then I'm up for it when I'm out, but I'd want a nice pay-day out of it and the video rights. Well...I'm not that fucking mad am I? A man's gotta think of his pension. I could lose a leg, arm or worse – hell I may get my bollocks ripped off. The lion's of Longleat would suit me down to the ground, in fact the Marquis of Bath was contacted on my behalf about the matter some while ago as a guy was interested in promoting it, that was 'til my release date was put back a bit by my hostage taking shenanigans. I don't know if the Earl of Bath was up for it, but it would sure beat watching the Queen's speech on Christmas day, wouldn't it, anyway I'm up for it when I'm out. I've already got the heart of a lion in me or so a lot of people have said. It would be the ultimate test!

Christmas was strange. I spent it with Jack and his sisters, but I felt bad because Jellybaby wasn't around. She'd decided to spend Christmas with the motorbiker and I was getting sick of being left out for some longhaired greaseball.

I was in the Moakes pub to drink my sorrows away and I met an old school pal from twenty years before. I couldn't believe what had happened since I'd last seen him – at 36 he looked more like 56! He depressed me even further, all he wanted to talk about was his HP and mortgage so I went for a walk round the estate, quietly hoping some gang of yobs would attack me, as I needed a good punch up.

Outside the local old peoples' rest home I stopped and looked through the window. Old folk just sitting there...grey and slow...fragile people with only their memories to keep them company. Fuck it! I had to get a grip on myself. I was feeling sorry for myself now! When Boxing Day came I went for a long run. It felt as if I was running away from my mind although at times it seemed like my mind was running away from me!

Uncle Jack took me to a lovely family to enjoy some nice company. There was a little girl - she was blind! She was beautiful, hair, face and smile – like looking at an angel. I held her head and touched her face and she smiled. This little girl had no eyes, I felt so sad, choked up! I've never forgot her, never, I never will! She was beautiful, only a kid of about six or seven years old. I felt how cruel the world is. I never lost sight of that angel's face and whenever my world crumbled in and I lost my way I thought of that kid. My life, my journey had been peanuts compared to her's. She was the hero.

The day before the New Year's Eve I felt at rock bottom. I was alone and broke and if there was one thing I needed right then it was cash. Not a lot –I'm not talking about millions of pounds here. I didn't need to go and do some Brinks type of robbery. Just enough to get me a stake together so as I could start something off. I didn't want a Ferrari or a desert island and oysters lifestyle, but a man does have to eat. I would have liked to been able to visit mum and dad with a few notes in my pocket, but not like this.

The fight had broken my dreams and while I'll always fight to live I'll never ever beg to live. If I could've got a boxing licence I'd have gone pro, but my age and with my past I stood no chance. My life was fucked.

If it had of been summer time I'd have found a job on a building site but it wasn't summer it was winter! There was nothing doing anywhere. The dole gave me a giro, a poxy few quid. That was no good to a man who needed to sort himself out. I stood outside the jeweller's shop, hesitating for a second. There was no other way, no choice. I was desperate and I knew what I had to do.

As I steamed into the shop I pulled out the toy gun, the water pistol I'd bought back in London. There were two guys and one girl assistant and I quickly got them into the back office, on the floor. 'Move and I'll blow your fucking heads off!' If only they'd known it was a water pistol! The manager opened the safe but he was slow so I had to speed it up, 'Come on or I'll pull the trigger in three seconds, hurry it up!' I filled up the bag and grabbed some cash and I was away without anyone getting hurt. I ran so fast down Wellington Street that nothing nor nobody could've caught me. This time my training had paid off. I scored for about £1,500 worth of cash and goods, which on the face of it would work out at just over £200 per year for the prison sentence I was to receive for this stupid offence.

The little blind girl's face flashed before me as I ran. I've seen her face everyday ever since, I'll always see it, it's like telling me, 'Hey slow down Charlie, stop and think for a spell, don't waste your life how you are – look at me'. Eyes are so precious! We all take it for granted, but I feel blessed from that little girl. She taught me so much that Christmas of '87. It was like I was meant to see her and she was meant to smile at me...like a message.

As we left the little girl and her family Jack and I walked, I said to him: 'Hey, Jack! That was the best Christmas of my life, that little girl sort of cured me of the last fourteen years inside.' If I ever did see an angel it was that kid, she melted me, made me so tearful inside, she taught me what feelings are about. 'Cos a guy loses that entire thing in jails and asylums, yeah, what a feeling. What a hundred psychiatrists couldn't do for me a little girl could, thank you. The only people who don't deserve eyes are filthy paedophiles or scum like the Yorkshire Ripper. Why should a little girl be born blind and a guy like me be so violent and forever in a cage? It's just too crazy for words. Nobody has ever hit me like that angel did - since or after. It proved one thing for sure! I'm no psychopath 'cos I love more than I hate. Psychos don't feel or cry – I do.

Nine days later, on the 7th January 1988 I was out for a morning jog when I saw a geezer approaching from the opposite direction. He was jogging towards me at a slowish pace, a great big bloke. As he got up to me he said 'Morning', I replied: 'Morning' whereupon he hit me with a left hook to the chin and as I went off balance he grabbed me in a headlock. Old bill appeared from all over the shop and that was that – I was nicked!

I'd had 68 days of freedom. It was probably 67 more than a lot of people thought possible and certainly, without my mum and dad, I would never have lasted one day. I was gutted; my world had fallen apart.

I gave the usual alibi of saying I was with a girlfriend, but it didn't work as the jewellery shop manager picked me out of an ID (Identity) parade. Another thing that got me caught was by chance the police stumbled across a photograph I had lying round. It was a one I had taken in a photo booth. I was holding a gun to my head, I'd written a message on the back of it: *Guns kill. So does love.* Boy, was I a clever fucker!

By staying out as long as I did I felt I'd achieved something and I'd met a lot of people who loved me for what I was. But as time would tell I'd neglected the one I loved the most and that was my greatest regret. I'd been so blind and if only I'd seen what I should've seen then I wouldn't be sitting in this cell today. But I've to put it down to fate. The next great test had begun.

The liquid cosh is designed to make you into a zombie, an automaton that's easily controlled. To take someone's liberty in exchange for a crime they've committed is one thing, but to deliberately turn them into a cabbage is surely worse, is it not? All of the doctors within prisons and establishments who've pumped drugs into my body, against my will, will one day have to answer for all what they've done. Whether that's for what they've done to me or to someone else it'll be brought to light. Hitler's concentration camps were used to experiment on those locked up within them; Saddam 'Insane', as I call him, was going to release germs into the air and he vandalised oil refineries during the Gulf War and then a guy called Molosovec carries out ethnic cleansing in Kosovo. What have they all got in common, they're all criminals so what difference is there between them and some, not all, of the doctors that'd forced drugs into my body?

The doctors not only let it happen to me, but they aided and abetted the staff in the special hospitals, hospital wings of prisons, in the Special Units (Control Units), and other parts of the evil British Penal System. No one tells you why you've got to take theses drugs, just that you've gotta take them or you'll be forcibly injected. If you ask any questions then you're accused of 'not co-operating' and risk further punishment.

My next move was to Park Lane Special Hospital, which is far less like a prison and where the screws/nurses treat me like a human being. Nothing has been accomplished by the treatment

I've endured. When I look back over the years they've all been wasted years. Doctors, trained people, who are supposed to understand and care for people, not tread them into the ground or slam a door into their face; only opening it to feed them, slop them out, and administer more drugs – it's a disgrace. They become job blind by it all and it's a case of them treating me with contempt. All what's been done to me has went unpunished, surely everything that I've claimed over the last 26 years can't all be lies and malicious, can they?

Prison is prison and can be accepted as such, but how can they tell you a hospital is a hospital when it's so obviously a prison where your clothing, your belongings and your cell are searched. Where you're locked up indefinitely in a cell 12' x 7' with bars on the windows? Okay, I'm not saying that they've got to be four star hotels with bowling greens and the like, but if you're accepted as a National Health Service patient then, surely, a little compassion is warranted?

Nurses in screws' uniforms with screws' mentality with prison keys dangling from a chain at the waist in time honoured screw fashion. I'm going to tell you something that not a lot of people know and that's when a screw gets to have served a certain length of time he was awarded extra links to his chain. So when you seen a screw with a long chain you knew he'd been serving for a good few years and he'd be more laid back than his younger colleagues. It doesn't apply to the screws of today, but it was one way of telling how long a screw had put in.

I've been to the hardest prisons in Britain, Risley (remand) to Hull, to Parkhurst, to Wandsworth, to Armley, to Wandsworth again! Walton to Wakefield, to Parkhurst again! Hull '75 for the riot! Parkhurst again – F2- Rampton to Broadmoor. I won't mention the others or the times I've been ghosted in solitary down the block and had visits cancelled after accumulating them for months. You're allowed (long term only) to accumulate visits and request to be transferred to a prison nearer home to take them. Your family can travel from miles away only to be told at the gatehouse that you've been shipped out. That's how it was for me – from pillar to post.

I'll only say jail was a picnic compared to what I got at Broadmoor. There I was entitled to nothing; everything can be taken away from you. At Rampton I went for eleven months with no exercise, no fresh air at all, locked in a cell for 24 hours a day and twelve of those hours I was not allowed a water container or a piss pot! NOTHING! Nothing to read, you have nothing. Have you ever lost the use of something essential for even a few minutes? The electric's gone off, the water's turned off or a light bulb's blown. It's no doubt been a pain in the arse for you. I've been deprived of a lot more than that for 26 years and at times I've only had a blank wall for company. No bell to ring, if they don't come in time with the pot, the floor gets it. I couldn't treat a dog this way.

The inmates are supposed to be ill, that's why they're in hospital, but they have to scrub floors and call the staff 'sir'. This is part of the psychiatric treatment? It's no less than the Victorian Workhouses in which the mad were put into. Nothing's changed, stop kidding yourselves that we're a modern day society with the best this and that in the world, it ain't so – not anymore.

They call the Japanese and the Eastern Block countries for having poor human rights when it comes to penal servitude, that's bollocks 'cos they want to start looking into the state of the places I've been to, I mean really look at them. These visiting groups that go around checking that none of the things go on that I've told you about are in and out in an hour, of course they aren't going to see what goes on when they've had to make a fucking appointment weeks before! Rampton 'Special Hospital' is run on one thing – FEAR!

I'm sticking to the subject of drug abuse for now. I could write so much about each stinking hell holes I've been in, but that will be covered in the future as there's just not enough space in ten of these books to get everything in I want to try to cover. A lot of people say 'Bring back hanging.' Well some guys would welcome this to end their torture and I'm sure if euthanasia was available then they'd be queuing up in these places except we'd get some judge saying that it was in their best interests that they should remain alive – well I can tell you it's a living fucking hell.

You can't win with these judges. I've just heard that a 15-year-old girl didn't want to have a heart and lung transplant that was needed in order to keep her alive. A high Court judge ruled that she must have the operation, even though it's against her will. In contrast to that we've got the parents of a five year old boy who've just lost their High Court case to have special treatment, that was refused, on the NHS to save his life, it just doesn't make fucking sense, does it. Over £5 billion spent on the peacekeeping mission in Kosovo yet no money in this country to save a little boy's life? What's the world coming to? Who's the minister for health?

I'm a diagnosed psychopath based on a snap decision by an overpaid, under trained doctor; the label must stick with me for the rest of my life. I've never killed anyone and I'm no more a psychopath than Hitler was a saint. No doubt these goons will read something into me mentioning 'Hitler' a few times, it's just that he's the worst example I can think of, but then again they'll say that was the first thing I thought of so it must mean something, yeah, sod all. I've got feelings, I love life, and I don't try to deny that I've been violent occasionally. If someone pulls a dirty stroke on me I don't run telling tales on them, not if it's one of my own. I would die before I would grass them up. I don't enjoy putting my fist in their mouth or using a weapon; I don't do it for fun.

I can make allowances for sick people, but in normal situations I can't do that as people are supposed to be normal in other environments, so what should I do, let them walk all over me? Broadmoor and Rampton will always be prisons to me, not hospitals. The drugs were for control, not treatment. My advice to anybody that gets caught up in this sort of thing is to fight it, believe in yourself and I can only hope that they would pull through and get off the drugs – 'cos they didn't work for me. Do you know of anyone that's been cured of mental illness, 'cos I don't. All these fancy named doctors getting paid for curing nobody and then when one of them real nutters who's on some sort of prescribed drug kills someone they blame the drugs! No one's been cured and no one's ever going to be cured from severe mental illness – which's a fact. Not one of them doctors can tell you that they've ever cured anyone of us, can they? Ask them!

I needed a break and wanted to get to a new jail, but I was told that none of them wanted me! It looked like I'd have to spend years on my own.

Prison breeds hate in a man. You can't walk away and expect everyday to be the same. You live an unnatural life in a violent environment. Some guys you despise, who you would never have to meet outside. Grasses, sex offenders, child killers – all the scum of the earth.

I'm a solitary survivor and if I had a little island or lived in a jungle then I'd be overjoyed. I'm nothing special, I'm nobody but I'm a true survivor. Years and years I've been alone. Solitary survival isn't one of those subjects you're going to get someone answering questions on in the next 'Mastermind' challenge, but if they did and I was allowed out for it you can bet all your housekeeping money on me to win.

You must go within yourself and search for the key. You may lose your mind – I did! But you must keep on searching. I'm still searching and I'm still dreaming. My dreams keep me free, I found the key once – I'll find it again. So will you, that's only if you want to. Nobody can find it but us. Until you find it, fight on and believe in yourself. Have faith in yourself. Learn to love yourself. Learn to like yourself and remember one thing and that's 'you're never alone'. Your best friend can be your shadow or the cockroach that crawls along your body in the darkness or the noises in the night. A cricket, a mouse, a rat, a door, footsteps, your own heartbeat – you're never alone. Silence is a switch in your mind. Like a yogi, switch off. There's a lot to do. I would often fill a sock with toilet paper, tie a knot and throw it against the wall. 'It bounces back'. I must have slung it a billion times. Count the bricks in the cell, I'd always come up with a different number no matter how many times I counted them.

What they try to do is to take away anything that you've got. I heard a story from a mate of mine, Joe Pyle, he went on to say how this guy in solitary had nothing, nothing at all except for this button that fell off a screws jacket. When he was banged up in his cell he would tinker around with this button and he became so good at being able to do things with it that it helped him pass his time. He would put it on his thumb and flick it up against the wall, he knew where it would ping off from and he'd catch it safely in his outstretched hand, flies, gnats nothing was safe, that's how good of a shot he'd become, but one day they caught him. The button was taken off him and his time became hard to do once again.

That's what they do though, the minute they think you've got something to pass your time away, bang, crash, wallop they destroy it. That's what happened to me at Whitemoor after I was sent their from Hull after taking my latest hostage there in February '99. I was shipped out from there and then and what did that lot at Whitemoor go and do, they deprived me of everything, completely everything. My art was taken away from me because I wasn't allowed any materials at all, not even a pencil or a rubber. I wasn't even allowed to send poems out. Okay I've got to face the punishment from the court for that hostage taking incident, more about that incident and all my other hostage taking incidents later on though.

They had me by the short and curlys because I'm a born again cartoonist and I'm the poet from hell on a mission of madness laughing all the way to the crematorium. So I went on hunger strike even though I was in a bad state physically as I'd hurt myself whilst on my mission of madness at Hull. I needed treatment for some of my injuries; I was denied treatment that I considered needed so it was all the more worse for me when they got me at my weak spot. I was prepared to die for my cause!

People had written letters to everyone from the Home Secretary to NACRO complaining about my treatment, not one of those places helped or took any notice so when these prison trusts and other voluntary bodies offer help all what I can say is they're a waste of space. The only organisations that are any good are the ones run by individuals like 'The Road to Justice' and 'Action Against Injustice'. My friend, Jan Lamb, ran 'The Road to Justice' although sadly it's shutdown due to lack of funds at present. Jan wrote to Jack Straw (current Home Secretary in the UK) on my behalf, but it was like pissing against the wind. My art was withheld and in a letter from Holly McLaren (Head of Residential at Whitemoor at Whitemoor) to a publisher she wrote: *'At Whitemoor a prisoner on the basic incentive level on segregation is not permitted art materials'.* She went on to write: *'Your interpretation of Human Rights Legislation and your accompanying advice is noted'.*

I was on hunger strike for 41 days before people writing in to me gave me hope and my solicitor, Martin Oldham, told me I'd be moving to Woodhill. Jesus went 40 days, but I bet he had a little help from the odd rabbit or two. Maybe I shouldn't have said that as I might get a hit put on me by the church just like Salman Rushdie, the author, has a one on him because of his book being considered blasphemic to another religion. I've a lot of respect for all religions no matter what they claim, but I know my hunger strike was hell so God only knows what Jesus' hell was like out in that hot desert. No one's got a right to stop you writing poems or drawing pictures, no one, yet they did it to me; that's how petty they were and that's what they're like.

I know of another man, Panda Anderson, he used to do step up's on a chair he had in his solitary cell. Then one day they took it away from him just so as he would have it harder in there, but he was tough and overcame it just like I've been able to do

I spend a lot of time training 'cos I never know when I'm going to need that explosive power. I've got to be ready anytime for anything, that's how the system's got me, they trained me over the years to be ready for the unexpected and I've become pretty good at responding to the way they think they can just push me about. 'Cos see the way them screws used to have a link added to their chains for so many years service, well...I get to beat them all and that for one gives me the edge over anyone thinking they can domineer me – my chain would be massive, if I had one.

I only respond to kindness and empowerment. Those stupid psychiatrists can examine my artwork all day long looking for answers. It makes a change from me looking at their squiggles of ink and coming up with an answer! There are no answers in my artwork for them. Okay they'll see that I'm the centre of attention at times, and why's that? 'Cos that's the only fucking person the system's let me really alone with over the years.

I do all sorts of training and then there's the repetitive stuff like push-ups, squats, sit-ups, running on the spot and plenty more. I sweat out my tension and it makes me fell better, at times, although my art's took over some of that and that's how the prison governor at Whitemoor tried to control me, more of that later. The average cell is twelve feet long by eight feet wide. Most of my days are spent walking up and down like a tiger in a cage. Doesn't that make you sad to see such a beautiful animal caged? I use that time as a switch off and I can imagine I'm in a field or walking through a beautiful meadow.

Letter writing is good too and therapeutic in a way. A release valve and a sure way of releasing anxieties. I'm not afraid to write how I feel. My imagination gets plenty of use. Some things though are personal and best kept secret no matter who I write to.

Reading has been a way of passing time and an obvious way, but in order to be able to do that you've got to have a book and at times I've been denied this most basic of human rights. A good book is one of the best time-killers in any prison condition. I treat each page with respect and go into a new chapter with enthusiasm; I can become part of the book.

On occasions screws at Rampton would attempt to frighten me by saying to one another ' Let's inject the bastard with an air bubble – or some petrol'. I got so frightened that I got someone to find out about the air bubble technique. It was thought that an air bubble would cause a seizure by stopping your heart. True, but the bubble would have to be a fucking big one, so I got over that worry, but not over the threat of being injected with petrol!

I look back on these hell times as being totally unnecessary. I'd get so confused and actually think that I was at home, I've even fell out of bed and slept all night in a pool of piss. I even went several years without being able to masturbate as I lost all sexual feelings, no matter what I couldn't get a hard on. The drug I was on at that time just switched my libido (sex drive) off. I had the life of a cabbage; I ate, slept and shit. No TV, no newspapers, no company, no books, I was forever tired.

My weight shot up and I would get out of breath just walking from my cell to the recess, I dribbled a lot, I trembled a lot and I dreamed a lot. I complained everyday, 'Get me off these drugs, I'm not mad, I don't need drugs!' But the more I complained the less they listened.

Since 1984 I've never had the 'liquid cosh'. Even though I'm still liable to become violent at times. When I was fully drugged up I soon began to accept that part of my life although I did fight it everyday. Soon you begin to accept what your life is. No matter who or what you are in time it just becomes part of your life. I suppose it's just like losing a limb or an eye – you get used to the disability. Well I got used to the liquid cosh. It's crazy to have to look back on those barbaric years. I've still taken hostages and regularly chin those that take liberties, so not a lot's changed, though I admit I'm getting older.

There are still times I get put into the strip cells, bent-up and restrained in the body belt. I suffered a terrible beating at the scrubs just after my father died; more about that in another chapter though, but there is no beating like the Liquid Cosh. There is no pain like it, there is no description for it – only torture. I won't say I beat those hell bent years, no man I know could beat those drugs! Face facts, a wild elephant gets shot with a tranquilliser, it falls and it sleeps. A man only needs a fraction to what the elephant needs to cosh him out. I've literally had gallons of those drugs pass through my heart and shoot up my brain. I've known many die both in Broadmoor and Rampton. Some young, some old, but 99% were all on drugs – 'none' had an option. In other words ' We the many led by the few...' and so on.

Today, I believe, they have an option. I don't think they're forced upon them – if so that's good. BUT, I'M WILLING TO BET SOME ARE STILL FORCIBLY INJECTED! Whatever, I can only thank God that I survived it. But what does make me puke, I don't smoke, I don't drink, I don't take any drugs, I always keep myself clean, and the bastards almost killed me with something I'm totally against. How can this be legal? Believe me now, it was illegal, but they got away with it for too long. We were the guinea pigs, we were the experiments – Holocaust relived. There was never no justification for it, how can there be? How can somebody inject a drug into another's body without their consent? How can somebody slip a drug into another's food without consent? Whether he or she's a dangerous criminal or a raving mad person, who has got the right to drug a man/woman with a liquid cosh applied by cold surgical steel into his/her body? If I done that outside then I'd be sentenced to 10 years if not life.

Look at these young 'uns who give their pal an 'E' (Ecstasy) tablet and the effects eventually kill the kid! The person who gave the drug is brought before a court for manslaughter. On that basis I indict the Home Office and the National Health Service of the United Kingdom for what had taken place. Just as ex-prisoners of war (POW) held in Japan have argued their case over the years for the atrocities carried out against them by their Japanese captors in the second World War I too will fight on against the acts carried out on me that I believe contravene all sorts of codes.

What about those warlords and dictators we here about? They are sought for War Crimes and have to be brought to book. Some of them have done less to their prisoners than the British Government has done against me. The Geneva Convention stops this sort of thing from going on in times of war, well I had atrocities carried out against me in times of peace. The Court of Human Rights in Strasbourg has set out certain rules that the UK and a number of other countries must follow, this country has failed several of those covenants!

I've been given a label and on it are written the words '*THE MOST VIOLENT MAN INSIDE PRISON*'. It's taken a quarter of a century for this to be stamped on my file. It's courtesy of a multiple lot of events that have given me this accolade.

ACCEPTANCE SPEECH FOR THE LABEL

My Lords, Ladies and Gentlemen, I'm so proud to accept this label. May I thank the prison authorities for all of their help in making this possible, oh and not forgetting Mr Home Secretary, Mr John Golds (Prison Service), the Minister for Prisons and the Health Secretary, thank you!'

Just assuming that the above was held on an annual basis then I reckon I'd win it hands down every year. I'm King of the Roofs, Master of Sieges, Supreme Lord of Cuttings and stabbings, Darth Vader of Destruction, Stylist of Attempted Murders and Guv'nor of Isolation. Who can beat that? There will not ever be another me in the system, if so it would take them 25 years to catch up to me. I hope what I've said has disgusted you all and made you ashamed of what I've become. A former hod carrier who fucked up his life and then was trained up to become what he is today – a total 100% thoroughbred institutionalised ballistic cheap thrill merchant for the world to laugh at! Remember this and remember it well, you all have to accept some responsibility for what I've become, therefore I'm owed some respect and peace – give it to me.

I'm not proud of this label, but I'm not ashamed of it either. Why should I be proud and why should I be ashamed? I'm just me, I don't see myself as violent and the label doesn't change who or what I am. The label doesn't make me worse; I'm just me. I'm a hostage of my own past. I'll probably have to die with this label; this is a fact of life. I know I've dug a big hole for myself, you don't have to tell me that 'cos I already know. I'm now trapped within the mythical character I've been branded.

I'm a threat to the system, a threat to Good Order and Discipline (G.O.A.D.), no prison governor trusts me, why should they, but an even bigger question is why should I trust them? I'm the man who can switch personalities within a split second. I can talk to a governor one minute and then take him hostage the next. I've become what I am over many years of madness.

Violence breeds violence. Once you become a part of violence it eats away into your body, like a cancer – it destroys all in its path!

You eat it, you sleep it, shit it and drink it. Every second of every day is violence. Every sound means someone could be on his way to commit an act of violence against me. A faint jangle of keys in the night awakens me to be ready for anything, I'm on guard, my heartbeat slows down so I can contemplate my next move and then it jolts into turbo boost ready for action. I've been moved so many times from one prison to another in the early hours of the morning so much that they've conditioned me to be this way, just like one of Pavlov's dogs I salivate at the merest ring of a bell! It makes you ill, it takes you over and it rules every thought!

You pick up a pen to write a letter, you stop and feel the pen, you look at the pen's nib and picture it embedded into someone's eye or you dream of stabbing it into somebody's ear. How come? Because the system I've been in has shown me all of this and more, things that the average and above average man couldn't contemplate for even one minute. Lord Longford, my pal, might be able to understand because he's had years and years of visiting prisoners. People think he's only ever visited the Moor's Murderess, Myra Hindley – bollocks. Frank has been visiting prisoners for over fifty years and visits many more than just that slag. Maybe, just maybe he can understand what I'm going through. All of you out there might slag him off for one reason and one reason only, but if only you knew half or quarter of what he does for other cons then your opinion would soon change.

You read a book – violence, you listen to a play on radio – violence, you talk to a fellow con – violence and you stroll around the prison yard thinking of violence. Violence is within, it becomes survival and it becomes a way of life. A con falls to the ground with knife wounds, he's dying. A crowd of cons will step over him not seeing; it's like he's not there. A man is dying before our eyes and we switch off, it's a way of life, it's just a death and we all gotta die. Some will stamp on his face and laugh, inside is another world, you've gotta switch off, you've no choice. The con in the next cell tears up his sheet and hangs himself, another breaks up his razor and cuts his own throat and another takes an overdose, it's one way out, but to survive you must be violent or act violent - dog eat dog!

I entered jail a young man of 21 years; my crime as you know was armed robbery. I wasn't so bad nor was I out of control, I've never shot anybody and I never killed anybody, but now almost three decades later I could put a gun into a man's face and blow his head clean off. Not because I hate him, but it's for the sake of it. There's a few billion faces in this world, what difference is a few headless ones gonna make? I could walk into a public lavatory for a slash, if a dirty old man walked in and upset me I could blow him away and go away and enjoy some fish and chips. I wouldn't even think about it. That's how cold and senseless prison life can turn a man into.

I hit a guy so hard in jail that I broke my hand, so I thought about it and thought why should I break my hand again 'I'll use a weapon.' Since that day I've used mop buckets, PP9 batteries, sticks, razors, you name it I've used it. I once cut a man for looking at me. This is how it gets to you. If he looked he may well have been weighing me up; maybe he was even plotting to cut me? I've survived attacks, it's not all been my way, but that's life – you win some and you also lose some.

I once hit a governor for talking to another con I thought the conversation was about me. I once took a governor hostage over a ¼ pound of mushrooms; I beat him up. It cost me an extra seven years, a busted jaw and a steel cage, but I'm not crying. Seven's been a lucky number for me as most of my sentences have been seven stretches! My life's been a struggle!

My world's been violence, would I change it, no! Have I regrets, no! I'm Britain's most violent man and it's stuck with me. They've created me and now they don't know what to do with me. Do they drop me in to that acid bath or what? The label should never have been stamped on me. I'll explain why. It's irrelevant if I am or not what they describe, but what they've done, I mean the Home Office, they've fed the press with this label. This label can only grow. Wherever I go I'm now a victim. Young cons look at me and say 'He don't look so tough'. Some maybe even want to fight me, it's like a gunslinger. He comes into town to kill their best, so he becomes the best. He stays the number one 'til another comes to kill him. Well that's how jail's become for me. Charles Bronson arrives, the cons are wary and I've got to watch my back. It's not paranoia it's just pure fact, I know how some of these screws work. I'm the man with the label, I'm the man to beat, beat me and you become me. On top of the cons I've also got the jailers. Some treat me with respect, some despise me, some will give me some trust and some won't give me an inch. It can be a very wearing and trying time, on top of the screws I've got the governors and nine out of ten of them hate me. They won't come near me and why should they? I've attacked too many of them for them to like me.

Violence within, it's a terrible way to live, I don't recommend it at all, it's forever on alert to be prepared, but it's a way of life I've known for over half my life. I'm probably messed up for all time, as I could never act this way outside, it's totally unacceptable. I suppose it's much like the Vietnam veterans, they all needed counselling you can't expect a man to fight a war and then come home as if nothing's changed. You can't expect a man to live with so much horror and not get some kind of psychological scars. Prison culture's no different than a war zone, it's unnatural and it's inhumane. Obviously over the years that I've been inside it's become more humane and it's easier, better conditions and more to do, it don't have to be hard, but that's for the normal con, for me it's actually become worse. When a label sticks nothing changes, maybe I'm mad but if I am then so is the system. I rest my case.

Singing – when low and depressed 'sing', sing loud, it's a great tension reliever and empties the frustration. It clears my head and I sing what I like best, my favourite hymn is 'Onward Christian Soldiers' although I know its never been in the charts or ever likely to be its one of those songs you blast away, even if a bad singer. One of my favourite songs when I went to a few night-clubs when I was out is called 'I'm alright now' – appropriate!

Food – prison food is stodgy, it's basically boiled stuff such as stews and curries. I've gone weeks if not months without chewing a good piece of meat. I've learned a great way of eating prison swill and enjoying it, even porridge! As you eat it imagine it to be something else – battered fish, pretend every mouthful is salmon, sausage is steak, carrots are strawberries and so on. Yes it's crazy but it works.

Dreams – they keep you sane. If you can't dream then your mind's not at rest as it needs to dream in order to solve problems, not a deep sleep, but a light sleep is what's needed to get that Rapid Eye Movement (REM). Dreams take me away from all of this and when I awake reality hits me like a nightmare!

Exercise Yard – always go out for your one hour's exercise as walking is free, you don't need a fancy health club to do this sort of activity and here in prison Her Majesty hasn't seen fit to supply me with a sauna or a spa. Even though I walk around in a cage I can switch off. The sky – breeze – birds – planes, it's all magic.

Suicidal thoughts - we all think of them, but only a few ever do it. Bitter people die unhappy, in or out of jail we all experience the bad times. The saddest thing of all is when someone young takes their life while in prison. Armley jail saw three young prisoners (YP's) take their own lives by hanging all within the space of five months, from May to October 1988 and then a further two hangings in the beginning of 1989, both were YP's. That creases me up inside, what pain were they going through, but here is neither the time nor the place to go into such things, as the family of those young victims will still be grieving. It's often said that my victims will still be suffering and their families will also be suffering. Why don't the authorities consider the families of these poor YP's?

Someone should have to answer to this disastrous loss of human life. So young and all over what and why? I wished some bastard would tell me. This book may stop somebody from taking their life; maybe these five young lads were under pressure, maybe being bullied, threatened or terrorised.

I've been to Armley; it's run with an Iron Fist. Some screws put a pair of steel capped boots on and feel they're entitled to kick the shit out of you. I felt their boots in 1985 so I write from the painful truth – Armley is a hellhole and for a young lad it's probably terrifying, so let's get straight to the point.

Survival – it don't matter how tough you are, how big you are or how strong. You can't ever survive too many beatings or so much bad treatment, we all have a breaking point, it's for you to realise enough is enough. Pen on paper is a good way to win rather than poking it into someone's eye.

But if you find yourself being dragged down to the strong box, out comes the body belt and in come the fists and boots, cover up best you can. Don't try and fight back against so many, remember faces, shout out names, your arms will be bent up, your wrists will be bent up, your ankles and toes will be bent up, you'll feel pain and to struggle would be more pain. Once they leave you strapped up try to remember times, names, faces, words said and cons who saw. Memorise it all as soon as you're out of the box get a special letter off to your solicitor and record it. Don't be afraid, as once the letter goes off you'll be treated okay.

A lot of screws are against the brutality, remember it's only the minority who are bad. All cons aren't labelled 'rapists' or 'grasses' are they, neither are all screws dogs. Some are simply there to earn a living and always remember this; these deaths can be stopped just as soon as the bullying is stopped.

The forces (Army, Navy and Airforce) is much the same, a weak minded lad who isn't used to being shouted at or being treated as harsh would feel lost, bewildered, emotionally disturbed and suicidal and the big mouthy sergeant major knows this. You've got to see it all through a sense of humour. If it gets too heavy, too much to cope with then there's only one way to escape it – chin the screw and get carried away. After the bent arms and legs and kicking the bully screw will think twice. At least you got the satisfaction in chinning the mug, you'll feel better, maybe some time after but I assure you, you will feel good.

Suicide is the last resort, it's the ultimate, it's fear, bravery, stupidity and insanity. Who the fuck knows what causes it, who the fuck is anyone to answer it, but it breaks hearts. These five young lads must have caused so much pain to their respective families and this was only from one jail. There are dozens of deaths every year, some very suspicious ones. I believe if we could be more understanding of people, care more for each other's ways, look out for signs of depression, anxieties and nervous disorders, pull them guys and girls aside and assure them that they are not all alone. A bully is a weak person and only looks for those that he or she can domineer without any resistance.

Others care, don't be afraid, we could stop 99% of cell deaths, sure if somebody decides enough is enough then nobody can help, but these five young lads couldn't have been at the point of believing life was all wiped out. They were victims of fear; it's sad but true we all fear something or somebody. I once feared cockroaches, I couldn't sleep thinking of them, as in the block they're all over, infested with them. Now I block up my ears and they crawl over my nakedness, as I accept them as part of this life. You've all gotta love yourselves, believe in what you are and in what you do. A rope or razor blade is only a double blow for your loved ones, be happy, think happy, act happy and it's bound to end up happy, only old people should die, not young ones.

Here's a right laugh for you, while I remember it. I was in Hull in 1975 and I was getting a little bit pissed off. I took one of my rages, it wasn't without good cause, as later on the whole prison erupted and the Hull Prison Riot happened. I was going for breakfast and I'd had enough. 'Fuck your prison, fuck you! I'm not having this bollocks, cop for this!' I slung my breakfast all over a screw's head and the little slab of butter we're given stuck to his hat where the badge was.

He wiped off the bacon and porridge from his jacket, but this little slab of butter stayed stuck to his hat! Even as I was escorted back to my cell this little slab of butter stayed on his hat. Laugh, I laughed so much I hurt my sides. He actually upset me, but I turned it all into a joke. Sure I lose time, sure I stay in the block, but silly bollocks is walking about with a slab of butter on his hat, even the other screws never told him, why? Well even they called him a prat behind his back; he certainly looked a mug that day.

Mad people are special beings, gifted – you can't buy it. I'm not talking about 'mugs'; lots try to act mad. You just wouldn't believe how many cons I've met in the asylum who try it on, they didn't fool me for one minute. I'm talking about 'MAD' as in 'mad' – the real McCoy! I'm mad, my madness is deep within, it's useless to ever treat it they way they've been doing it.

Only once did I ever come near to being brought out of it and that was at Belmarsh. The governor came to see me everyday and Dr Ghosh was called in to see me regularly, she's a lady and a half is Dr Ghosh. But fuck me, if I only didn't go and blow it all when I took them Iraqi air hijackers hostage, but more of that later on. I had my reasons for doing this, but that was the time I was nearly pulled back from beyond and do you know why? Because I was treat like a human being for once, since then though it's all been up hill.

Drugs, therapy and talk are all useless, unless you've got a caring person on the other end of them. When I was forcibly injected I could feel the hate being injected into me; it transferred from the person on the other end of the needle. Now give me a nice warm-hearted person doing that in a loving caring way and maybe you're beginning to see what I mean. What's the use of me talking away to anyone if they're mind has wandered onto something else, yeah, I can sense this straight away. I've only ever found a few genuine people that gave themselves to their job.

I'm happy as I am as long as I'm 99% under my own control. Okay, I accept that I've got to be kept behind closed doors, but give me someone who cares about me and I'll die for them, they could tell me to jump off a building and as long as I knew they cared for me I'd do it, I'd do it because I know they wouldn't tell me to do it if it could harm me – trust. But please God, be my witness, I'll die mad.

Flashbacks come to me, like when I was mopping a floor in Full Sutton prison. A governor comes walking towards me; he had a file of papers under his arm, a smile on his face, he had 20 maybe 30 paces to reach me. My brain raced, 'Look at this cunt, who does he think he is – flash fucker'.

Ten Paces!

'Whose is the file he's got?' 'Who's he smiling at?'

Five paces!

'Morning Charlie', he says.

One pace!

I picked up the mop bucket, which was full of dirty water. Whoosh! - All over him. It's madness every day with me; it's why I'm so unpredictable.

Another incident that flashes through my mind is an incident that happened in Parkhurst. I banged up (stayed in cell) this night feeling depressed, as I had problems with life outside and problems with life inside. There seemed no solution, I brood a lot, I get wound up and I explode. I got on my bell and a night screw comes to my Judas hole, 'What's the problem, Charlie?', he asks. I say, 'I want to come out!' He says, 'No way, it's night time and nobody gets unlocked except in an emergency'. 'This is an emergency! My pot's full of shit and I need another shit – open up', I say. He runs off to see security and they come over to unlock me, silly sods!

There's no shit in my pot; I only said it to get out. I walk with my pot over to the recess. At least ten screws watch me, I throw my pot over them and I smash a bottle I've got in my hand – they all run! I'm shouting at them, I start to smash the lights and I pull out the sinks and pipes. When I go into destructive mode there's no stopping me, I'm a steam train!

It's well after midnight, cons start banging on doors and shouting. I'm the only con out of his cell. I run riot on my own and I'm enjoying myself. The M.U.F.T.I. squad are on their way to sort me out – shields, helmets and batons. I'm alone, I'm always alone, but I'm a survivor. I end up even more alone in the box, trussed

119

up like a Christmas Turkey. The mad man's in the box again, which has been my whole adult life – in a box.

But the piss pot trick worked, which reminds me of a story about Androcles and the lion. Anyone heard of Androcles, he was the guy that was meant to be thrown to the lions in Roman times because he was a Christian, as that's what they did in them days.

The story goes that one-day Androcles was walking along and he came across a lion, the lion was limping badly and Androcles noticed that a very large thorn was in the lion's paw. Very bravely he approached the lion, calming it with soothing words as he approached. Amazingly the lion didn't attack him; Androcles pulled the thorn out of the big cat's paw.

The story goes that when Androcles was thrown into the arena in front of the crowds that had come to see the spectacle of Christians being fed to the lions that the very same lion Androcles had taken the thorn from his foot was the very same lion that faced him in the arena; they recognised each other.

Here though I take over the story and finish it off my way. The lion allows Androcles to approach him, at this the crowd become silent as they've never seen such a feat of bravery from a Christian, it becomes entertaining for them to watch as Androcles strokes the mane of the big cat. Just as the crowd start to cheer the Christian on the lion eats Androcles and the crowd go wild and love the action, baying for more.

So the lion gets set free to appease the Roman gods. Now the lion goes up to a thorn bush and pushes his paw into a big thorn and hides in the long grass. Soon he sees a Christian coming along and he goes into his routine of limping in front of the man. The man being a Christian believes that God will protect him from harm so he goes up to the lion and goes through the same routine as the previous Christian, cooing and talking gently and he goes to remove the thorn. Just then the lion says 'Sucker!' and eats the Christian and he finishes off by saying: 'I'm not going through all of that palaver in the arena again, fuck that for a lark'. And with that he goes up to the thorn bush and pushes his paw into another thorn! I'm not saying my piss pot routine was as clever as the lion's thorn routine, but the screw was just as much of a sucker as the Christian!

For those of you who don't know what a box is it's a cell within a cell, no windows and no furniture, it's got two doors to get in by.

It's used for the most violent of cons and is meant to cool them down, but it can also act as soundproof for when the bastards want to give you a going over. A lot of kickings are meted out in these places, but that's showbizz folks.

Every jail I've been to, I've been in the strong box. I've lay in these strong boxes naked for days and the only means of telling the time is by the meals – like a fucking battery hen! More folk complain about the rearing of battery hens and the conditions they live in, but I'm overlooked though because I'm just a sad case.

There's no sky, no conversation; it's you on your own. At times I'm fed through a flap in the door. The old jails like Wandsworth, Wormwood Scrubs, Leeds and Parkhurst are infested with cockroaches. I would watch them marching in; army like, in search of crumbs – poor bastards. I would leave some in the crack by the door and watch them for hours. The bulb's on for 24 hours a day, which in itself is torture, as they're messing up my body clock.

I've heard about this thing called 'Jet Lag' and how people's body clocks get fucked up by just being a few hours out of synch, imagine mine being constantly 24 hours out of synch? That's how they play it!

You get monitored constantly through the Judas hole, 'clink' and it opens, no sooner does this happen then 'clang' it gets slammed shut, fucking knob heads. Those cockroaches gave me something to occupy my mind with. You could say I'm a professor in cockroaches. I've had the things crawling all over me, waking up with them in my hair and on my face – fucking terrible.

I recall Wakefield's 'Special Cage', which houses 'special' cons. I should know, as I am one of those special cons. You don't know about this cage do you? I'm not surprised, as it's not something that the Home Office would be very proud of in the treatment of fellow human stakes.

'Monsters Mansion', that's Wakefield prison. Monsters like three times child killer Black is in there and I've heard Stone's on his way there soon. He's supposed to have attacked a young woman and her two daughters, only one survived – a little girl. They were just out walking along a country path when this guy attacks all three of them. Stone's going on about how it wasn't him, he's stood his ground even though he's been cut up at Frankland prison. Either he's as mad as I am or maybe there's something in it. I know monsters and how they go on and Stone isn't going on like a typical monster. You don't front it out amongst a lot of long termers in a northern prison like he did for no reason. Stone's got one problem though and that's as long as he's got this tag on him it makes him a target for every straight con and that includes me, yehaa, it's nonce season, yippee! None of the nonces though are put in the cage, they're all on a wing together; Wakefield's full of them.

Fuck China and these other places – listen to this. The outside door of the 'Special Cage' only opens at meal times when your meal is pushed in under the cage then it closes back up. The only other time it opens is for your one-hour's exercise. Then both doors open and you step out to no less than ten guards and a dog.

You are then searched with a metal detector and then marched the 20 yards out into the exercise yard, which is approx. 30 foot long by 15 feet wide. It's a steel cage monitored by electronic CCTV cameras. This is your one-hour of 'fresh air' – the other 23 hours will be behind two doors with stinking stale air. Whilst you're out on the yard the security will spin (search) your cage.

So what's life like in the infamous cage, as so few have ever got to see it apart from those imprisoned within its confines – only a handful have ever got inside of it. Let's see the Home Office hold their head up in response to this! Let me tell you first, it totally cuts you off from mainstream prison life, it's silence beyond comprehension, so silent that you think you're deaf! It'll be the nearest thing you can get to a coffin.

She's claustrophobic and at times she can squeeze your heart so tightly you feel it's the end! The light is unnatural and dull, the air is stale; full of carbon monoxide from the waste output of your own lungs, she's infested with cockroaches – it truly is the belly of the beast! The only visitors you get are rats, mice and vermin.

Spiders – I've never seen so many, but they're my friends. I love to watch spiders, I've watched them for months and I like to watch when a fly gets caught up in a web, then the spider leaps out and sedates the fly and goes on to gently wrap it in its silken web – so beautifully. Later on the spider will return, when she's hungry, and suck the liquidised blood and guts out of the fly. You can see the spider swell up and I swear I've actually seen a spider smile after a meal, I'm sure of it! I do love a predator, spiders are the most fearless of all predators, some of the females eat their mates after sex has taken place, typical ain't it. Still I know a woman that does that, but that's another story, now where was I.

Yeah, the cage! It's actually two cells smashed into one, she's got her own shower, toilet and basin in one section. This is all to make sure you don't have any excuse to ask to come out of her, as she's been designed for total isolation – so nobody gets to see you and you don't get to see anybody else.

There's a cardboard chair and table, but try sitting on a cardboard chair, even though it's compressed and strong it wobbles about under your weight, I'm 17 stone and even though these chairs are designed for big men, after long periods you get a bad back. I've even fell off it many times, as it buckles up beneath my weight.

She's got a window with two sets of steel bars and a steel cage covered with a sheet of plastic, probably made of kevlar. The sky cannot be seen, all what you can see is a wall plus the window's level with the ground outside, as you're in the cellar. So at night if you stand up and look out then you'll actually see cockroaches run by at eye-level.

The sewer is directly outside and you can smell it; as well as hear it running the raw sewage through its pipes. When there's a blockage you can imagine the stench as it serves the whole seg block. At times the shower has flooded when the sewer pipes have become blocked and it's stunk my cage out. They got the civvies (civilian maintenance workers) in to sort it out when I was out on the yard.

The cell's about 18 feet long by about 15 feet wide. One wall has a bulletproof observation window rather like the cell in the film 'Hannibal the Cannibal'. There's an office on the other side of this window, which has a curtain drawn across it on the office side so that they can peep anytime. There's also a Judas flap in the outer door for them to look in, but the cage door would not give them a good vision. So how does a man keep sane in such a medieval place, who else has experienced it? Well...there are two cages in Wakefield prison; they were built back in 1985 especially for con killers. (Killers of fellow inmates.) People like Bob Maudsley, Johnny Paton and big Fred Lowe.

I was one of the first to go into it in 1993 and I've been back three times, but what a lot of people don't realise is that Wakefield had 'Special Cages' back in the '70's. But they were only normal cells, no shower or basin. They just stuck a cage door inside the outer door, so they never had to open you up to feed you and you only got one shower a week so apart from your one hour's exercise you was in total isolation – I was also in those cages as well!

But back to the 'Daddy' of all the cages, would it sound insane if I said I loved it in there? Could you accept that or would you say I was mad or making it up big style for sensationalism? No, it's true – Charles Bronson loves the cage for the following reasons: Peace, solitude, self-imposed routine, I can entertain myself by doing my cartoons, solitary fitness routine, constant availability of shower, the screws respect me, peaceful sleep, singing's a pastime I can enjoy and it's like I'm not even in prison – I'm on my own island.

Hell, I even won a Koestler Award from inside that coffin. Everybody else has the help of teachers, classrooms and computers; all I've got is a hole in the earth. All I had was a pen and pencil and I won a Koestler Award. Some have said: 'what could Bronson achieve if he were not in a cage?' 'Probably fuck all', is what I'd say. Simply as my life would be more stressful on a normal landing with screws wanting to kick seven bells of shit out of me when things go wrong. I despise prison politics, drugs, I detest paedophiles or grasses, I hate fascist governors on a fast accelerated track to nowhere fast and silly screws. I dislike crowds and bullies. I just don't like prison life.

I can't see how cons can sit and watch TV or work in workshops sewing mailbags or living in dormitories or sharing cells or going on visits and making fools of themselves by kissing and cuddling beyond what's considered normal. I'd sooner be on my own, in my coffin. Hell, I don't even need a gym; I don't need none of it. I've got myself; I'm a lone survivor – like the spider. Fuck with me and I'll suck your brain out. Some will say, 'Bronson's mad, he's done too long, he's had too many blows to his crust (head). Well I'd say 'sure' but it's the system that created me – I'm only what they made me.

They isolate men like me as they fear me, then after 26 years or so they try to see if I can cope on normal wings and then I snap and grab a hostage or half kill someone for looking at me or for just coughing near to me. Cons respect me, as they know that 90% of violence I've dished out has been against the system apart from the Iraqis, but I don't like Iraqis so I make no excuses. I got into trouble for them rats; I should've snapped their necks and got life, as I'd have felt better for it. I'd love to blow Saddam Husein's face off his head; in fact I'd love to cut it off slowly.

Solitary – multiple years of this does no one any good. Imagine locking a dog up for years, no natural light or air and feeding it through a flap in the door of its cage. The RSPCA (Royal Society for Prevention of Cruelty to Animals – UK based) would prosecute you for cruelty.

So what should be done with me, is there a cure? The authorities should start by no more lying, no more false hope. I should be told how it is and what will be, then I should be given some peace and proper contact with the outside world. I once worked with some kids that came into the prison for remedial exercise, give me something like that to work on.

I once went into a shop in 1987 and stood there not knowing really what to say when I'd asked for a bottle of milk and the assistant said I should go and get it out of the fridge. No way was I going to go into that fridge; it was the shop assistant's job to bring it to me. That's how much things had changed since I'd last been out 14 years previously. I had no idea things had changed so much, it was the fault of the authorities for releasing me straight from cat 'A' back into the wild.

The other matter is that sex is freely available in prison, if you're homosexual. I'm not one of them. I've got nothing against them so long as they don't involve me in it. So when homosexuals can demand condoms from the prison authorities for their little games then surely I, as a heterosexual, should be allowed some contact with a female for sex. As it's discriminating against heterosexuals to allow gay relationships to blossom in prison. I might just get my lawyer onto it, as it must surely contravene some European directive?

Let me help kids, bring them in ten at a time, let me tell them what a shit life prison is. Let me tell them the truth, as I know I can help them, they'll listen to me. Out of every ten I know I could stop eight of them from ever turning to crime. I've got a big following of youngsters, how do I know? Because I've contributed some articles to 'Zimmer Magazine' and they've a big circulation on the south coast of England. Lots of clubbers read it and I've had some positive feedback from teenagers. I've also contributed to 'Fat Boss' magazine which is aimed at the young black community. I'm not jumping on the Stephen Lawrence case here because it doesn't matter to me what the colour is. Since I've been a black man for a day (details of that further on) I know what it feels like and that's no different to being a blue, green or white man.

All the police can do is help turn them into criminals and I'm not going to qualify that with long chapters on rehabilitation and preventative measures, but it's true. Allow me some trust, stop treating me like an animal, why can't I have some compassion, I'm not a stinking paedophile.

They fight to let Myra Hindley out, well I'd stuff her in the Wakefield 'Special Cage' where the bitch belongs. She's got everything I never had. Maybe if I got all her nice treatment I'd not be like I am today. Why don't people fight for me like they fight for her, what've I ever done to society that justifies such barbaric treatment. I'd never harm your kids - Hindley kills them! So why is her life so cushy? I'd wish my 26 years of hell on that evil bitch. All the brutality, all the loneliness, all the pain, all the emptiness and now I'm so fucked up I just don't feel human anymore.

Hindley falls down in Durham's 'She Wing' and cracks her hip then the whole fucking world knows of it, poor cow, pity she didn't break her neck. Me, I have to wait weeks for an X-ray if I've damaged anything, get my message, what I'm saying is that these governors and prison bosses are nonce lovers.

You're being betrayed, wasn't that what prison was for, to lock them away forever and to make them suffer in pain, you could've fooled me.

I'm a fucking animal and because of that they whip me like one and chain me like I'm a freak – do I deserve to die in a cage like one of them animals in a zoo? Cos if I do then let's see some of our notorious sex killers die in the same way and then I'd be happy knowing they got what they deserved. Let's stop all the pussy footing around.

What about that Dennis Nielsen, he's suing the Home Office, do you know what for, I'll tell you for why, because he's not allowed pornographic mags, that's why! Am I mad or is it the system? I'd give him a kick in the bollocks so hard that he wouldn't need a porno mag, he'd be using boot polish to clean his teeth! The beast killed 15 young guys, so why ain't he in a cage?

What about (Ian) Brady (Moors Child Murderer) he's got a computer, TV and video in his cell while I've got a fucking piss pot in the corner and a cardboard chair in mine! Brady gets £25 a week to spend while I only get £2.50. Brady wears his own clothes while I have to wear rags. He tortured and killed kids - I love kids.

Brady and his accomplice, Hindley, recorded those little children while they was being tortured, I've heard one of them tapes, maybe if you heard one then you'd change your mind about me being inside here. I couldn't ever listen to anything like that ever again, my heart still cries even now. Maybe one day those tapes will become public and get played. Do you know why they recorded them things; it was so that they could get off on it when having sex, fucking cock-sucking motherfuckers!

He's never to be released and neither will Hindley ever get released, but I might be lucky. I know at least 1,000 men who would target Hindley if she ever did get out; they'd shoot her dead. You've got lovely ladies like Lady Diana and Jill Dando ending up lying in the gutter dead, what makes Hindley think she's any better. If she lived 10,000 lifetimes she wouldn't ever be able to come anywhere near undoing her wrong and come anywhere near to being loved as Diana and Jill are.

Look at Reg Kray, he admitted killing one man, he and Ron were willing to take it on their own toes, but no the police weren't having any of it, they wanted the lot of them. What's it achieved, nothing! Reg killed a fellow gangster who threw his weight around and terrorised people because of that Reg's has done 32 years. Look at many of the sex killers, they serve half the time he's served and then they go and kill all over again, what a crazy stinking system this is. Who would you rather have as a neighbour Reg or Brady?

I admit what I am and that's a very complex and, probably, still dangerous and definitely unstable in the conditions I'm in. Isn't it time for the authorities to say 'We've treat Bronson terrible, let's now show him some compassion. Let's send him back to the asylum and help him get back some sort of humanity. Let's help him mix, let's give him a nice room. Let's see if we can get him back outside before his mum dies'.

Yeah! That's my view, but I'm still in isolation, my bed's a concrete plinth raised six inches off the ground and my furniture is still cardboard, my visits are ½ an hour two times per month. My dear old mum would have to travel a round trip of some 500 miles just to see me for ½ an hour. Mum's nearly 70 and she's been into hospital for tests so I've refused her to come and see me. Why should she come here to see me just for them to take the piss out of her, she's a decent lady so why should she be punished just because I'm her son?

I mean Sutcliffe (the Yorkshire Ripper) was going to be sneaked out to see his dying father, that was 'til the press heard about it, but can you fucking believe it, someone like him who mutilated all them prostitutes been allowed out of prison for a day. I was refused permission to go to my dad's funeral and then again refused for my gran's funeral back in January of this year, '99. Can you see why I get so angry with them?

I'm only allowed eight photos and six books at any one time; I can't wear any decent clothes. I have to wear this 'canary suit' as I call it. Big fuck off yellow patches on it so as the screws can see more easily, at least they can see. My eyes have been damaged due to all the bashings I've had and from being kept in dimly lit conditions so I've got to wear shades as any bright lights knock me for six.

I don't get to see any other cons, I'm looked up for 23 hours a day, I'm not allowed any cassette tapes and I can only use the phone once a week. For fuck sake! This is 1999; it's as bad as when I first came inside in 1974. I say give Brady and Hindley some of what I get and hopefully those two scum will do a Fred West and we can have a party. Anyway what did make me feel a little bit better is when I got the chance to spit into Brady's face through a cell door flap that was left open one day as I was being marched past it, what a shot!

Sadly I have to end this chapter here even though I could fill it ten times over, I'm sure you're as keen as me to move on to the more interesting bits, if you know what I mean?

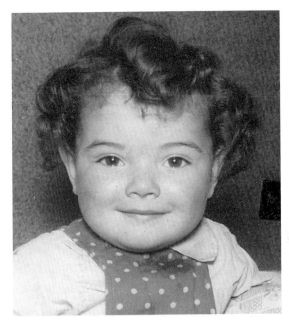

Charlie aged 18 months

Charlie aged 3 with Auntie Pam

Left Charlie aged 3 with brother John   Right Charlie aged 3 with brother John

Charlie aged 12 helping at his cousin's birthday party (next to window)

Charlie released in 1992 and his friend Mark

Left to Right Dave Courtney and Freddie Foreman 1998

Diana Dors
I met her in Broadmoor
when she visited me,
she was a lovely lady

Charlie Bronson

Jenny Eclair

Lisa Faulkner

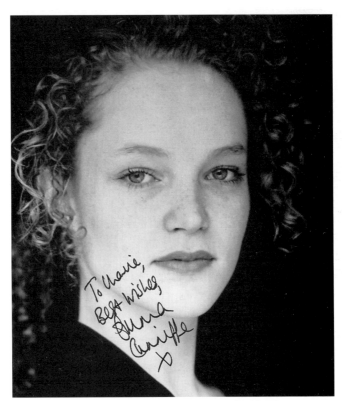

EMMA CUNNIFFE

MARTINE McCUTCHEON

Charlie in Belmarsh Prison 1994, with some of his Artwork

Charlie inside in 1991

Charlie with his Bird Joey
in 1991

Charlie out of Prison

Charlie and Eddie
enjoying a drink
when Charlie
was out
in 1992

Dad in India in 1945

Charlie & his cousin Loraine on a visit

My Brother John and my Mother

Charlie's Father aged 30

Charlie's Mother

Charlie and his Son re-united

Charlie's Mother and Father in1993

Reg Kray 1986 Parkhurst. The message reads:
Charlie, God Bless, Your Friend Reg.

2nd left Frankie Frazer, right Ray Williams 1998

From left to right Chris Lambrianou, Roy Shaw, Joe Pyle,
Johnny Heibner, Joe (Junior) Pyle, Freddie Foreman 1998

Joe Pyle right, Jimmy White second left 1994

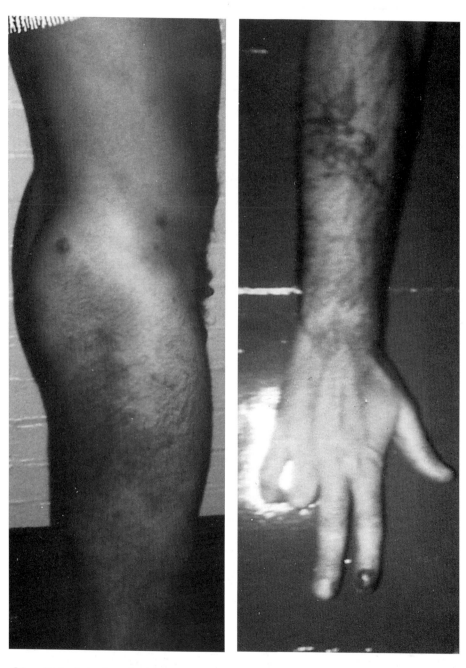

Charlie's Injuries from the attack in Wormwood Scrubs

Charlie and ex-girlfriend Kelly Ann Cook

Jan Lamb
Charlie's ex-girlfriend now close
friend, with Harley

Linda Calvey - Black Rose
Serving Life for murder. Charlie's
ex-girlfriend

Joe Pyle at his home with Harley 1999

Tony Lambrianou with Harley, at his home

Dave Courtney
in the Firestation Pub London
with Charlie's Mascot Harley
1999

Kenneth (Panda) Anderson
at his home with
Charlie's Mascot Harley 1999

Lord Longford
at his home in Hastings
with Harley 1999

Charlie's Girlfriend Joyce Connor

5

I was now in Woodhill prison and it was 26ᵗʰ May 1993. I'd
stopped speaking to the screws over one of my visits being
stopped. One of my civilian friends was due to visit me. James
Nicholson was turned away from the prison and this was the final
kick in my teeth. The way I saw it they deliberately and blatantly
upset me - and upset I was. There are only a few things that the
prison authority can fuck about with that will bring a con's temper
out of them and one of those things is visits along with telephone
calls, food and wages. Fuck about with them and then anything
can happen and the prison authorities must accept full
responsibility for their actions, ask any con! My head was so bad
over this I couldn't sleep or relax. A liberty had been taken.

Loraine, my cousin, and her husband, Andy, shot up to see me
to try to smooth it over but when they left I just felt bad. You see
at that time I was on remand and that made me innocent 'til I was
proven guilty. Here I was kept in solitary and denied a visit, who
the fuck do these people think they are, messing decent people up?

This Wednesday began as any other ordinary day. My bowl of
porridge, a good shit and a shave and out in the yard for an hour's
workout with my medicine ball. Young Kirk Barker came out with
me, as he was good at throwing the twelve-pound ball at me none
stop for half an hour. Kirk's one of the good guy's. After our ball
workout I began my push-ups and sit-ups. It was pissing it down,
but I love the rain, it's refreshing. The hour went by smashing, I
felt okay, then it happened all hell broke loose.

As I left the yard to go back to my cell I saw the library officer,
for reasons even beyond me I'd lost my self-control. I ran at him

and grabbed him around the neck in a Japanese strangle hold. I screamed out to all the screws: 'STAND BACK OR I'LL SNAP HIS SPINAL CORD!' Even Kirk froze and nobody came near me. I dragged him back to my cell and banged the door shut. The siege had now begun.

I sat him in the chair facing the door and I stood behind him. The first screw to look through the Judas hole was Mr Reed the SO (Senior Officer). I still had my hostage in a neck hold. I shouted to the SO: 'ANYBODY COMES THROUGH THAT DOOR AND I'LL KILL HIM! DO AS YOU'RE TOLD AND I'LL LOOK AFTER HIM!' My demand was short and sweet; 'I'll release my hostage for a blow up doll, a blonde one'.

I realise this must sound insane, maybe it is, personally I don't give a fuck either way. My reasoning for my demand was reasonable to me at that time. My world consists of four walls and a closed door. I can't associate, I can't play games, I can't go into other cons' cells to play cards and I've got to sit on my own. As according to the authorities I'm too dangerous, too unpredictable and too violent to mix.

So the way I see it, if these faceless people can segregate me indefinitely and stop my visits then I want a doll. It will be company for me, something to cuddle up to at night, I could tie her to my back and take her for a jog on the yard and Loraine could fetch me some nice clothes for her.

I suppose a lot of people will say he's gotta be fucking mad! Well like I say, maybe I am. How would you be if you lived my existence? It's empty. My way of protesting at my segregation and the way my friend was refused in to see me was by making a stand against the authorities and asking for something outrageous and easy for them to give me. Well you'd have thought they would've wanted the situation resolved quickly and for the sake of a few quid that they'd have went out and bought one for me so as to end the hostage situation. But we aren't dealing with the brightest of people running this lot so you'll have gathered by now and this part that follows proves my point.

Anyway I demand a doll, just an ordinary one. Which I could've understood if it was a deluxe model, but it wasn't. My hostage turned out to be a smashing bloke. After the first hour we both got on well. I know what you're going to think here, and that's that the hostage won over my confidence to get out quickly –

bollocks. I can see when people are trying to pull one over on me. 'Come on Charlie, just pop your head in this little loop, we won't hurt you, we promise' and all that crap. No! No one can pull one over on me, maybe my own kind in a bit of frisk (joke) but not the authorities or hostages. So when my hostage and me start getting closer I know it's genuine. I gave my hostage my word that I wouldn't kill him.

He asked me! 'What if they don't give you the doll?' I didn't answer that. Soon there's trained special negotiators outside my door, they done two-hour shifts. The other cons on my side of the block were all evacuated to the other side. Police were in, riot screws and governors. Woodhill had its first siege since it opened up and I bet you won't see that in the Guinness Book of Records.

All I wanted was a blow up doll! For 13 ½ hours it went on. Tension! Fear! Excitement! Emotions! Threats! Shouts! Demands! Still no doll. I find it all mind boggling that the authorities can sit back for 13 ½ hours over a simple demand for a doll as I made it clear that I would release him once I got the doll. So they were responsible for this poor man's mental torture.

I must say it now, I respected the man. The only time he lost control was when they read him out a message from his wife. This even made me sad, but it's often a ploy to try to bring the hostage taker and the victim closer to bond them together so it makes it harder for the hostage taker to hurt their victim. I know all the ropes as you can see there's no flies on Charlie Bronson, but I let them play their little games anyway, as it's good practice for them.

The hostage situation was taped by the negotiators so as to be used as evidence. I can now give you an extract from what was actually said. I think it only fair that you are let into this part of my world. There are two of us talking, a prison officer and me, here goes:

26th May 1993 – 5.30 p.m. (7 ½ hours into the siege)

CB (Charlie Bronson): 'I want my family here mate'.

PO (Prison Officer): 'Yeah, but Charlie that ain't gonna happen until this is all over, mate'.

CB: 'Well you can fuck off then 'cos this is gonna go on for weeks'.

PO: ''Cos they won't let anyone in mate'.

CB: 'Well you can tell the governor to fuck off. I said – FUCK OFF'. I'm not leaving this cell and he's not leaving this cell. Bollocks to the lot of you! My sister (Meaning my cousin Loraine, but I call her my sister as I consider her my soul sister.) either comes here and I see her outside there or there's gonna be dead fucking bodies mate, I'm sick of it.

PO: 'Alright Charlie, alright mate.'

CB: He's starving this man, fucking starving. In fact you can fuck off, go on FUCK OFF.' (My hostage had nothing to eat.)

PO: 'Alright'.

CB: 'Oy! Listen here, cunts; I'm doing the fucking messages here, not you. I give them when I fucking say, not when you cunts say. Cos I know you bastards, your full of shit. You starve this fucking man all day. You can starve me for ten years, it don't matter to me. You get my fucking sister up here, never mind all your shit you fucking slags.'

PO: 'Sorry, Charlie, I'm doing my best mate'.

CB: 'I'm not interested, you're not trapping me mate. I wanna see my family.'

PO: 'Not the intention, Charlie.'

CB: 'I wanna see my family right. End of fucking story, fuck the Board of Visitors'. (The Board of Visitors are a set of visiting magistrates that can hear your grievances, and if those problems haven't been resolved then they might eventually do something about them. The system isn't worth a candle!)

PO: 'Alright'.

CB: 'Listen you cunting Board of Visitors, you've been standing there for five months and you don't even know me, you've never asked me, you just keep me in solitary all the time, well I'm the gov'nor know, well fuck you Brodie. (Brodie Clark) Don't you come your shit with me mate, fuck ya! You get my sister up here 'cos I wanna see her, not you or the Board of Visitors – my family. You ya cunt, you stopped my visits, you've stopped my phone calls, you're a cunt and if you're man enough then come into this cell and we'll let Andy go, alright cunt! You bigga enough? So lets have a fucking swap, now youse get my sister here, 'cos I wanna see my family and you can get the cakes there and all. I'm having you in the European Courts for torture, mental torture. That's what you are, a fucking Nazi. And I'll tell you something else, you're a cunt and you ain't telling me, pal, I'm telling you. Tell ya mate I'm gonna do one of the cunts talking, talking, trying to trap me that's what they're trying to do, but they ain't fucking trapping me'.

PO: 'Not trying to trap you Charlie'.

CG: 'Bollocks! I'm gonna tell you something now'.

PO: 'I'm listening, I listen, mate'.

CB: 'I'll tell you something now, I'll fucking tell...'

That's an extract for you. In all there's a lot of hours of that siege on tape and I could fill a few books with it, but there's more important stuff to push on with, for now that is.

The note that I allowed my hostage (Andy Love) to write to his dear old lady, in reply to her note that I allowed in, shows how the authorities didn't give a toss about him and how Andy didn't feel threatened by me. Here's an extract that goes in my favour and shows that I'm not as bad of a cunt as they'd have you believe.

EXTRACT FROM ANDY'S LETTER TO HIS WIFE

Sweetheart,

Thanks for your message it really helped. I'm okay except that they are not feeding us (Proof that they didn't give a damn about Andy's welfare.) or telling us what's going on. This may go on for some time, but I don't think I am in any immediate danger.

Keep the kettle ready, I'll leave it up to you decide to tell my mother or anyone else.

I allowed him to write his wife a message, which is more than the authorities allowed me when they stopped me writing to my mother for three weeks when I was in the loony bin.

Another extract from a note that Andy wrote to the prison officers outside of my cell follows. In it you'll see that Andy asks for food, yet the authorities didn't respond to his request. I didn't make Andy write the note!

We really would appreciate something to eat. I haven't had anything for 24 hours now. What is going on out there and why, for Pete's sake, isn't anyone telling us. Can we talk to someone in authority? Charlie isn't completely unreasonable and is aggrieved at the way he's been GOAD'd (Governor's Order and Discipline rule) while on remand. He'd like to have some hope of contact with other inmates in the future, e.g. in CRC. Please can someone come and talk with him soon?

On the same sheet I wrote the following.

Governor Sue Shilling,

Andy and myself are both disgusted. Andy is starving; my demands have not been met, why? It's time you showed your face and let's talk business. It's nice to be nice.

Chaz

At 11.00 p.m. I released him unharmed. I shook his hand and wished him well and I told him to sue the Home Office over the way they ballsed up the situation and would you believe that they still didn't give me a blow up doll! I truly feel disgusted at the way he was treated by his own people! They put a doll before his life, but I firmly believe that they wanted me to do him harm so that they could have the perfect excuse to kill me outright. Now can you see what I'm up against? They were willing to give up one of their own in order to kill me! The faceless ones that sit behind a desk just never gave a shit for this man. I would've thought that a doll was a good swap for a human life. Why doesn't someone ask them why they wouldn't have it resolved?

Once they got him to safety they come back for me. I was put in another cell. I must say now there was no violence although I was all geared up for it and ready to go into action. But since they refrained from such a messy thing I too co-operated and refrained. This part of it was dealt with professionally. One female screw in particular called Sara (Sarah) was a big influence in me calling it off. She's a real human and through her words and honesty she did keep me cool, good woman. She done two shifts outside my door, talking to me for four hours in all. Every word she said I listened to. So thanks Sara Irvine, wherever you are.

Andy Love obviously had to make a police statement as charges were going to be brought against me for this hostage taking situation, but surprisingly Andy was a man of honour and in his statement he said that towards the end of the siege he felt that I wouldn't harm him, his exact words were: 'As the hours went by I realised that wasn't likely to happen... As time went on he said to me he would not harm me... He really just seemed lonely and wanted company and was concerned as to the possible outcome of his forthcoming trial.'

The following day, the 27th May the police were back in photographing the cell and taking statements. Not mine, I won't talk to them until I see my solicitor. The van arrived for me and off we went - me in a body belt as we sped along the motorway. I wondered to myself 'Am I really insane, am I ever going to walk free again, am I going to die in a cage and why me? I truly don't know the end not now, but there's one sure fire thing I do know and that's that I love this world so much, I'll always dream for freedom. No matter how deep I bury myself or how deep they tread me down I'll climb back up with or without my doll. What other way could I make such an impact, I didn't do it by half!

The van drove straight towards the block and I immediately recognised it to be the segregation block of Winson Green prison. There was plenty of screws waiting, some I recognised. The screws in the van were all Parkhurst screws that had picked me up at Woodhill as they'd dropped a con off there. I travel all the time in my job and it's usually a part of the job that I wear a body belt as this lot are real kinky sods, but the real reason is that I refuse to be cuffed up to anyone ever again.

Once we all got out of the van I was led to D-wing and taken to the category 'A' landing where another load of screws were waiting. Here they released me from the body belt and I was taken from the cell and told to strip off, which I did. They told me that I couldn't wear overalls. I said: 'Well it's the same bollocks as last time, I'll wear fuck all'. So they quickly gave me the overalls. Fancy them trying to get one over on Charlie Bronson! The reason I prefer overalls is simple. They're loose and I don't like tight clothes, they're made of better material than prison jeans and I like my own choice. Big deal you might say, but bear in mind that long term prisoners are allowed that little bit more of a deal out of the prison system and don't forget that I was only on remand at this time!

I was then taken to cell '3', as cells go this one's a blinder, it's a long one and good for pacing up and down in. Four steps forward and four steps back. I like to evaluate the size of the cell as if the light goes out and I have trouble with the screws I can feel my way round the cell immediately. If I was to be in a fight situation and something was put over my head I would be able to know where the nearest wall was to push off with my powerful legs. The cell also had a good window.

Although its got two sets of bars and an outside steel cage, the window lets fresh air in and I can see the hospital wing and other cons walking by. Most importantly is that I can see the sky. I love watching the sky especially at night.

Winson Green was still mostly piss pots at that time. Some wings had been modernised with a toilet and a basin in each cell, but at that time my toilet was a piss pot and my basin is a plastic bowl. My world is still isolation and at least six screws have to unlock my door, not because the door's so huge but because my reputation precedes me wherever I go, it's bigger than any fucking door, that's for sure. I may as well be called Attila the (Hun) Bronson, Lawrence of (Arabia) Bronson, King Kong Bronson, Billy the (Kid) Bronson, the Incredible Hulk you name it I'm it.

The wing was mixed with convicted and remand prisoners, which is unusual as remand prisoners have to be kept separate from convicted prisoners due to certain privileges being granted to remand prisoners that convicted cons don't get. As far as I was concerned I might as well have been convicted 'cos I got fuck all extra to shout about.

The slag in the next cell to me had killed his wife and kid; I'd found this out on my first day. On the same landing was young Jackson, he's only 21, just got life for stabbing a gay. Two have just arrived for guns; they were pounced on by the Flying Squad, no doubt set-up. Sams is opposite my cell. Michael Sams was up for trial the following week for the murder of Julie Dart and kidnapping Stephanie Slater. He picked up £175,000 on a railway bridge for ransom of Stephanie, a Birmingham estate agent worker.

Sams has a wooden leg and it was this that helped get him caught. Do you know how he got the ransom money without getting caught? He told the people dropping off the money to put it on to a tray balanced on the edge of a viaduct. Unbeknown to the undercover cop who put the money on the tray Sams had a piece of string tied to the outer edge of the tray, which he pulled from below the viaduct. Since it was so misty it helped him pedal off along a path without being seen with the cash. He swore blind he'd not murdered anyone and he'd only been in it for the kidnap money, but when he was convicted of murder I managed to get his wooden leg and I hid it.

The landing above us is segregated as it's full of rule 43A protections – bad, evil, monsters. Plus they're all doubled up in cells so all of them are pumping each other's arses. My pal Billy Wilson is down below us. Billy and me were in Wandsworth and Parkhurst together some years before. I chat with him out of my window most nights.

Just out of interest the rule 43 protection given to sex cases has been abolished at HM prison Durham at time of writing, now in 1999, offers no protection to those seeking sanctuary on 43's. Everyone's mixed there and already it's led to a few people getting cut up, one of them's suing the Home Office because of this mixed policy, but that would suit me right down to the ground. Molosovec carried out his ethnic cleansing in Kosovo, which was totally out of order, but give me a chance to do some sex case cleansing and I'll clear the lot.

The exercise yard here for us category 'A' is a cage, it's not a lot bigger than two cells put together. Really it's disgraceful and inhuman plus not a blade of grass in sight, all concrete wherever you looked. Obviously the sex cases that are category 'A' don't come out with us on exercise; we don't see them, not that we want to, as they are the scum of the world. I would end up snapping there fucking necks if they enter my space, they're vermin.

They've given me my medicine ball and a mat and every day I get it in my cell for one hour to train with. So at least I've some pleasure. The other cat 'A' prisoners watch T.V. and films, which I am obviously not allowed to, as I can't associate with other cons, prison rule.

Loraine and Andy phoned me up and that cheered me up no end. I learned for the first time from them that they were actually at Woodhill when the siege took place. They're so loyal to me and I love them both. I'm only sad that I keep bringing bad news to them.

Since I've been in Winson Green I've been experiencing strange dreams and I'm having fits of laughter. I start laughing and can't stop but I'm laughing at absolutely nothing. Only the other night I woke up with a bad gut, it was early; 2.00 a.m. and all was silent. I got out of bed and sat on my pot and had a good dump. My red night light's on, the window open and here I am, 41 years of age, sitting on a potty – I started laughing. I was still laughing a good hour after. The night screw came to my Judas hole three times. I laugh an insane laugh, I'm sure I'm losing my mind.

I've been having bad dreams lately and I've become depressed over them. They're unnatural, gloomy – no hope dreams. Horror! I see myself in a grave and faces I know are shovelling earth on top of me - they're laughing. I'm thinking a lot, deep thoughts. The other night I watched the sky for hour after hour, just thinking, who am I, what am I, why am I, Who cares? I feel and sense I'll never love again. I don't write this in a self-pitying way, I don't believe in self-pity. I write this in factual form not fantasy or how I'd like it to be remembered. How can I ever live a normal life again! I can't even stand a person breathing on me or touching me, so how the fuck do I build up a relationship?

You might think I'm a no hoper and a loser and that I'll never get back to normal life, but what's normal life? Who likes being touched and breathed on, go and stand close to someone in a queue and start breathing on him or her, see what they do – pick someone big? I'm fucked up bad psychologically, I crave only for excitement and I thrive on a challenge.

This is reality at its best. The cage is closing in on me, and I'm only a remand prisoner – classed as innocent until proven otherwise. I'm a man that's been to war for so long it's altered my whole way of life. What do they expect me to be like, a lamb? I know that I'm not normal and here on remand I can feel insanity creeping back, I can feel it in my bones.

June 8th 1993 – Today I saw Maggie Morrissey, my brief. (Along with Milton Keynes police detectives.) Obviously they interviewed me over the siege. It was no comment all the way. They've interviewed thirty witnesses and it's now gone off to the Crown Prosecution Service. It's a never-ending circle. The machine's in motion and right now I'm caught up in its works. This book I'm writing seems endless. The end though is inevitably my burial.

As I throw my twelve-pound medicine ball, Bertha, about I smile to myself and wonder what comes next? Maybe it's best left a mystery. Maggie told me today that my trial date for the Luton business would be September 6th at Luton Crown Court. So I see it that I'm being messed about as it was supposed to be in July. I call it the 'Ice Game'. They put us on ice and try to melt us. It's all one big fucking game. Originally it was designed for the gentry of this country to empower themselves by travelling around and sentencing serfs and vagrants to whatever punishment. It gave them a hard on and was the first Viagra tablet ever invented. It's no different today. Wouldn't you like to have the power to give someone a five or seven 'stretch' behind bars, of course you would, we all would. It gives us a feeling of power! I wonder where the van'll take me next and when? I know for a fact the slags won't ever melt me – I'm un-meltable.

I received a wonderful letter today from Loraine. She tells me that Andy misses me a lot and they both want me back out to start a fresh life. September the 6th will surely be the decider. If somebody up there likes me then maybe a miracle will happen.

22nd December 1993 – Detective Constable Baskill of Humberside Police charged me on the following indictable (to be tried only at Crown Court) offences:

Charge One – Charles Bronson, at Milton Keynes in the county of Buckingham, on 26th May 1993, assaulted and unlawfully and injuriously imprisoned George Love (His first name is Andrew.) and detained him against his will. Contrary to Common Law.

Charge Two – Charles Bronson, at Milton Keynes in the County of Buckingham, on 26th May 1993, with a view to gain for himself or with intent to cause loss to another made an unwarranted demand of an inflatable doll, a cup of tea, weapons and a helicopter from Sarah Irvine. Contrary to section 21 Theft Act 1968.

September 6th 1993 – Luton Crown Court with Judge Rodwell, prosecutor Matthews, my barrister; Izzy Forshall and Patrick Felix; my co-accused and his barrister; Saunders.

The cat 'A' van arrived from HM prison Bullingdon at about 10.40 a.m. We're forty minutes late. My barrister and my solicitor, Maggie, were none too pleased, but truly it was nobody's fault as we hit traffic. Even though we had a police escort with flashing lights and travelled some of the way on the hard shoulder of the motorway we're still late. After a quick chat with Izzy and Maggie I was led up into the dock along with Felix and six screws.

Straight away I spotted Loraine and Andy up in the public gallery. Also Maz and Andy and of course the one and only Kelly-Anne. Kelly looked smart, but it was obvious to everyone that she was pissed. Firstly she shouldn't have been in the public gallery as she was to be a witness! Secondly she was told to get out, but being pissed she came back in so it destroyed any chance of having her as a witness. Truthfully, she was just a fucking pain in my head and I'm glad to say that she was just a thing of the past. I also noticed my pals Lord Longford, Julian Broadhead and James Nicholson. I noticed Frank (Lord Longford) turn around to say hello to Loraine, he stood up and his trousers fell down! I'm not kidding; they fell down to his knees. Frank's a tall slim guy, but years ago he was a bit stockier – he needs to tighten his belt.

After the twelve members of the jury were sworn in it had come for the time to make our pleas. The charge of 'Conspiracy to rob a bank' was put to us. Both of us went 'not guilty'. 'Going equipped with intent to rob'. Both of us went 'not guilty'. 'Possession of a shotgun'. I went 'guilty' and my co-accused went 'not guilty'.

The wheels of justice had begun to turn, the machine had been switched on, it was like a chess game; move by move. We were all the parts, we were all drawn together by some mystic fate or so I believed at that time. Every single person in the courtroom was a part of my fucked up life and it was my life they were playing with. Twelve members of the public will decide my fate. I hope they believe my story or I'm fucked. Truly fucked!

The prosecutor started, and in came the Crown's witnesses. No sooner had one cop finished giving evidence another one would take his place. Then Izzy tore into them like a vulture tearing out a dead lion's heart, all five foot two inches of her – fearless. If she wasn't a barrister she could have made a good S.A.S. officer. Directly behind Izzy sat Maggie, my solicitor. Maggie is fast, smart, and misses nothing. She is also a nice human. I had a good duo, a great team.

Then my co-accused's barrister tore into the prosecution witnesses, like a piranha tearing away a buffalo's hide, he, also, was good. This was a battle, the fight of my life. Felix was twenty-six years of age; he could afford to loose and go to jail, as he would come out young. For me, well... I can't afford a defeat.

I sat in the dock for three and a half days just listening to all of the Crown's evidence and I can honestly say that three quarters of it was bullshit - fabricated lies. A couple of cops were seen to be either lying or exaggerating. It was mostly crap. They even produced a video film of a 'Group 4' delivery van bringing money to the bank, it had no relevance to the case what I could see. It certainly looked good for them but bad for us which was obviously the reason for showing it.

Thursday afternoon, at three o'clock, I was called to the witness box once I had sworn on oath. My story blew the jury away, it blew the cops away, it blew the screws away and the judge – yeah it blew every fucker away. It's how I am, a mystery man. No fucker knows how I tick and no fucker will ever understand me. I can't even work myself out, so how can you?

Man you should've seen their faces, their eyes, and their expressions. I wished that I could relive that moment by a photo or a film. I'd blew there machine to fucking pieces and the were shell shocked by it.

I wasn't going to rob no bank or no van, that shotgun was going in between my own teeth, it was my funeral. Felix must be the unluckiest dude in the world – he was driving along and out jumped a guy with a shooter and jumped into his car and told him to drive. Felix was my hostage, either he drove me to where I said or he would drive no more, as his brains would get blown out all over his nice clean windscreen, he drove.

The bank - there never was to be a raid. Two shops up from the bank was a hairdresser's shop, that was my target. My plan was simple – wait in a car opposite the shop, wait for Kelly-Anne to go in to get her hair done, rush in and bang in front of her. You may ask WHY, lots of reasons - I was depressed, she fucked me up, I saw no future and I'm born mad. Whatever my reasons, I blew that courtroom out of this planet! Even whilst being cross-examined I stood above them all. Neither names nor addresses leave my lips.

I'm stuck in this machine but I'll escape it – my way! My number one priority is to see Felix walk, so I used all my energy on him. All the time I was in the witness box I felt Loraine's eyes beaming into the back of my skull, she truly gives me energy and strength. I felt her presence in that courtroom like a butterfly feels the breeze to help it along. She is an omen to me, a lucky star an irreplaceable human. I'll be fucked without her; I'd cut my throat to give her my life.

Loraine's youngest son Darren had shown up in the public gallery on the day of my evidence. He's a good kid – seventeen years of age, a right good looker, all the girls run after him. He's a cheeky bugger, full of spunk and plenty of bottle, I love him. She has two other sons, Jamie and Leigh, and they're smashing lads, all film stars in the making.

Friday the 10th of September and I went in the box again and again I blew their machine up, I'm a machine smasher, and I'm the part that won't fit. They'll try to smash me into place, screw me into place, but I won't fit, it's useless as I'm just unfittable.

Felix was next up in the box; it was hard work for him. I could see his wife in the public gallery; I could almost feel her pain. It looked to me as if she was praying for Felix to pull it off. It obviously hurt me to watch them both as for them to loose it would be more tragic than for myself. I could do no more for them as I had probably done more for them than most villains would ever do to help. So I wished Felix well. He never spoke too well, as it was hard to hear his soft voice. He had been told several times to 'speak up'.

His story was a complex one, as he had named people and those people all had to come forward to back Felix's story. Some were helpful and some weren't, it's swings and roundabouts though. As far as Charles Bronson jumping in Felix car – Felix could only say and did only say, "the guy was truly insane!"

The week had ended but it obviously wasn't over yet. We all had to start the machine back up on **Monday 13th of September**. It was now the speeches and the summing up; all the evidence was over and done with both for and against. It was a wait, the sweat was on and the ice block would melt. For me this week was worse than others, it was the worst week of my life, as not only did I have all of this case to go through but also my dad had taken ill at the same time – he had lung cancer!

Loraine and Andy had broke the news to me on **Thursday the 9th of September**, I was happy that it was them who had told me. That very Thursday night, back at Bullingdon jail in the seg unit I was allowed to phone home. I spoke to dad and my mum and afterwards I returned to my cell. I turned out the light and buried myself under the blankets then I broke up inside. When I awoke on the Friday it was the beginning again. I had cried myself out last night and the battle goes on and it did.

After the day of **Friday the 11th of September** was over, Felix went back to Bedford on his luxury coach whilst I got back into the category 'A' van surrounded by six screws. We sped off (well as fast as a van could speed) towards London. I was going to Belmarsh instead of Bullingdon, which suited me, better. At least I could get a few days of training in as I was full of tension, the week had drained me and I had to prepare myself for the Monday ahead.

We arrived at Belmarsh and I was in cell number '4' in the seg unit of the category 'A' unit. This was my third time at this prison in a month. I'm sure that I must have hit the 'Guinness Book of Records' as I don't think any other prisoner had hit a prison three times in the same month, if so then tell me who? I'd travelled over fifteen hundred miles in the past six days; this would take it out of anybody. The cost of this was coming out of the ratepayers' funds - your money!

The van had arrived again at Belmarsh on **Sunday the 12ᵗʰ of September** after only two days and I had to be returned to Bullingdon to prepare for the following day's trial. I can't really work out the prison management's theory, as Bullingdon is an hour and a half drive to the court in Luton and from Belmarsh it's only an hour's drive. So why the fuck do I get moved to Bullingdon on top of this travelling. This machine is well insane, more so than myself!

The weather was terrible; it rained and rained and rained for the entire journey. The four screws and me in the back of the van could barely see out of the windows. I must admit that it was a relaxing journey as the other two screws in the front put a tape of the 'Eurythmics' on – I love the voice of Annie Lennox. The song 'Must be talking to an angel' played and I had a smile on my face as the van made it's way to Bullingdon. I just hoped that my angel was still with me.

The van pulled up at Bullingdon seg block and all of the lads were at their cell windows shouting out to me, 'All right Chaz', 'How are you?' and so on. I shouted back 'I got twenty-eight years!' Everything went silent, it was a mass of silence so loud that you could hear it, I then broke the silence by shouting 'Only joking' and I began to laugh. The lads had lifted my spirit when I seen them all at the windows, I felt wanted.

The entire mob were waiting once I got inside of the block – screws, PO's and so on. I was given a meal whilst the escort were taking me out of my body belt. Then later I was returned to my cell and I had a chat to the lads out of the window. I settled down to write some letters then I killed the light and hit the sack, as I had a big day to follow. I'll tell you one thing, if I lost the trial I believed that I would loose my sanity. Fuck me, I really felt I would. I bet that Felix wouldn't be doing much sleeping that night in Bedford jail.

Monday the 13th had finally arrived and the trial was to continue. Matthew's the Crown prosecutor had his speech first, which went on and on and lasted for fifty minutes. Izzy followed and only took thirty minutes and it was fantastic, she's one magic speaker. Saunders, Felix's barrister, took his turn last, this was the longest, I didn't think you could get any longer than the prosecutor but here we did with an hour and twenty minutes!

The afternoon was the turn of Judge Rodwell and he made it clear to all that he was dead against me, the only thing he didn't say was that he hated me. Izzy said afterwards that it was the worst summing up that her ears had ever heard and she was shocked. I'd obviously hit a raw nerve with this Judge and it didn't look good. I couldn't believe it when it came to half past four and the Judge ended with, 'This court is adjourned until tomorrow'. He still needed more time to sum up, this guy was after blood and it was my blood that he wanted.

Loraine and Andy had visited me every day in the cells below the court, they gave me support and clean clothing. Today when Loraine came to see me I could see her face had changed from the other days, her eyes seemed very cloudy and dull; she was unhappy, sad and hurt. If I was to lose she would take this worse than anybody. She'd prayed that I would win. It will break her heart, as she knows what it does to me. Andy was also to take it bad, as he loves me like a brother. Loraine is something so special to me, she's like the sun; I can't go on without her shinning some warmth my way. We're so close.

Kelly-Anne came twice, the first time pissed out of her skull and the second time she was abusive. It was totally out of the question that she could ever give evidence even though here help was vital to me. She's just a pathetic waste.

What the Judge had said was nothing compared to what Izzy said to me: 'If you get a guilty on conspiracy to rob it seems as though Judge Rodwell is looking to life you up Charlie!' My head pounded and the words were rattling around in my head in slow motion as she said them, I was in shock and it would've been plain to see. A life sentence, life,life,life – I swear I never thought for one moment that the charge carried a life sentence, this was one blow that I didn't expect. Izzy went on to say that my evidence had terrified them all, the way that I'd shouted and the whole way that I'd conducted myself. 'They think that you're just a freak'. I told Izzy: 'I am only what I am and that is me'.

I hoped for my mum, dad, Loraine, Andy and everyone I'd let down, for there sakes, that I didn't loose the next day. I believed that they wouldn't see me again. I wouldn't be able to accept life; life imprisonment for me is murder. I didn't deserve life, fuck it, would you have accepted it? I needed the following day to arrive to resolve this situation.

That night I lived in hope, hope that I'd get a 'not guilty'. This night felt like the longest night of my life, as though the following day was just not going to arrive. 'Life sentence' must have bounced from every part of my mind. I was more concerned now than when all of those cops had guns in my face. I sense and feel danger and I've got the sign. I tried to picture the faces of the people in the jury and I remember them studying me as I watched them. I was thinking are these people against me and about to turn my life inside out or are they with me and on my side. I wished that I knew but this was something that I wouldn't ever work out or know until I was back in front of them.

One of the females on the jury had smiled at me several times but that could be interpreted in many ways and I was unsure of which way. Was it fear or was it to pacify me or was it to say you're going to get it? My head was spinning and spinning so much that it eventually sent me off to sleep.

Tuesday the 14th of September had finally arrived and the van pulled up into the courtyard of Luton Crown Court at 10am. I was tense; it had been a silent journey all the way. Fortunately all the screws knew me well so they left me deep in thought. I changed into my decent clothes and had ten minutes with Izzy and Maggie before I was up in court for 10.30 am.

Judge Rodwell finished off his summing up and the jury was sent out. The sweat had now begun, I felt numb all over as this life sentence was still rolling around in my head like a roulette ball.

I studied Felix for a spell, he looked tense, ready to explode studied his wife in the public gallery – she looked on edge.

Loraine and Andy looked tense. My Uncle Bill looked worried – then in she walked, Kelly-Anne. I stood up and shouted: 'GO HOME, GET OUT OF MY FUCKING LIFE!' She looked to be pissed, she left.

I was taken down into the belly of the court whilst the jury decided our fate. I was in the belly of the machine, deep in the middle of it all. It wasn't just the prison authorities who were wondering at what the outcome might be. It was the police, the screws, the Home Office and fellow cons. A lot would dearly love to see me go free. A lot would dearly love to see me caged. The screws with me were all decent sorts. One in particular, a block screw from Woodhill, had actually been with me everyday all through this. (Darren) He gave me a lot of moral support regardless of what he thought about my chances.

After three hours the judge called us up and told the jury that he would accept a 'majority verdict'. The pressure had become even more so, it showed on everybody's face. Izzy and Maggie came down to see me, we spoke in great length. Izzy actually looked very concerned and flustered. Obviously she takes all her cases very seriously. Maggie looked worried. Loraine and Andy wanted to see me, so did Bill. Loraine and Kerry, another one of my relations, came to see me first, we put our hands against the glass that separated us and put our hands as one. It's never nice at the best of times to have a visit behind glass. I would've loved a hug for love.

Then Andy and Bill come. Andy had my ring on, a big gold ring with the initial 'M' on it. He wears it for luck for me. Then it happened, it was time. The time was now! Fuck me. I was now feeling like battering a wall or punching a hole through a door. This was murder! The courtroom was silent. All eyes were on the jury foreman, a young man in his 20's. My eyes were fixed on his mouth. My brain was telling me all was okay.

'Do you find Charles Bronson guilty or not guilty of count one, Conspiracy to Commit Armed Robbery?' "Not guilty". A loud sigh of relief could be heard from the public gallery! I looked over to see a sea of faces, all smiling. Felix also got a not guilty on count one – another loud sigh.

'Do you find Charles Bronson guilty or not guilty on count two, Intent on Robbery?' "Guilty". Fuck me, my heart lost a beat, my pulse rate went sky high, my world collapsed – I felt numb. Not because of the guilty verdict but because worse was yet to come, the sentencing from this judge that held me in disdain. 'Do you find James Felix guilty or not guilty of count two, Intent to Rob?' "Not guilty". Felix looked as though a slab of concrete had been lifted from his back and then thrown on his head. I grabbed his hand and said 'good luck'. He had tears in his eyes! A young man, 26 years old, a wife and two kids. I felt happy for him.

Judge Rodwell seemed to have changed in his demeanour and said: 'Mr Felix, you are free to leave this court'. I was 'guilty', so the jury said. I was the danger man, the one who needs to be in a filthy stinking cage. I'm the man who's lived and breathed prison all his fucked up life! Guilty! Guilty! Guilty! I look guilty. The word 'guilty' reverberated inside my head like an echo in the Alps!

Izzy spoke mitigation on my behalf, a nice short speech. But a good honest one at that, which sunk in. Every single word she said I digested. I saw the tears well up in Loraine's eyes. I saw the look of despair on Andy's face. These two human beings truly understood me. These people had come to court for me, to give a show of strength and solidarity; I wasn't some lone wolf. I'd underestimated the love in people's hearts. I'd let a lot of people down, me...well I didn't matter because after seeing the hurt I'd caused it brought me down to earth – with a thump. I'd a team fighting for me, real people, real life. All that had gone wrong in my life was my own fault and now I could see the people who had been injured from my wrongdoing.

Judge Rodwell seemed to take great delight in going on and on and on. It was obvious he didn't like me. Judges have to do a job without fear or favour, but when vindictiveness comes into it then I feel it goes the opposite way to showing favour. He said I was a danger to society and prison was the only place for me. 'I sentence you to eight years on count two and two years for the possession of a shotgun!' Both sentences were to run concurrently – it was all over.

The headline in the 'Luton on Sunday' rag read: 'Charles Bronson had a death wish'. The article went on to say how 'that crook Charles Bronson wanted to blow his brains out in front of the lover who rejected him – not rob a bank'. Basically they had it right and that was I'd met Kelly-Ann Cooke way back in 1988 as I've already covered. She'd been unfaithful to me after I'd been sentenced for that jewellery shop job back in '88.

So here I am back in the unit on my own, just 'til Sunday then I'm off back to Bullingdon as I face another trial for the hostage taking situation, I've got it all to face, but in the meantime I feel relaxed here amongst familiar faces that aren't going to try to kick the crap out of me. The screws are good to me, I get double grub, I get treated descent and I've no aggro here plus it's peaceful.

Saturday morning comes, I wake up fresh, I had breakfast, went out into the exercise cage, had a run and done my sit-ups. The sun was out. The screws had a game of badminton with me – it was a good laugh. In the afternoon we played scrabble, they've done me the world of good and there's respect. I can't slag a man whose good to me – I never will. Some of the screws here are good men, obviously there's arseholes, but I've not chinned one in three stays, so it speaks for itself. Plus I won the scrabble.

There I was, fresh from court, with an eight stretch if there was any reason for me to crack up and take hostages then this would've been good enough, but I don't work like that, see. The screws could've decided to keep me at arm's length, but they didn't, they embraced me and looked beyond what they could see and found another human being. That's all I ever ask, but you see the Home Office employ some funny fucker's in the prison service, many of them deserve to be behind bars with me for the bad they've done to me and others in their charge.

I'll tell you something now! As I write this chapter I can feel the silence. It's 7.45 p.m., my door won't be open 'til 8.00 a.m. Twelve hours away! Right at this moment if I had a wish I'd wish for my world to go back to November 9th 1992 when I walked out of prison. I swear I would've taken another road. As this road is hell, I can't get off it!

Just before you go off into the next chapter I thought I'd better warn you that it starts back in '92 before I was released. There's a particular reason for that, which is to give you some background up to what happened to me in this chapter. I know some you clever clogs will say I've done it arse about face, but that's a risk I take.

6

Leading up to my release in November of 1992 I was in Lincoln Special Unit. When I first came to this place, through the doors that led onto the unit, I sensed a feeling of intense awareness; a screw sat behind bulletproof glass watching my movements. The first con I set my eyes on was fat Joe Purkiss, I've always liked Joe, he's not the brightest of guys but he's got a big heart. I first met Joe in Parkhurst; he's also ex-Rampton. His fat face lit up as I gave him one of my infamous hugs; Joe never changes apart from his belly getting bigger. He soon had a cup of tea brewing up for me. The other two cons on here at this time were Martin Clifford and Paul Flint.

The unit's so small it's impossible not to get under each other's feet. Straight away I got the only cell without a bed, this was the cleaning cell with buckets and old furniture stored in it. Joe and me painted it out and I moved in without a bed, who needs a bed, a mattress on the floor suits me fine. In the daytime I like to stick my mattress up against the wall so as to have a lot of floor space. A bed's too bulky it takes up too much room. I don't have tables or chairs, I sit on a blanket, it's how I like it.

My pal, Peter Hale, taught me how to sit correctly, it's posture - chairs are bad for backs. I got all my photos out, some I framed and hung on my walls, it looked homely, the screws were friendly and the atmosphere was relaxed so it seemed okay. I saw one of the cons playing pool with a screw, the con must have been embarrassed, I saw him later, he approached me about it to say that the screw was okay, I told him it was his business.

There's a woodwork shop, its three cells converted, a TV room, a multi-gym and an exercise yard; 30 foot X 12 foot, all caged in. Here we've our own library, washing machine, computer and fridge. All sounds good stuff but is it? It's observations, like guinea pigs in a laboratory experiment. It's difficult to explain my feelings on it, but I got stuck in and got my routine worked out. In the first two weeks of being there Joe went to Armley for accumulated visits to see his mother. Paul went down the block over a protest about not being able to go back to a London jail so as to see his kids and Martin went over the hospital.

Tony Steel came on the wing. So Tony and me were all alone and the next week flew by smashing, no problems. But little were we to know that another week was all that was left. Tony and me worked out together, played pool, ate our meals together and watched TV together and he's one of the best guys I've had the pleasure of doing time with. I respected the guy, as here he is with three life sentences, never killed nobody and been locked away since he was 18 years old. He never whinges or depresses other guys, at night I got back to doing some oil painting, I knocked out some of my best work ever, all in all I was getting it together. Joe comes back from Leeds after only one week. Leeds soon got fed up of Joe, so Tony, Joe and me were all plodding on.

I was expecting a visit from a friend and I asked our governor, who at that time was Governor Prat, if my friend could come on to the unit to see how I'm doing, how I'm living and to see some of my art. Plus, Joe and Tony wanted to meet him as I spoke to them of him. Prat said it was okay, so all was set. I bought a strawberry gateau, no big deal to people outside, but in here it's a luxury. Bear in mind our wages are so little it barely keeps us in smokes or tobacco, obviously I don't smoke so I can do it.

A senior Officer (SO) came and told me: 'It's in the book for the 30th of March'. It was all fixed for him to come on to the unit. Five days later on the 30th at about 11.30 a.m. I was eating my dinner with Tony and Joe. All of us were in my cell sitting on the blanket on the floor when a screw put his head around the door and said: 'Charlie, do you know your visit today is in the visiting room?' 'What!', I said. He never got time to answer. 'FUCK OFF, cunt, away from my door!'

I asked Tony and Joe to leave and we all got banged up in our own cells over dinner as we always do. I was fuming, raging, my head was pounding, 'What the fuck are they up to, do they want me to blow up, are they nuts, shall I rearrange the unit, World War Three, tear the place apart', I thought to myself. For a good hour I paced in the cell the like a tiger, my breathing was heavy. Then the door unlocked and the screw stood there as he spoke, I surely never understood a word he said as I was looking at Governor Prat at the side of him. I asked Prat why he was upsetting me and all of the arrangements that he had agreed on some weeks earlier. I hit him in the face, 'Go on, Fuck off!', I said.

It sure never made me feel any better; in fact I was more upset so I slammed the door shut: 'FUCK OFF!' Tony shouted, 'What's up?' I told him I'd hit Pratt and we spoke for a while, twenty minutes passed when Tony shouted that the MUFTI (Minimum Use of Force and Tactical Intervention) were out on the landing with shields, helmets, overalls, the works – World War Three style.

Nobody spoke to me, the door came flying open and they ran in behind shields, the force of it smashed me to the back wall. I tried to fight it, but what can one man do against that? It took them longer than they'd planned to get me secured in lock holds, wrists, arms, neck, legs, ankles and of course as usual one hero grabbed me in my plums, there's always one, isn't there? I accept all of this; it's all part of the game and with my history they come in fast. I would've liked to have been asked to come out.

So as I'm being carried out of the unit, through other wings having my wrists bent up so much that I'm in agony I soon find myself back in the block and back in the box, where the body belt comes out. It was obvious this belt was a size too small for me as it took them ages to get it on me. Once it was on I felt uncomfortable. It was too tight on my stomach and the cuffs were digging into my wrists, I was in trouble.

I was in pain, there was blood on the floor, I could taste blood and feel it on my face, my head ached through blows I'd received and my left eye had blurry vision. My wrists were in agony, but why am I in a restraint belt, it wasn't necessary to put me in a belt, even in a nut house loonies are only put into a straight jacket if they explode. Had I exploded, no way? Also why leave a man in a belt that's too small, all of them knew it was too tight. I crawled like a snake to the door, rolled on my back, obviously I'm bollock naked as they had tore off my clothes.

So here I am lying on my back bollock naked, strapped up in agony and smashing the metal soundproof box door with my bare feet, screaming to come out of the belt. They took me out of it the following morning at ten O'clock. Although in the early hours they come in, all because of a Scottish screw, a night clocky, who could see I was in agony, he got the hospital down and security to loosen off the cuffs, but even then it was still too tight for me. I truly witnessed both my wrists swell up, I watched my fingers go blue-white and I felt the numbness.

On top of this the belt was so fucking tight I felt it digging into my sides. My breathing was heavy, I was sweating – fuck me! I was terrified, I didn't suffer with claustrophobia, but I did now. 'Help, get a doctor!' Me shouting help is a miracle, me shouting for a doctor is just insane! I can't describe the agony so I'll say no more.

In the belt and out of it I asked the governor and a member of the Board of Visitors to get the police as 'its torture'. I wrote to the police and my solicitor, but six days later I was still waiting to see the police, obviously this lot didn't want the police in too lively, what with the cuts and bruises and the state of my wrists.

My friend civilian, Julian, visited me three days later and he noted my injuries, so I was now considering my next move. The kicks and punches mean nothing, but leaving a man in agony in a belt too small is not ever going to be acceptable by me. I must make a case of it, as truly I wouldn't want this happening to anyone else.

9th April 1992 – I'm sick of it all. Ten days I've waited to see the police and to get photos taken of my injuries plus I'm depressed badly and I've got throbbing pains in my head. This block is about to explode, I've got to get out or I'll be going in the box.

16th April – I've just come out of the box, not a word's been spoken since I went in. A terrible bad time for me mentally, deep depression's set in this time, deep anxiety, hate plus three fingers on my left hand are paralysed and numb. Could be a trapped nerve or a fracture. I never slopped out all the time in here. I've had absolutely nothing to read and nothing to see but four walls and a door. I've got no bed, just silence. This morning my door opened and big Mick Fillingham, the screw of the unit, the only screw who I respected, good man, has told me via the governor that I'm to be moved to Long Larten soon. So I've decided to come out of the box, so I've at least achieved something. I had loads of letters just handed to me, which I'll answer later today. I feel good about going to Larten; maybe this is the one, the lucky one, God willing.

Dave Dudley and Johnny Richards are in the block cells; they're two good guys. They've been filling me in with the news of the last week. People outside just don't understand what life's like inside of a box. No windows, little air, no bed, no news, no talking, stinking pots' stale piss, stinking cockroaches, flies, sweat, it's a filthy stinking life not fit for even a dog. But isn't it better to go into oneself rather than explode and destroy? I feel better now that I'm moving on to better pastures. I hope the new governor won't get too edgy or be too fast to put me down; I feel I can win now. If I fuck this up then maybe I'll end up getting certified mad all over again, as enough is enough.

I've good friends at Larten, Alan Byrne – who you may remember was the guy I mentioned earlier. It was his name I had on my back in the unlicensed boxing bout previously mentioned. Charlie McGhee and Stevie Waterman were there so I was looking forward to seeing them all. I've never been told where I'm going so soon before leaving a place, so I'm to leave in two weeks. Well this is it, lets go at it full-hearted, it's head down and forward. I'll see this Number One Governor in court for torture or they'll pay one way or another. As in 18 years of imprisonment I've never spent such a claustrophobic painful night as I did on the 30th of March, I'll never forget it, I'm not being hateful over it or saying I'll be revengeful, I'm just saying I'll never forget it. I wonder what happened to my strawberry gateau?

Torture is the cowardly way of evil it was a shameful day to all of them and many screws are disgusted it happened at all. It goes without saying why it was done. They'd already beat me; I'd accepted it. The belt was unnecessary and overreacting, but even so if a belt then at least it should be a belt of the correct size. I'm 14 ½ stone (at that time) and they all knew I wasn't ten stone.

They fought for over ten minutes securing it to me, knowing it was too small and they left me; knowing the outcome. Yes it was a sad day, after all I've had done to me this has got to rank alongside one of the most evilest! The thought of their eye at my Judas hole spying on me naked strapped up in agony and hearing

153

me shouting in pain being left sickens me. My mind tells me a dog can't be treat this way.

Am I really the mad rabid dog who they all fear, as surely only fear would make them react so cruelly? As far as Governor Prat is concerned I don't believe he would have justified my treatment, as basically he's a good man. I don't hate him, but it's as if I hit him with an axe or cut his throat. I haven't seen him since, I hope I do if only to see his reaction towards me. I don't think he dislikes me either, right or wrong, who gives a shit? A slap in the chops is part of life, it probably put him on his toes, he's probably a better man for it, after all not many men can say they took a hook from Charlie Bronson.

It livened up their jail, I lost, so what? If the mugs hadn't fucked my wrists up in that belt then we could've put it down to one of life's upsets. Another chapter I never needed, but it's only truth and no more, who can say different, on oath it's all the same to me, God knows how they'll escape this one, probably by producing another body belt, probably say I was so violent. I don't even wish to know what they'll say. I can only say my part and feel a proud man. I'll say this much though, if it wasn't for this deal I'd be in this box and leave this box for another box as I was slipping down a big black hole and I swear I believe these knew it. Insanity is a terrible thing when one loses control of it.

26th April – I saw two detectives, I had waited exactly 28 days to see them, what a fucking liberty. Obviously bruises had gone, lumps had healed up – crafty fuckers.

29th April - An old man walked off a visit today and he dropped down dead before he got to his cell, Jesus Christ, the sooner my van comes to collect me the sooner the fucking better.

30th April – I went out for my hour's stroll in the cage today, the weather was lovely although at times cloudy and showery. The wind was fresh, but it felt lovely, as soon as I done my first lap I come across a pigeon in a lot of trouble. I'm no vet but it was obvious this pigeon was in trouble. The only part of its body that moved was its head, slightly. I picked it up and it was trembling, the poor sod had a leg missing and one of its wings was broken. No doubt it got caught up in the razor wire somewhere, it was in agony, I looked at its eyes, I could almost feel its message – 'Kill me, don't leave me this way, Charlie'. I put it on the concrete slab and trod on its head – instant death. I must admit I felt bad over it, but I couldn't leave it like this as I carried on walking my, mind felt weird, strange feelings came over me. I've been feeling bad thoughts for some time, as screws talk to me I'm only half listening, another half of me is studying their jaw and I'm wondering, 'Can he take a hook?' Strong feelings of violence, I once had these feelings years ago, they're really negative thoughts, all in all it's been a weird day to day, a bit like a dream, as if it's not real. The only positive thing I done was put the pigeon out of it's misery.

1st May – today was supposed to be the day I applied for more remission to be restored, almost for certain I would've got another 100 days back, which would have put me out for September 1992 – only four months away, but sadly it's all fucked now. That last hook has cost me a lot, also today I've been told that Julian phoned to say he's visiting me on the 6th, I believe I won't be here, I also believe these know I won't be here. It's only a feeling I have, as by all accounts, according to these, I was on my way Tuesday gone, but violence broke out at Long Larten so the governor put it off 'til it all cools down a bit, this is what I was told.

So a week will be gone by Tuesday, it'll be interesting to see, but I truly feel I'll be off by Tuesday, I hope I'm wrong, as a visit with Julian before I go would be respected. I've not seen the cops since and nothing's been told to me, it will all come out in the wash though.

3Rd May – just been informed the cops are seeing me Wednesday afternoon, the 6th. Hope the filth have done their homework so as to nick these Gestapo. I had a thought, in January '88 I was arrested, charged and remanded to Leicester jail, on arrival I had no choice, I was put into the punishment block and told by the governor I would remain in his block under G.O.A.D. for all my stay in his jail. My thought is that if I was a black guy then could he have got away with this?

5th May – the cops arrive today, strange, as it was booked for tomorrow. They've gone away to fax my statement and it's now up to the DPP. Probably take months before I hear anything, so it's these cunts roasting for a change, not me. Julian's up tomorrow as he also has to see the cops before he sees me. I'm looking forward to seeing him, as I must surely be away anytime now. Every time I hear a vehicle pulling up I'm racing, ready to go – tense times.

This morning I lost my head and ran out onto the landing bollock naked, shouting and howling, I even squatted down to shit on the landing, but my bowels were empty. These upset me over bringing a doctor to my door, but fortunately no harm done. The cops are trying to get an outside doctor to examine me, as they need a doctor's report – I refuse to be seen by a prison doctor.

They had the chance to help me out of the belt, proves what hypocrites they all are to leave a man in agony, but soon as the heat's on they come running like good little boys. If I ever seen one of them outside I'd string them up for what they done to me. I'd truss them up just like I was and leave them in agony, wouldn't you want to do the same? I don't say this in a bitter twisted way. I say it in a funny way, as believe me I'll laugh when I do it. I was fucking gutted over Jimmy White losing the snooker he played so well. Let's hope greener pastures wait at Long Larten.

Here I am, innocent 'til proven otherwise, here I am being sent from a court to be remanded and sent straight into solitary, how can this be justified. There are five punishment cells in Leicester block with a population of 500 cons, so why me, yes, why was I put into the block from day one? If I'd been abusive or arrived aggressively it could be justified, so why this treatment, murderers, rapists and bank robbers don't get put into the block like I do, is it a phone call from the Home Office? 'Bronson - alias Peterson – is on his way, get a cell in the block prepared, watch your roofs, watch your security, watch him closely!' Is this the way?

I was eventually released from Gartree on 30th October 1988. Where did it all go wrong? In order to find that out I have to take you back in time from before where the last chapter left off. It might sound odd doing it that way, but it's important to the plot if you are to fully understand the situation. The last chapter ended in 1993 and here you find me back in 1992, the time I said I wished I could go back to.

Kelly-Anne Cooke was a pain in the arse but we had a connection and you know the times when someone gets to you and you just can't put your finger on it, well it was the same thing here. When I tell you about her you'll probably say I needed my head examined for taking up with her. It was through my Uncle Jack that I became involved with Kelly-Anne and as I've already explained we had a sort of thing going between us, but it abruptly ended in '88 only to restart up in 1992. Just flashing back in time for a moment to when I said (at the end of the previous chapter) that I wished I could change my world by going back to November 1992, well here I am. And for the entire world I still can't change that period – how did it all go wrong?

I was in a pub in Laisdowne on the Isle of Sheppey round about Christmas time doing a bit of business when a mutual friend introduced me to Jan Lamb. Jan and I were immediately attracted to each other, she was a voluptuous 30 something with eyes that I could die for. We got on great right from the beginning and Jan commented on my sense of humour, which is what I think won her over. Jan had to have a sense of humour to be on my wavelength – luckily for me she had that. I asked for Jan's phone number on another matter, but I'm sure she knew what I was after. After a few days I phoned her up asking if she'd like to go out for a few apple pies. We met up at the pub, but I managed to get Jan to come back to a caravan that I was staying in. I said she'd have to see what it looked like. As we walked back through the rows and rows of caravans I found they all looked the same, rows and fucking rows of them. I'd forgotten the row number hadn't I? So I tried to look cool, making on we were just having a gentle stroll when all along I just wanted to get her into that bleedin' caravan. I spotted a red pair of curtains hanging, wasn't that my caravan, thank fuck for that. 'Here it is Jan, my girl, good ain't it?'

No sooner had I opened the door I was pulling it closed behind us with. I saw that look in Jan's eyes that said more than words ever could, 'Well girl, now you're here we might as well have a shag, so get your kit off and give me a fucking one', as I said it the cheeky grin I gave Jan made her laugh. Writing it here sounds a little too over the top and anyone knowing what sort of person I am would understand that this was a reaction to getting the come on from Jan, otherwise I'm reserved.

We were at it for hours, as I'm a fit guy and I kept it up for some time. Jan was wearing a leather skirt before we started and that was a real turn on for me, leather does that to me. Talk about the 'Karmasutra Sex Guide', it said nothing about shagging on the cooker, on the sink, in the shower, on the kitchen bench, on the floor, on the step of the caravan in fact anywhere was suitable for me, even on the beach. One night we were at it on the beach and people were walking along looking at us, I shouted to these voyeurs: 'WHAT'S A MATTER, HAVEN'T YOU SEEN ANYBODY SHAGGING BEFORE?' They quickly went away, I was in stitches at them. Both Jan and me would laugh at the places we'd had a shag at. I'd tell Jan to get her kit off whenever I felt like a shag - she obliged. I think we had the right chemistry and for this short while we created a chemical bang that both of us would remember with fondness.

I used to play 'Led Zeppelin' songs all of the time, I'd bought Jan some cruthchless nickers. I'd tell her to get them on and get her to sit on me my while I moved and gyrated to the music. Can you picture that, shagging away to Led Zeppelin; it was fun though, it always was. We just couldn't keep our hands off each other. Yeah, I was sure making up for lost time.

I told Jan that I had to go and see Bertha. Jan said: 'Who's this Bertha?' I told her: 'Bertha's my world and I don't let anyone bad mouth her or hurt her'.

I asked Jan if she wanted to move in with me, 'Get your gear together and move in with me?' We had a great laugh together, but when I worked out and did some training Jan used to get a bit annoyed at me saying I was doing too much.

One day Jan asked me where her leather skirt was? No, I hadn't hid it to wear for myself; I'm not like that. I told Jan that I took it to keep Bertha warm. Jan wasn't too pleased, as she knew it was something I liked her wearing a lot. 'How could you give it to this Bertha when you like me wearing it, what the hell's wrong with you?' I showed Jan to the cupboard and opened the door and there was Bertha sitting in the corner with Jan's leather skirt cut up so it would fit her.

Jan's eyes opened wide in disbelief, 'A fucking leather ball, you've got to be kidding'. 'No, Jan, not a leather ball a medicine ball!' Jan was beginning to dislike Bertha, I could tell, as Bertha would start turning up in all sorts of weird places, on the roof of the caravan, underneath it, in the bin and under the kitchen sink. Jan even said: 'One of these day's I'll burn that bleedin' thing!'

Jan was becoming more obsessed and jealous over Bertha and told me I'd have to choose between her and Bertha. 'No one will ever stop me having my Bertha around'. 'Right then I'm off, you can shag Bertha because I'm leaving'. To this day I've still got Bertha.

I used to rub her down with wax to make her shine, mind you I told Jan that in my eyes she shone all the time. I used to enjoy giving Jan a rub down with oils, but that would be telling you too much if I was to go on about the rub downs we gave each other.

Jan and I lost touched for a while and then she'd heard I was back in prison and she wrote. We've always remained close friends and write to each other all of the time, we've become closer and real good friends. I still remind Jan of Bertha by doing cartoons for Jan, some of which show me in bed with Bertha, but Jan knows it's only a joke and I was maybe a little too obsessed with training.

Jan was complaining about my training, so I told her that it was a good job I was fit, 'What do you want, some unfit sod that can't keep it up?' I remember one night I was so full of energy that I went outside and started to lift rocks up and down, but they weren't heavy enough so I started on the caravan next to mine. I got hold of the tow hitch and gripped it in an underhand grip and lifted it off the ground, up, down, up, down...'What the hell's going on' came the shout from the inside of the caravan I was lifting. Opp's! I dropped it and sneaked off back into bed with Jan. I didn't think many other people would be using the site near to Christmas time.

On 2ⁿᵈ of January 1993, after only my second Christmas out of prison in nearly twenty years I was charged with conspiracy to rob, possession of a firearm and GBH. (Grievous Bodily Harm) Kelly-Anne had taken up with a wrong 'un - a prick called Jim. A gun and a wig were found in my jacket and as for the prick called Jim I gave him a knuckle sandwich for a number of reasons, he deserved it. Maybe Kelly-Anne will tell the world all about it one day. I faced a number of charges and because of my reputation I faced five years in jail. Here I was on remand again because I decided to act as judge and jury against one of Kelly-Anne's pricks.

I made an appearance at Luton magistrates' court from my remand cell on 11ᵗʰ January and was further remanded for four weeks! Loraine was there and my cousin Darren, a lovely lad. I never got a chance to speak to him though. I half expected to see Kelly there so she could jump up and tell everyone it was a bad joke, but she wasn't. I'd guessed that she'd probably be on the piss – drinking vodka. It's been a week of mental stress for me, all I did was give this Jim one good punch, but because I was wearing a ring it caused a bit more damage than I anticipated. Usually it only took one punch to put an average guy away for the night, but with me being away for so long I didn't realise that the added bonus of a ring on my hand would do a little more damage like breaking his nose.

I kept waking up at night seeing Kelly and I still can't believe I'm locked up again after only a matter of 30+ days of freedom. I recall Kelly turning up at court on 2nd January and not looking at me, she left in a red car, which I believed was a cop car! I'm becoming paranoid and think back to the time I was arrested in '88 and wonder if Kelly had anything to do with it then, although my mind is too split to even think she had? The prick, Jim, comes back into my mind, he tried to strangle Kelly and was abusive to me, he deserved all what he got, but I didn't deserve this. I was only acting in Kelly's favour.

Jim to me was a sicko, a fucking rat and a mug. Kelly had this gun to protect herself after Jim had assaulted her at Christmas time in '92. I'd had trouble with Kelly myself and we ended up having a big row where she attacked me and I instinctively lashed out – slapping her across her head. I hurt Kelly's ear and felt guilty afterwards, although she brought it on herself as it wasn't in me to hurt a woman, but what do you do when a woman attacks you? It hurt me knowing I'd slapped Kelly. Kelly made a mug of me in front of others in a pub and flaunted herself in front of others - she had these fantasies!

After I'd punched Jim's nose in I helped him clean up the mess, but he ran to the police and I was lifted. They found the gun and wig in a jacket in the wardrobe so I faced extra charges on top of the GBH charge. I was back inside on remand, back in the block and back on cat 'A' at Woodhill prison. What the fuck was going on, am I truly insane! Big Dennis Campbell is two cells away; he's what you call on a lay-down from Whitemoor. Dennis is good solid stuff; last time I saw him was in Parkhurst. I had four stab wounds in my back and I was being stretchered away to St Mary's Hospital. I shouted to Dennis: 'I've stabbed myself'. I'm like that; I always like to leave with a bang. Although in actual fact I hadn't stabbed myself, but more of that later.

My life's been insanity from the day I left my mother's womb, I screamed so loud even the doctor got nervous. I believe I was born a 'danger baby', a cat 'A' baby. What I mean by that is that my path and destiny were already marked out for me, I'm simply following that path. All my childhood was crazy, all my teens were crazy, my adulthood I've lost and as Ron said, 'Madness is a gift of life'.

Professors of psychiatry have told me that I'm unique. I always get my victory and if it means waiting then so be it. I waited twelve years to serve a guy up who upset me. I cut his arse up with a Stanley blade, me and Stan got on well. The big fat rat screamed like a baboon. I am what you could describe as a special type of madman as nobody knows what I suffer from; no one's been able to agree on a diagnosis. It's been debated that I'm an epileptic, but I say bollocks to that. The police were mad enough to charge me in the name of 'Bronson' so you tell me who's really mad, even though they knew my name was 'Peterson' – small minds.

In five years I counted that I'd chinned 22 screws, it speaks for itself, I'm a problem. I'm sick of it, fuck all's changed with me. No sooner had I been back inside and I've already chinned a screw and just before coming here I chinned a prisoner at Luton Police Station, so I'm still on my toes. Young guys see me as the prisoner to knock out, knock Bronson out and get a name. It's really very silly, as to get a label like mine and catch up to me they'd have had to do as much time as I've spent in solitary to get anywhere near to what I've served and the places I've been.

I'm no threat to fellow cons, I don't lock the cell doors, I'm not a fucking gunslinger. Some of the stories going on around about me amaze me. I've supposedly tore out eyes and ate them, fuck me I'm a vegetarian!

Anyway here I am back inside and I'm not happy. The cunts don't want to give me bail, so I'm not pleased. Big Dennis reckons I'll get two charges dropped, so do I. The GBH charge is the one that's worrying me. I hit this guy so hard it had five years worth of anger in it and he stopped my right hook like a bullet. He was in the wrong place at the wrong time. I caught him in Kelly's flat, he's a ponce, a silly bugger, but whatever he may be he'll never look so nice as he did.

I'm against violence, but in extreme cases violence is necessary and the only answer. Jim's got five brothers in Luton and I say they're all scum too, as if my brother grassed I'd smash him as well. In a 'good society' the lot should've waited for me down an alley and got their retribution. Ron and Reg Kray taught me a lot about being a man, I consider them both to be gentleman and both never moaned and now Reg has to get on with it without Ron, he takes it on the jaw. I was privileged to have met them and I remember when their mother passed away, I was at Broadmoor with Ron and I cried at the passing away of such a good lady.

I'm really a loner, I've very few people in my life, I've hardly anyone I can express myself to. I've only ever been able to fully relate to one person and that's my heavenly cousin, Loraine. Loraine has been the reason I've survived all this hell; she comes to me like the angel she is. She's strength within my soul and a comfort at depressing times; she's my soul sister. I once cut her out of my life, but she still come to me and whispered, 'I'm sorry Mickey', I forgave her, I had no choice.

I seen for the first time in over nine her before I was sent here on remand, sadly it was at our Auntie Pam's funeral, which was such a great loss for us all. But when I looked into Loraine's eyes I felt so warm, there was an angel looking back at me. 'You made it, Mickey', that's what she said. She could melt butter by just looking at it. I once saw her walking on air, crazy but true.

Whitney Houston is number 1 in the charts at present (1993), but I always rated Dolly Parton's 'I will always love you' as the better version, maybe I'm old fashioned. I've done some singing in my time, mostly through cell windows. I'm told that 'My Wonderful World' number is as good as the great Louis Armstrong's original, a psychiatrist told that to me. I once broke out with an Elvis number 'Jail House Rock' in a Parkhurst church service – I got banned.

My crazy mixed up woman Kelly Anne is a chronic alcoholic and right now I feel she's a pathological liar, maybe it's just the way I'm felling. We're not in love and at times I don't love no fucker as no bastard could love me in the way I need to be loved. Kelly Anne doesn't love me - she needs me. My idea of love is cuddles, lots and lots of cuddles – all night cuddles. Where the bodies gel together with sweat, cuddles that are so powerful it feels you're both actually one person.

My ideal lover hasn't been created or we just haven't met. I'll never find her, as she's only a figment of my imagination. My dream is to cuddle up to my lover and enter her and stay inside her all night. No sound, no noise, no movement. Just us together, as one, it won't even be sexual intercourse, in a strange sense it will be spiritual for both of us.

A silent, still, sleeping fuck, no orgasms, no ejaculation, just deep within. What a way to die. If some arsehole crept up and finished me off as I slept with my love then it would be a great ending, but my lover don't exist and never will. Maybe just as well as my obsession for her may drive her over the edge. Kelly and me are more like brother and sister and at times I feel we both have serious mental problems.

My last night of freedom (this time) she slept in a bed with Carol, a known lesbian and I slept on the settee. Me, a man whose been denied love for almost two decades and I've gotta sleep alone whilst two sexually active women cuddle up together. It should be me getting cuddled. Fuck me, I may as well be back in a stinking cell, (that's how I felt) alone, confused and hurt. Life's a bitch, really. All I done was break some scumbags nose. Maybe I'm truly meant to be on my own. All this love crap does bug me, what's love? I obviously still feel lustful when I'm close to a young pretty girl.

Kelly keeps telling me to bring a pretty girl back to the flat, but I can't even chat them up. I'm lost, but now I wonder if it's for her satisfaction or mine? I like Kelly, as she's dangerous, I love dangerous things. She's capable of turning out all my lights, at times she actually puts me on edge. I respect her loyalties when she's sober. I'm in jail right now over her nonsense, but I can't or will not hate her, as she's crazy, hell-bent. I love madness at its best, violent mad, I'll walk this rap, you'll see.

I could get bail in a week, God willing. Prisons don't want me, mental hospitals don't want me and the police outside are petrified of me. No fucker wants me, I don't want myself, I think a lot about death. Death at times takes over all of my thoughts. I sense a very violent end to life, but as long as can fight back I'll be prepared for the ending. After all, what's death? It must be serene, peaceful and eternal sleep; we all need a rest at times. Fuck taking my own life, no way, ever. I tried once, never again, once in 40 years ain't bad.

Kelly is retracting all she said in a statement against me, the police gave her drink before they interviewed her, the filthy scum will go so low to put me away for good. They don't want me in prison and as soon as I'm out they'll do anything to get me back in away from their doorstep, I can't win. Luton for me hasn't been lucky; I have to forget the place before it puts me into a hole. I'm on a desperate avenue, prison put me there and Luton's been bad news for me.

The date's arrived for my court appearance at Luton and I ended up with a fine for the assault and the other two charges were dropped what a result. All of my hopes had happened and here I was walking the streets again, a chance in a million, I felt good, but it wasn't to last.

I was set up in a crime I was to become involved in and unwittingly the man that set me up was the one that put me on to the job in the first place. There I was all togged up in my gear ready to do another big heist and I'm on my mobile talking to the man who set me up. He asked me if I was near the place and was I ready to do it. No sooner had I confirmed all of the details then the police pounced and at that time I was in a car with a black guy, his surname was Felix.

The whole world and his friend had joined the police force by the look of this as they surrounded the car I was in and they all pulled guns out on me. I later learned the only reason they didn't blow my head off was 'cos I had this guy with me. Would you believe that my cousin Loraine's husband, Andy, was also pulled into all of this? It got straightened out in the end though.

Felix along with me was nicked, the guy who set it all up had to be congratulated on how he did and he will not be forgotten for his deviousness. I was remanded and Felix got bail, no doubt something to do with his colour. So when I was up on the **26th of March 1993** I had a plan that night as I lay in my cell. I'd decided that if Felix was granted bail 'cos he was black then I would surely qualify if I was also black. Out came the tins of black boot polish. I decided that I'd rub them into my skin before I went to sleep, save me doing it in the morning, this was at midnight. I awoke the next morning and my body heat had melted the black boot polish into my skin, yep, today I was leaving Woodhill a black man!

'Racial Discrimination' flashed through my mind as well the word 'boredom'. With my co-accused (an innocent man) being a spade (black) I just had to make a point for the court. When my door unlocked the screws here just didn't know what to say or make of it. I collect my breakfast at 8.30 a.m., I go out for a walk in the cage for ½ an hour with my pal, Kirk, whose the block cleaner. As I'm walking up and down some black guy from a cell window shouts to me: 'Hey, brother!' This guy thought I was a spade!

The van arrives to take me to court and seven screws, none that I know, get out, I'm cuffed up- no words are spoken. It's a silent journey to Luton magistrates' for this preliminary hearing in which I might be granted bail, although I had a snowball in hell's chance of being granted it.

I'm deep in thought about the case and I'm wondering if Kelly will be there and if Loraine and Andy will be there, what will they think? Will they think I've finally flipped my lid, well maybe I have? I felt tense and edgy, but I also felt violent within me at the same time. A strange feeling of depression hit me like I was being dragged out of my senses.

I had a statement with me to read out to the court. If I was refused to read it, well...I never knew how I'd take it! I'd be upset though. On arrival the Luton cops couldn't believe it nor could Tim Green, my solicitor at that time. Tim got me my previous acquittal, a great man, also with him was my friend, Frank Longford (Lord Longford to you). Frank could not believe it, he's an old man and he must have seen some sights over the years and obviously wouldn't have shocked so easily, but he was shocked! His eyes aren't the best at times, but he looked dazed, he's a good man and I respect him a lot.

Tim never liked the idea of me reading my statement out also he said it might not be allowed. 'I'm ready, allowed or not', I said. My co-accused, James Felix, is a totally innocent man and my statement will prove it, plus I'm innocent of any conspiracy. I was cuffed up to a screw and then led into the courtroom. Where to my delight I saw Kelly, Loraine and Andy. James Nicholson (the Prince) was also there and my Uncle Jack's family, I felt quite emotional and here was me ready to give my maiden speech.

Felix's brief was not ready for the committal, he was mumbling something about the papers. I rate his brief like a bat with no wings, a fucking idiot! As this was to be the committal the bastard got me upset as I wanted to be committed, we had the papers so why fuck about, let's get this poxy trial on the road. All this remand does my nut in. Back and forward to court all the time like a yo-yo. I want the trial to go on so as to get it finished with.

I was watching Kelly for a good minute; her hair looked nice, she was dressed smart, she looked bloody lovely, but our eyes never met. She was 20 feet away; it might have been 20 miles. There was nothing between us anymore if there even had been at all. I felt empty, seeing Jack's family brought memories flooding back, I really felt alone.

Loraine and Andy's eyes were on me, I love them both and I know they love me. Loraine looked her lovely self, but their eyes couldn't take in what they saw – me black! They looked stunned, so did Jack's family, the Prince looked bewildered, my co-accused even looked baffled, the magistrates' looked shocked and the whole court was really in a state of shock! A bigger shock was coming as if I couldn't read my statement I now knew it would result in violence, as my breathing was heavy and sweat was running down my back. A true sign I was about to fly and bear in mind no words were spoken between the screws and me since we left Woodhill.

The atmosphere was electric - I was tense. Tim, my brief, stood up to explain about my request. I shouted out, 'I either read it or I'll be upset'. Silence! Whispers! Eyes! 'Granted', came the reply. Phew!

It took me ten minutes to read it out, as I read it I started feeling emotional. I looked across to Kelly who was now looking at me, as 90% of it was on her, asking her to marry me!!! I told the court that I'd fight ten of Mike Tyson. Swim up Niagara Falls; fight sharks just for a cuddle from Kelly Anne. I went on to tell them that I've eaten more porridge than Goldilocks and the Three Bears.

Not a whisper was in that courtroom, all eyes on me, 'Thank you', I said. 'Thank you for listening, God bless the Queen and my Kelly Anne'. I was remanded for a further two weeks. Now the amazing thing is I blacked up the previous night. Would you believe a miracle happened, fate! Unbeknown to me somebody else was going through the press, 'The Sun'. The Queen was on the front paper – BLACK. Her photograph was in negative form making her look black! It almost fucked my mind up, her black - me black! The odds on this must be one billion to one, fate. I've no need to lie as it can all be checked out and confirmed by everyone who was there.

We travelled back in silence with a police escort. The morning was insane, truly mad, just another chapter in my life of confusion. I'm now seriously thinking of standing trial as something else! Why not have shocked juries, what's wrong with that? These trials are taken far too seriously especially when it's my future at stake. God knows why I do these things, as I don't know why myself - fortunately no damage done and nobody hurt.

I pulled another crazy stunt at another trial but I suppose I can tell you about it here while I remember. I was being messed about being moved from this place to that and was due up in court on a different matter to the one I'm telling you about here. I decided to go to court bollock naked, which I did and while I was in the holding cell I was told that my cousin, Loraine, was coming down to talk some sense into me. I sat there with a towel wrapped around me. She said: 'You either get your clothes on for the court or I'm off and I won't be at the trial, are you listening?' I took her advice as she made sense in other things that she said, as I said she's my angel.

Back to the black Charlie Bronson, Kelly smiled as I walked out of court, I'm sure I saw a tear in her eye, but then again she'd have to be a heartless bitch not to feel any emotion after all I said. I just hope it sunk into her head and gave her some sense of hope back, as I love to see her smile. I was proud she turned up, God only knows if she'll ever change, then again God only knows if I'll change. But one thing's for sure, I'm glad to be white again, fuck me it don't arf take some getting off, that boot polish!

As for Kelly she had further problems in her life as the Social Services had become involved with regards her children. Hopefully they've grown up safe and well.

Maybe you want to go back now and read the previous chapter to take it all in 'cos it sure as fuck seems complicated.

7

Taking hostages for me has become a dangerous game. They want me to fuck up, they want me to take another one, it would suit them fine for me to take one a day, take a hostage a day to keep the penal system away, but do you know what the outcome would be – death. They'd shoot me and it would be a case of shoot to kill!

I've got to tell you about one particular hostage-taking situation because it's special, very special. My best siege of all time is the one in which I took a governor hostage; it was the best one for pleasure. Governor Wallace at Hull Special Unit became my fly, wrapped up in my web.

April the 4th 1994 just after breakfast I made my move. Deputy Governor No 2, Adrian Thomas Wallace, became my hostage. He upset me, he was arrogant, big headed and had to be right all of the time, no matter what. He upset me over some little thing, which multiplied.

There were only four cons on the unit, we were all considered too dangerous to put on the wings with other cons. There was Ed Slater; a lifer, Paul Flint; a lifer, Tony McUllagh; a double lifer and of course yours truly. I told them all to stay out of it 'cos 'I'm gonna wrap Wallace up!'

He walked into the unit like a lord. I pushed past the other guys in front of me as soon as I saw him and grabbed him by the neck. There were screws about but I'm so fast that they didn't see it coming, whoosh! I pushed Wallace towards the wall and put my forearm under his chin from behind him, I pulled his head back and applied pressure to his throat. 'Don't come near me or I'll snap his neck', I shouted to the screws. I chinned Wallace and dragged him backwards into the TV room, I kept my back to the wall and once in there I tied him up using his own tie to do so. I sat him down on a chair in the middle of the room facing the door while I barricaded the door with tables and chairs.

I spoke to one of the screws, Roy Kirk, through the windows, 'He's nothing but a bastard and nobody likes him!' I told Wallace that I'd snap his neck if he moved. I noticed he had a personal phone! (Security) So I called them up and said, 'I want a fillet steak, French-fries, mushrooms and a tin of dog food for Wallace. The mushrooms meant a lot to me 'cos I had a ¼ pound of them nicked from my cell and I know it wasn't cons. At the time Wallace did fuck all about it. This part of the siege wasn't mentioned in his subsequent statement used in evidence, poor memory this guy has?

He was lying a maggot, 'Please, Charlie, please don't hurt me'. None of that went into his statement either, proving what an arrogant sod he is. He had this blue pin striped suit on while I was dressed in tracka (tracksuit) bottoms, a vest and prison boots – worlds apart. I slapped him across the chops a couple of times and this knocked him to the floor, it was just to show him who was boss. I grabbed him by the neck like I was holding a puppy and threw him back on the chair and told him to 'Fucking shut up'.

I kept telling him he was a bag of shit and how I was gonna kill him. I was starting to get really pissed off and told Wallace that police marksmen would be brought in and if I was gonna get it then he'd get it as well, as they wouldn't give a fuck.

I rifled through his pockets and put all the stuff on the table in front of him and then started to chuck it all over the room, none of it was any use to me, credit cards and other shit, his money; I tore up! I pulled his keys out of his pocket and with a yank it ripped his trousers down the leg, a new fashion style by the House of Bronson, he looked really cool in this little number.

He really got to me this guy and as I spotted an iron I felt like taking it to his face and reshaping it, a bit of plastic surgery never goes in wrong, but I'm not a cold hearted bastard although I came close and held it to his head I threatened to stave his head in with it, but I didn't. Doesn't that show you the type of man I really am? I could've done it, but the look in his eyes, the fear, the terror and the tears stopped me.

169

I swung Wallace around in the chair he was in, turning him away from the door and the windows, as he was seeing too much for my liking. They're a crafty lot this mob, winking and twitching to each other. The room was about 10 feet square, I kept pacing up and down making decisions and kicking furniture around that was getting in the way.

I told Wallace to shut up, but I had to ask him to get on the radio he had on him and I gave my demands to him. 'Tell them that we're to leave the prison together and if there's any SAS or Royal Marines in the prison that they'd better shoot us both'. Wallace complied and he also told them that I'd done jungle warfare and I wasn't fucking about'.

Roy Kirk was still watching through the window during this time, I was becoming bored with it so I turned the TV on to the pop station and turned it up full blast, yeah, this suited me down to the ground. I asked for a cuppa' and being the gent I am asked Wallace if he wanted one too, which he did. Wallace shouted to the screws what we wanted and shortly after the tea arrived, I moved the barricade just enough to let the cups fit through.

This Wallace fella's a clever guy, he asked for his hands to be untied so as he could drink his tea; I obliged. His free hand, I told him to keep in his pocket. I'd told them that I wanted my demands met by 11.00 a.m. or Wallace would get hurt.

I despised Wallace because he's power crazy, he hates cons and he's a coward and I'll tell you why soon and then you'll know why I made that remark. Also I'd been writing to a female inmate at Durham's 'She Wing', Avril Gregory, a lifer. It was agreed that a one-day visit would take place at Hull or Durham prison for the pair of us to meet as I'd been writing to Avril for a while. Who agreed to that visit – Governor Wallace and the guy in charge of all of the CRC units in this country.

Great, I was built up to this visit, Wallace and Goulds had agreed fully to this visit going ahead. It'd made my day and I was really looking forward to meeting Avril and then you know what, the fucking bastards cancelled it? You know what they told me, that it was some problem at Durham! I knew then that I'd been lied to by these bastards once again, I'd fell hook, line and sinker for it all over again. I took it calmly, very calmly as there was no point in being awkward over it as I'd need time to think what I was gonna do.

When you're banged up with people you get to feel that they'll stand by you and you all work as a team. But as I took Wallace hostage I heard Eddie Slater and Paul Flint saying 'Come on Charlie, there's no need for this, come on – not this way Charlie'. What a fucking mob of turncoats.

Roy Kirk was my personal officer and I even worked out with him in the gym and I had my own special diet that the others on the unit also followed. There was 34 screws to look after us four, I'm not kidding, work out the wages spent on that little lot in a month and I bet all of your debts would be paid off and some more! I started to trust Kirky and credit where credit's due; he started to mix with me. But I'm use to how they go about it, although I sensed something different about him, like he cared.

This man called Goulds told me to apply for accumulated visits down south and I would be transferred so here I was having all my hopes built up again, a move was on, it looked good, but guess what, yeah, I was knocked back again at the last fucking minute. By now I was starting to lose it.

I was supposed to go to Belmarsh so I could be closer to Loraine and Andy, Wallace loved it when this was stopped, fucking arsehole. There's one thing to get a KB (knock back) but when they gloat over it then that deserves a slap. Wallace stopped equipment coming into the unit from the education department; he upset Eddie Slater one of my fellow cons over a claim for lost property. I cleaned the unit spotless, I worked hard to achieve positive things, but he never once respected it.

I tried to smash one of the windows in the TV room so as to be able to speak to Kirky, I tried with wood and then I bashed it with the iron and would it fuck go. By this time I was losing it badly but Kirky indicated he would remove the small glass from the room door, 'why didn't I think of that?' Kirky was shouting at me to calm down, 'It's this cunt's fault', I told him. Wallace was put down by Kirky's words, but I knew he was trying it on with me and that was starting to get to me, as I'm not an idiot and I know you don't get to be a governor without having some brain cells in your head.

I wrote a note saying I wanted to speak directly to Goulds and to get a phone so I could call his London office. I demanded a blow up doll, but a one with blonde hair, not black. I was starting to worry about the SAS as they drill through walls so I strapped a chair to the front and back of Wallace, clever eh? I grabbed him by the neck ands we marched to the next room, another TV room, as we had two rooms that accommodated two TV channels, one for each room.

'I'm in charge, I'm gonna die today and if anybody tries anything, they'll join me!' I got Wallace on the door and tied a sheet around his neck and I asked for two more cups of tea, it's thirsty work this hostage taking malarkey. I sat at the back of the room, behind Wallace, the lights were out and the TV was on, it gave me some cover as I stayed in the darkness as the light from the TV glared at them looking in.

As I said earlier, I like to sing to get rid of tension so I started to sing into the radio, I told them I wanted this song recorded and for it to played at my funeral as I knew I was gonna die that day, I was prepared for it coming my way. I sang 'I believe' and I belted it out, it was my swan song or so I thought! This steak and chips was taking a fucking long time to come, the room service stunk – they weren't going to get a tip that was for sure.

I was behind Wallace and I wanted a piss, I pissed in the waste bin. I knew Wallace would be thinking that I'd pour it over him and it was that which gave me even more pleasure in not doing it. His day would've been made if I'd done it, but by not doing it kept him in suspense. I was playing mind games with in reverse with him, to really humiliate him I should've pissed over him but I saw it as a waste of my piss, why piss on a dog. I read in Wallace's statement later on that he'd thought I was going to sexually abuse him when he heard my zip opening, what a fucking pervert, here's me wanting a piss and all he can think about is sex.

I heard all the other screws coming over the radio and it was starting to do my head in so I told them to close the prison for the day and go home. My blow up doll hadn't arrived so I got Wallace to get on the radio and ask for it and I wanted it dressed in a black skirt with black tights. My last hostage situation, when I took Andy Love, my demands weren't met so here I was again simply asking for a blow up doll, but when that failed to turn up my demands became heavier, I wanted an Uzi machine gun with 5,000 rounds of ammo.

I had the keys to the whole damn prison and I wanted to know which key fitted what door, I had to get out of that fucking room somehow. I wrapped the sheet around Wallace and me, as if anyone was going to shoot they'd have to have fucking x-ray eyes to see through the sheet so as to get a clean shot at me.

I got back on the radio, 'I know I'm gonna be shot by one of them fucking coppers' bullets, make sure you send a recording of that song to my solicitor in London'. I then started singing some Christmas songs and hymns and for good measure I tore the TV from its stand and smashed it to the ground near Wallace. I was getting claustrophobic and my life was running past me, and it's not like they tell you, all what I could see was liquid cosh, beatings, body belts, pain, kickings and worse – hell!

I had to get out of this room it was starting to kill me, I pushed Wallace out and I kept my back to the wall, we're sheeted together, I headed back for the first room we'd been in, fuck knows why? I grabbed for the handle, but we started to fall over, as I was off balance.

Footsteps come running and I was overpowered, Wallace was snatched from me like a baby. 'Alright, its over', I said. I was cuffed up and still on the ground when I felt an almighty smash, like my brain had exploded, what the fuck was it? I twisted my head around and from where I was held I could see Wallace's foot coming in landing for a second time, it made contact with my jaw, crunch! You'd have thought I was eating boiled sweets from the noises that were coming out of my jaw. He kept kicking me in the face and body.

Wallace's statement was a load of lies, he said he got to me before the other screws come running, how the fuck could he when he was sheeted in with me and I was under him on the floor and the screws were only a few feet away from us? Wallace went on to say that he was grateful that he'd been dragged away otherwise he felt he'd have done some harm to me. Look! A man of my size isn't gonna lie there taking it from a fucking arsehole like Wallace, am I? I was fucking cuffed up and held down for him to do his dirty work on me, like a coward does.

Guess what else Wallace said in his statement? He said he felt as if though he was being pampered and didn't want all of the hassle after he'd went to the governors' office. The first two screws to jump me were Kirky and David Lloyd Jones, Jones mentioned nothing of Wallace kicking the shit out of me, and neither did Kirky. Jones conveniently lost his notes he made immediately after the event saying they were left in the TV room, fucking liar. I had the shit kicked out of me and Wallace's statement confirmed it when he admitted kicking me, yet not one of the other statements mentioned this? A screw called David Purvis jumped on me as well and his statement didn't even mention the kicking I got?

In a conflicting statement issued by Wallace he went on to say that as we went down "I whacked him one". He went on to say "I thought to myself 'He's still there', and I can recall Roy Kirk on him and I whacked him again and then there were a lot of officers on top of him, and I can recall George White shouting 'get out of here'. Dave Purvis then grabbed me visibly..."

Wallace, in this statement, admits whacking me and says that I was held by a screw when he did it, the truth of the matter is he kicked seven bells out of me while I was cuffed up and held down. He was right though when he says I was held. If I hadn't of tripped this day then who knows what the real ending would've been! Maybe it was to have been a marksman's bullet.

Cutting a long story short, when it all came to court, I pleaded not guilty to the Andy Love hostage taking at Woodhill, in a trial that lasted less than two days. I didn't dispute any of the facts and I was given a total of eight years to run concurrent. On the Wallace hostage taking I was given a whole load of domino numbers that amounted to a total of 15 years, which included the Woodhill sentence and one earlier of robbery where I had a loaded sawn off shotgun, remember – 1993?

Well it looked all roses and there was noting left for it but to get my head together for some serious thinking. What did come out of it though was that Judge Laurence Marshall, who tried my Woodhill hostage case, asked that he be kept informed of my movements as he was concerned at my being moved some 28 times in the space of only 21 months! Judge Marshall of Luton Crown Court said he would be asking Probation Services to keep him updated so that he could monitor what was happening. Since then I've been moved quite a bit, yet I can't see Judge Marshall paying any interest, that's how it's always been – people making the right sort of noises and leaving it at that. Another let down, if a judge can't do as he says then how can I ever expect a prison governor to?

While I remember – I was lined up to fight Lenny McLean for £10,000 winner take all purse it fell through, not my fault though!

8

This is one of the chapters that most of you have been waiting to get to. It's all about sieges and different hostage taking situations. As far as possible I've listed them all in order of time. They aren't all listed, as there just hasn't been enough room!

1976 – Wandsworth, I had just arrived at the seg block, this was the toughest block in the country at this time and they loved to give it to guys like me so I gave a bit of my own. In one week I assaulted five, it cost me a lot of remission and eleven months in isolation, but they dropped me well out after that. Sometimes it pays to suffer for a spell and reap the rewards later – peace.

1976 – Parkhurst, this was a violent year for me, it was very difficult to escape my reputation, I'd now built up a notorious image. No man can run from himself and keep his dignity so I had to fight my way through my sentence. This guy had grassed on a pal of mine so I had no option but to serve him up, and serve him I did. He had the same option to do to me which I done to him, in fact he got the first thrust of the knife in, but that's about all he did get in. The scars he wears are a strong reminder not to open his mouth in the police station ever again. Some need to be cut up to make an example to other would be canaries.

1977 – Wandsworth, one of the hardest fights I ever had was in the recess on 'D'-wing. I fought a big jock who was as tough as iron. The fight lasted a good half-hour. In these days most screws would turn a blind eye to a fistfight, that's they way it was in the 70's. It was a good fair fight, we were both still standing and we shook hands after. I was pissing blood for a week after, I lost teeth, I got cut and my ribs were like jelly, what a battle, I never did see jock again, I hope he got out and made good of it. Max respect to the man. I bet they still talk about it.

1986 – Wormwood Scrubs, when I smashed my fist through bullet proof glass I never expected the consequences. I nearly lost my arm, I was rushed to hospital with my wrist tendons hanging out, I had also severed my main artery, later on I had to have a skin graft and another operation. I was doing one arm press ups for six months after, I almost lost my bleedin' arm. I don't recommend this, take my advice don't try it.

1988 – Full Sutton, I was in serious training and this big black dude, who was a very ignorant type of guy, was forever interrupting conversations and showing disrespect so it was odds on he was a red hot favourite to upset me, and he did just that. I caught him with a peach of a left hook; it caught him on the button. He was a big guy, but he went up like a kite on a windy day. I was quite proud of this hook, which I rate it the best ever that I've thrown. It's only a shame it wasn't ever caught on video.

1990 – Gartree, I hit my hat trick with screws up on the wing. One upset me and I just let go at them all, they were going over like skittles, it reminded me of a cowboy film like the old bar brawls, but it don't mater how many you bowl over they just keep on coming, you just can't win in prison, take that from me, 'cos it will cost you your life and your freedom.

1991 – Winchester, it only took days 'til I blew it. I ran into the SO's (Senior Officer's) office and took it over, I phoned the numbers on the desk and told whoever it was 'Get me a Kentucky meal'. Yeah, that's how crazy I was at this time, I'd do anything for a delicious meal. I never ever got that Kentucky; all I got was a bigger headache.

July 1992 – Here I was in Parkhurst over on the beautiful Isle of Wight, but enough of the sales pitch. On arrival I was put into the block and told that there might be a chance that I could go up on to 'M'-wing if I behaved. Danny Reece was the block cleaner so I asked if I could go out on the exercise yard with him, we worked out together, he's as strong as a bull, then Keith Ritchie came down on the block with a bag of goodies for me and the lads; sweets and biscuits, but the screws wouldn't let him give them to us, so I stripped off and pressed the bell I was going to run out and get their office and shit on the carpet. They must have known that I was up to something. Again they overreacted and brought in the heavy mob.

My door was flung open and in they came, we had a rough and tumble for about ten minutes – they love it...well so do I. But I can't ever win, they overpowered me and in the box I went.

Looking back at it all seems amusing, but it's not at the time and I certainly don't recommend it. I stayed in the box for a week. Danny Reece was putting cheese rolls and milk through the flap in the bottom of the door. In all the prisons and all of the blocks that I've been in no block cleaner has ever done this before. Every day Danny came to the hatch to shake my hand, he doesn't like to admit it but he's got feelings, he's a tough fucker - loves me to bits.

So off I went to M-wing, loads of cons I knew worked there, Kevin Brown, Tony and Pete Coulson, Mickey Rielly, Dennis Campbell, Vic Dark, Jerry Parker, Rupert Tibbs, Keith Richie and Big 'H'. I ate, good, trained good and slept good the time was flying by – I was winning. Most nights from 6.00 to 8.00 p.m. I trained on the wing, alone. I was feeling good.

Mr Marriot, the Governor, was obviously terrified in case I went off my rocker again, he came to see me often and I assured him I was okay. Big 'H' was a good pal to me, but then they moved me to Whitemoor, I missed him a lot. I was still allowed to see Gi Gi, my head was better than it had been for years. Don Swinton, a psychologist, helped me a lot, a good man who I respect. Then I had a brainwave; years ago in the 60's big Frank Mitchell built a fishpond down by the football pitch on some waste ground. At first they all saw it as a big joke, I was going to build one as well.

Governor Marriot's a man I class as a Governor (I give him a capital 'G'.) with balls. He was subsequently slung out of Parkhurst over an escape; he was made the scapegoat. I was behaving myself and I just asked him if I could make a pond, he, at first, laughed and thought I was joking. I said I was serious/

A meeting was held and a couple of days later he called me up to say permission was given, my reason for this was simple, all my years in prison I'd never done nothing in prison but smash it up.

A fishpond represents peace, and a con with a troubled mind could find some comfort in a pond, just to sit down and watch the fish swimming could be a relaxing thing. Let's face the facts, it's better than watching walls and fences, ain't it? I was going to do my own design, a figure eight with a bridge; it was all in my head and coming to life. They gave me a pickaxe, shovel and a fork and I went to work. I began my pond, my monument of peace.

The first day I dug deep, about eight feet, some screws were looking worried, but I assured them that I was fit enough, I just wanted this pond to be the best fucking pond ever. I wanted to leave it for my fellow cons so it could live on and so people would finally say that 'Charlie Bronson's got his act together'. It wasn't to suck up or for parole as I never got fuck all off these people. This pond was my own idea and I felt great.

On the second day Cliffy Moody arrived, so I let him help me. The third day I ended up in Saint Mary's Hospital with multiple stab wounds in my back. During the time I was building this pond some smart Alec decided to take the credit for it and became jealous of the pond. I smashed his jaw in three places and got on with the job in hand. But the thing is when you're a face in one of these places you get a lot of people wanting to suck up to you, he had plenty of people wanting to do that and more. His cockney mates were watching, about eight of them so I says to them 'What's your problem?' 'No problem, Chas, honest.' I turned to walk away, the worst thing I could've done with this mob of cowards and wankers. I won't name any names, but everyone knew what happened, I'm no grass. One con said that he'd done it all by himself saying that he'd 'stabbed Charles Bronson'.

The surgeon said two knives were used with different sized blades. I was having words with a con, others joined in, men that I knew and respected, some were genuinely trying to stop the fight, when I was being pulled away I was stabbed in the back.

I was left alone, I knew that I was hurt bad, my breathing was painful and blood was pouring out of my wounds, I still managed to walk back to M-wing, poor Cliffy was devastated. I collapsed in my cell and I saw the faces of all my family passing before me, I felt sure I was dying. Big Bill the Bomb (Billy Williams) came running in, he stuffed up the holes that the bastards had put into me, Bill saved me that day as he had once saved me outside.

The face that I will always remember was Big Dennis Campbell's looking down at me from one of the landings. I shouted up to him 'I've stabbed myself, what a way to get off the wing, eh!'

Later I fucked off the police, 99% of cons would have used it to get compensation, to help get parole and get out faster or just for the sympathy vote – not me. Later they brought me back, cuffed. I couldn't even walk, but they still cuffed me.

They put me in the hospital wing of Parkhurst, Gi Gi was allowed to come over and see me, he was mad over it, so were a lot of others. He told me that a lot of cons feared me, that was why they done it and that my back was the only way.

After Gi Gi left I had words with a screw and smashed the hatch off my door and slung everything out on the landing, as I destroyed my cell all of my wounds opened up and claret was everywhere. The pain shot through my body, they sent the heavy mob into me. A man with holes in his body, what sort of people are they?

I was bent up and put in the box, this was the same box I was certified mad in back in 1978, it was still just as rotten and dirty, it hadn't altered in over 14 years. I fucked all of the doctors off and wouldn't let them in the box, they spoke to me through the hatch and I spat at them. Mick Connell, a screw, came to see me; he told me that they were worried in case the wounds became infected. I told Mick I was shitting blood. Then Don Swinton came to see me; he was disgusted to see that I was slung in the box in my condition. Through Don and Mick I took some anti-inflammatory tablets and put some antiseptic on my wounds – I was in a lot of pain. Don done a deal with the doctors to put me up on the high risk landing, once I was up there I showered and let the doctor examine me, he prescribed some drugs and changed my bandages twice daily.

Colin Robinson was on this landing and so was Bob Maudsley. Bob had killed three cons, one in Broadmoor and two in Wakefield. It was good to see Colin again, but most of the others were a pain in the head. One of them in particular was heading for a clump; he was upsetting me.

Mr Marriot came to see me, I genuinely believe, even now, that he was saddened at what had happened to me. For the first time ever we were getting somewhere, he stuck his neck out for me. Mr Marriot gave me something that not many other people had – trust. I would like to think that I'd never let him down this time. Another governor, Joe Whitty, also took chances, but more of that in my next book called 'Legends'.

He told me that I would be moving on soon and that he had no choice in the matter, as no one knew whom it was that plunged the knives into me. I wasn't very pleased about all of this I lost my pond. I get stabbed in the back and here it was me that had to be moved, so long Parkhurst.

January 25th 1985 – At Park Lane Special Hospital I gave a guy a good turning over 'cos he propositioned me in a letter asking that I have a gay affair with him. Mervyn Horley was aged about 36 and he was with me at Broadmoor and when I eventually landed at Park Lane there he was – fucking stalking me. I should be in the Guinness book of Records for being the first person to be recorded as being stalked in the UK. I've said a few times, but I'll say it again and that is I've got nothing against homosexuals as long as they keep their goings on to themselves and in the right place and at the right time – sounds like a 'Martini advert'. This was the note he wrote to me:

Dear Mick, (I was known as Mickey Peterson way back then.)

No offence meant, but I would like a 'gay' relationship with you. I do 'French' only. I did french with Alan Carter. He said this is better than sexual intercourse. I love Des Adams. I love him. He wants me for himself.

Signed Love & Peace
Duchess

I don't even care if I become a gay icon or have a gay following, but the minute anyone tries to impose their sexuality on to me then that's the minute I snap. I saw Horley being with some other nutters being walked to the workshops, I ran towards him and set about him, he went down like a lead balloon. 'That'll teach you to write those stinking letters to me, you fucking pervert.' I remodelled his face, just a little bit for him, that day.

I used to call him 'Holli' at Broadmoor; he was a known queen way back then. I had a broken bottle with me and I grabbed Holli around the neck with one arm and then with the one holding the broken bottle I used it to stab away at Holli's hands that were up in front of his face, he knew what was coming off. Some of the larger splinters of glass snapped off as I dragged the bottle down the side of his face, luckily for him he was wearing one of those Parka type coats with a hood that he had up, as it was a cold day.

I was shouting at Holli 'I'll fucking kill you, you bastard'. I wasn't interested in doing the staff who jumped in to pull him away from me. He'd taken a liberty – I was no queer and am no queer. I made another lunge at him, but by this time he was dragged away to safety. I shouted after him, 'Nobody sends that sort of letter to me'. I was shouting at the staff, 'What would any of you do if you got a letter like that?' There was more claret (blood) than in a wine cellar.

I was charged with this and went to court and had three more years added on, I was almost out and the slag had me doing another three. Eleven fucking years and now it starts again!

1985 - Walton prison, it was the summer of '85. This was one of my greatest days and I look back on it with a smile; this was a dangerous mission and a lethal climb. Walton jail's five stories high, it's an old jail with old drainpipes and rotten guttering, but I made it and for three days and nights I was free. I demolished two roofs. The Scousers threw me up sweets and water bottles. I love the Scousers, even though Jack Straw doesn't, they've got a great sense of humour. From up on this roof I could see crowds gathering outside the wall. They were shouting up to me 'Jump, Jump, Jump'. See I told you they had a sense of humour.

Liverpool jail was the last hanging prison before it was abolished in the mid 60's. I sat up there in the silence in the early morning, looking over at the old death cell trying to imagine what must go through a man's head when he's waiting to walk his last few steps. Just how many men swung below me? How many of them were innocent? I wonder.

I looked over at the hundreds of cell windows on the other wings, here slept 1,600 men, all crammed up like sardines and there I was free as a bird. But only a fool knows the end, more years added on, more solitary, more pain, there's no end. A sense of power a feeling of invincibility let me tell you now, a man don't know nothing unless he kisses a rainbow, it's beautiful.

1988 – Was the year, hell I was so upset, life was pulling me down. I just had to break free from the prison madness here at Leicester prison, I needed to escape from myself, I needed my own space; a man needs to be free from so much crap. Even though I was still in the prison seg unit it was still driving me mad, they were pushing me over the edge, so up I went. Where better than

181

the roof. A place of thought, a place where I belong (The Birdman), a place nobody can touch me, a place I can be free.

This was a time in my life when certain people outside were causing me serious grief, so bad was my head I felt like diving off, crushing my skull. I was losing it, losing faith, I was going nowhere, I was a lost soul, I was locked out to the world, but the problems of other people's worlds crept into mine and I felt helpless. I learned a lot up on this roof; I learned a lot about others and myself. They don't mess with the man no more 'cos one day they know I'm gonna walk out and that's why they don't mess or so I thought! They turned on the light and I saw the light, I came back down a stronger man, that's how prison life is, - unreal, crazy and dangerous and that's why I love it.

1990 - Parkhurst, this was one of my mad moments. The prison van had arrived to take me to the second furthest northern prison in England – Durham (Frankland). That's one long journey from the Isle of Wight to Durham! I said to myself 'nah', so I thought fast 'what should I do?' Ten on to one is never good odds, they're just gonna jump me, wrap me up and throw me in the van. So I played it cool, I walked out of the seg unit with smile, once at the reception gate I made my move.

I broke free and legged it past them all; I even beat the dogs. In seconds I was on my way up to the roof. I'd done it again; even I couldn't believe it, so imagine how they felt below, sick and gutted. In no time at all they were all below, trying to sweet talk me down. The governors, the doctors and the board of visitors, all the usual parasites. I shouted down 'get my pal Valerio Viecci out of the SS unit and I'll come down peacefully after a ten minute chat with him'.

Valerio was the mastermind behind the Knightsbridge £60m robbery. I hadn't seen him since '88. He was a good friend to me; low and behold they brought him out to see me! I come down, we had a chat and away I went happy as Larry at seeing my pal. A moment like this really makes life worth living. We ain't got a lot in prison, but those that are staunch amongst us are like a brotherhood. I would have demolished that roof at the drop of a hat if I'd never seen my brother Valerio. They were lucky don't you think?

1990 - Frankland, man, was I fed up. I was so bored I was dangerous and when I become bored nobody's safe. It blew up on the exercise yard, I spotted the deputy governor so I grabbed him then made a run with him slung over my shoulder a bit like a fireman's carry, but it wasn't to save him. The 200 cons on the yard let out a shout 'Yippee!' It was like a football cheer, it made me lose my plot, I almost lost it, it was a bit like a dream, was it real? I made it to the wing and ran in, I kicked open an office door and shouted 'Everybody out!' So there we were the governor and me. That's how it happens, a second of madness, a loss of control and the dream is reality, dangerous or what? Well that's how it works with me; nobody knows the inside of a madman's head.

1991 – Wandsworth prison seg unit. When my door opened I couldn't wait to get out on the yard 'cos '91 was to be the greatest fate of my life. I was going to demolish Wandsworth prison all on my own. I'd just lost my Uncle Jack, he was like a father to me, I knew my world was never to be the same again. I wanted to destroy the roof and myself, I had now had enough of the prison madness, it was time for some serious action. Wandsworth's probably the most feared prison in England, it's basically isolation at Wandsworth seg block, one lasted eleven months, but I don't mind it 'cos I love the peace and solitude. The routine suits me, but this day had caused me a serious brain disturbance.

Once out on the yard I leapt over an iron rail and jumped on to a drain and pulled myself thought the barbed wire and up I went. I could hear the alarm bell and whistles going below, but this just starts the adrenaline pumping. I made it up to the third floor only to get stuck. The drainpipe had a large tinned duct over it rather like a collar or an umbrella; this is bolted against the wall. For well over an hour I tried to pull it off, I hit it nutted it and even kicked at it.

My fingers were bleeding and my strength was running out, I could no longer hold on to the pipe, I slid down defeated. A tin umbrella stopped the Wandsworth destruction and I was only a matter of feet from victory, but it may as well have been miles away. I was told later that I'd knocked out all of the bolts but for one! They said that if I had hit it one more time I'd probably have knocked it off. It took me a long time to get over this defeat. I was never put in that yard again. They built a cage just for me; hell if it wasn't so crazy it couldn't be true.

1991 - Full Sutton, I was walking around the yard with a con, we was chatting away and minding our own business when a team of civvies walked out looking at us, we felt like two monkeys in a zoo pen, 'Who's that lot?' I asked the con. 'Don't know...', he said, '...but they look official', I nodded. 'Watch this', I said. I ran over and grabbed one; the rest ran off. It turned out I'd grabbed a trainee probation officer in the jail, he retired the very next day.

September 28th 1993 – This date's very significant and is leading up to a set of events that will cause controversy within the establishment, wait and see, read on – please. The letter started, 'This is my second day in hospital at Swansea, the treatment is going very well and the doctors seem pleased to the way I'm responding to it, son. They tell me that I'll be home next Wednesday or Thursday after they've finished the radiotherapy treatment. Then I have to go back at a later date for tests to see if it has got rid of the cancer in my right lung. I'm not getting any pain just now, son, so don't you worry about me. I know I'll come out of it alright. Your mum is coming to see me tomorrow, I'll feel like a new man then won't I?'

My dad had cancer, he was optimistic about life and he was my hero. Mum wrote to me when dad was out saying he was getting on fine and has lots of friends calling on him. I recall when I was a bad little boy and when I ran away from home and...I just broke down in myself, as I knew that this was serious.

August 12th 1994 – Lord Longford come to see me today. The last time we met was up in Wakefield jail through the bars of my caged cell. Today's visit was a lot better than that; it was relaxed and sensible. The screws weren't making a mess of themselves by being all over the place.

Frank Longford is a very old man and no way could I or would I harm him, why should I, he's a friend, so we had a cup of tea and a nice chat. I told him I'd denounced all acts of violence and become a better man, well at least 'til someone upsets me. We discussed my up and coming trial over the Woodhill siege, which I've already gone into, we touched on many subjects. I'm quite impressed in how well of a man he looks for his age. He's so fast and witty and on the first visit he did a press up for me, amazing! He's truly a lovely old boy, but he gets bad press over certain issues already mentioned, but who am to judge him, keep at it my old friend.

September 23rd 1994 – Wormwood Scrubs, I just come in from the exercise yard this morning, I'd done my press ups and sit ups and was feeling okay. Then I was called into the office to see the number one governor, he handed me the phone; it was Loraine on the other end. 'Dad passed away last night at 10.20 p.m., he's gone'. Then my world caved in. I'm only glad it was Loraine gave me the news 'cos I love her. Loraine spoke for a while, as I couldn't get my words out.

When I come back to my cell and the door shut locked I felt empty, alone, alone like never before. I was a little kid lost at the fairground shouting for his daddy and there, all the time, he was right behind the child. He's gone; I've lost him! It was 9.00 p.m., ten hours have passed by since Loraine told me. As I write this it's difficult to see through my tears, I'm choked up, I'm so messed up in my head it's so hard to believe it. He ain't coming back; maybe I'll catch up with him later. Eternity is forever, God bless you dad, I miss you so much.

September 24th 1994 – I spoke to mum and brother Mark on the phone, I'm so proud of Mark, he's a good strong man. Mum's voice was full of pain, sadness and confusion. It hurt, hit me hard, I got a lump so big in my throat it almost choked me. I wanted to hold her, tell her I love her and assure her that she's not alone. It's hit me bad, I feel I've let my family down and I should be there. Here I am in a stinking cell with a crowd of screws outside my door, every time it opens, watching me, searching me and fearing me. Some just do a job, some try to do more and some don't exist in my eyes. Mum says he passed on peacefully, with no pain. That's nice to know.

September 28th 1994 – Mum and me both decided that I wouldn't attend dad's funeral, which was today. The main reason being that this lot wouldn't give me low key security. There would be massive security if I were to go out. Mum don't need all that, I funeral is a day of respect, not a day of power and force. So today when my family and friends are showing respect to my dad, I shall be sitting alone in the Scrubs chapel, and I mean alone.

I didn't need no hypocrite vicar sitting with me; one had witnessed me getting turned over years ago in the block and turned a blind eye.

An escort of screws marched me over at 2.45 p.m., no words were spoken. The Scrubs chapel is no doubt the finest church in the system; it's really a very beautiful place. I sat alone while the screws stayed well away. Obviously they were there, their eyes were in my back. I heard one cough and I heard another's key chain move. They were there alright, they've been there all my life and no doubt they'll be there for the rest of my life. I made a plea, days before, that I didn't want to see no sky pilot (vicar). I don't like prison sky pilots, I've never respected false people. If one had of walked in I may well have taken him hostage, that's how I felt. None walked in; I was alone, alone with my family. I pictured my mother's face and prayed she would be strong, I pictured the times when we were a happy family, dad was a good family man, and we couldn't have had a better dad.

The sun shun through the chapel window and the rays hit the table where candles were on and at the back was a painting of Jesus on the cross. I sat there feeling warm and contented. At 3.30 I got up and walked out. The escort walked me back to the block and the sun was shining down on me, this was my dad telling me to be strong.

September 29th – I had just about had enough now, all these blocks, all the senseless moves and all the secrets. I don't know if I'm coming or going, I told them days before I wanted to go into the strongbox the day after my dad's service. In fact I wrote it down so there would be no complications, basically I said 'I'm sick of it all, sick of the lies, sick of you lot, sick of not being able to go the gym, sick of the isolation and I'm going into the strong box so as to be alone and I'm not coming out until you lot tell me what's going on'.

My door unlocked at 7.30 a.m., I walked out, naked, 'Right lets go', I said. There were a good ten screws, none I'd ever seen before, which I felt was very strange, I noticed the block screws all standing well away up by the offices. 'You're not going into the box', one said. 'I am!' I said. A voice came – 'Jump him lads'. They punched me, kicked me, twisted me up, beat me with sticks, put me in a body belt and left me bleeding, bruised and beaten in an empty cell. It was an unprovoked attack on a naked defenceless man.

All my life I've been involved in violent incidents, I've always given as good as I got, violence breeds violence. A lot of my beatings were an eye for an eye, but this attack was a set up, totally unnecessary and totally unprovoked. Plus it happened at a time that I was at an all time low in my life. It's one act of cowardice I'll never forget they actually made a terrible mistake and I've got all their faces clocked. (Remembered)

October 3rd – Wandsworth, I arrived here block from the Scrubs, where for the last four days I've not been allowed out of my cell. My injuries are severe that the screws inflicted on me at Wormwood Scrubs. Lumps, bumps and all my fingers and toes swollen up. (Photographic evidence supplied for the readers of this book.) I've phoned my brief and Loraine, the Scrubs will not be getting away with it, the cowardly bastards. Loraine is taking it higher than just the prison governor. I've a trial three weeks today and they still won't allow me to settle or treat me like a normal con. They're low life scum to do this. Somebody in the Home Office must be really getting a buzz out of all of this. The shit will be hitting the fan soon; questions must be answered.

October 4th – I saw my brief today, she's disgusted with it all, the police are coming in, photographers and an outside doctor. The Scrubs heavies took a liberty. (As at present time of printing this book 22 staff at Wormwood Scrubs have been charged with criminal acts of violence against prison inmates at Wormwood Scrubs – proving my case beyond a doubt.)

I've not dropped my case and I will be pursuing the matter further to expose these cowards employed by Her Majesty's Prison Service under the control of the Home Secretary of the British Government and I demand a full police investigation into my side of things since the things have come to light at present day in September of 1999.)

Now we'll see how good they are in court as I'm having them all nicked for torture, no good rats, brave fuckers ten onto one, that's the strength of them, maggots. I've legal documentation to support my case. I was seen on 4th October 1994 by my solicitor Margaret Morrisey and she recorded the following injuries that I accuse Home Office Employees of inflicting on me: Bruised red and swollen cheek bone, bruised left eyelid, bruised right eye, cut inside lower lip, bruise in middle of upper lip, graze to right hand side of chin, swollen left temple, lump and bruising behind right ear and that was just to my head! Other injuries were recorded on most other body parts. Look at photograph of my damaged hand!

Extracts from legal papers drawn up by my legal team

A prison officer who chose to remain anonymous telephoned Margaret Morrisey. The account he gave Ms Morrisey in his calls to her was that 'Mr Bronson had humiliated a Deputy Governor named Gareth Davis by calling him a "tea boy" and demanding to see his boss. The same officer had decided to set up a confrontation with Mr Bronson, had recruited a young and inexperienced control and restraint team, had briefed the team that Mr Bronson was making outrageous and unreasonable demands (when in fact he was following custom and practise in his case), and had further briefed them to humiliate Mr Bronson in order to take him down a peg or two in the eyes of the other prisoners'.)

The prison officers that carried out the assault on Mr Bronson used the following remarks: "hit the bastard", "we'll teach you", "your mum's dead", "smash his hands", "you won't work out with Belmarsh screws again", and so on. He was put into a restraining belt, but it was taken off to shouts of, "get the small belt". There was then a struggle to squeeze Mr Bronson into the small belt, during which he became unconscious.

He woke up alone in an unfurnished cell, very tightly belted, with swollen wrists and fingers, vomit on his body and blood on his body and on the floor. He was in pain, felt as though his chest was on fire, his breathing was heavy and he believed he was having a heart attack. The belt was removed after about nine hours. Mr Bronson spent the next three days in this cell and on Monday 3rd October was moved to Wandsworth.

The following extract taken from my legal papers shows that the medical records show the lack of concern from the prison medical team

At Wormwood Scrubs it seems from medical records that Mr Bronson was visited by a doctor at about 9.45 a.m. on September 29th 1994 in order to decide in accordance with procedure whether he was fit to continue to be restrained. The doctor's notes records:

"Because of this man's violent state he was unable to be examined. Looked through the cell window. Lying on the floor, restrained".

Nevertheless, shockingly, the doctor recorded his view in the register of Non-Medical Restraints that there was,

"No clinical contra-indication to continued restraint."

The next day Mr Bronson refused to see the same doctor, who described him, memorably as,

"Lying comfortably on the floor".

It has been Mr Bronson's way over many years of prison confinement to give a wide berth to the Prison Medical Service. These two visits explain eloquently why.

We have two current accounts of this incident through official prison service channels. According to the 'Report of injury to inmate' form. "Mr Bronson refused to return to his cell, assaulted a member of staff and had to be restrained". According to Sir Derek Lewis' (Former head of the Prison Service who subsequently wrote of me in his book: 'Hidden Agendas'. He only mentions my sieges, not once does he mention the atrocities carried out on me by the men under his charge!) letter to Sir Graham Bright, MP, "When he was unlocked for breakfast Mr Bronson headed straight for an unfurnished cell and pushed aside a member of staff who barred his way. He was restrained by staff, placed in a body belt and returned to his own cell...!

September 1996 – Belmarsh, Yeah, I'm often asked, 'Chas, did you really get the Iraqis to tickle your feet?' The answer is, yes. The bunch of evil slags hijacked a plane and flew to Stanstead airport with 203 innocent hostages, women and kids – terrified they was. Then whilst at Belmarsh jail they bumped into yours truly. Filthy fucking terrorists, these Iraqis give me a bad head. Simply put, I don't like people that terrorise a planeload of women and kids and then threaten to blow it up.

I also never liked the way they went on whilst in Belmarsh Unit – flash twats. Walking about like royalty in new track suits – political, too political for my liking. Look at the way Gadaffi's held back for them that planted the bomb in that plane that flew over Scotland. Look how many years it's taken to get them handed over! Okay they're from Libya, but life's life.

One of the slimy, greasy twats bumped into me, didn't even say sorry, so I bumped back into him with a right hook – bang, lights out! Next day it kicks off big style...bang, crash all eight of them, only one of me. (As I've no time for gangs.) What one man can't

189

do, ten men can't. They were only Iraqis, so I went in on them like an abattoir worker.

After ten minutes I had three of them tied up like Christmas turkeys. After fifteen minutes I had the whole jail on a razor's edge. Some called it the 'siege of all sieges', 'Bronson's last stand', but I don't get into what it was or wasn't, I just go by the facts. One of them had shit his pants, so he went under the bed into cold storage with a blanket over him to stop the stench – pooh! Well the other two…they just reminded me of 'Pinky and Perky'. (Cartoon pig characters.)

Me being Britain's number one hostage taker and all that, I know the way the prison negotiators work, they try to wear you down, but not with me, I just do what needs to be done. 'Get me an apple pie, fast!' Oh yes I do love an apple pie, these Iraqis to me they're a lot like Japs – slippery customers and torturers at heart. One's gotta be careful with these dangerous characters.

My mum has always taught me, don't talk to strangers and my dad taught me to attack "if you feel endangered". Hell, these were terrorists; I'm only a blagger. What was I doing in a barricaded cell with such evil men, hell they could've killed me so I kept them all tied up? I belted them a few times just to let them know who the guv'nor was, not that I enjoy hurting people, but these were real scum. I'd sooner have a pot of tea and an apple pie, but how can I trust these filthy swine.

The hours ticked by and I was so fed up, the pratts couldn't even talk English, they're all the same these foreigners. They come over to our country and can't even learn English, pratts. I took my boots off and untied one of the Iraqis and put a noose around his scrawny little neck. 'Right', I said, 'Fuck about with me and I'll choke you to death, tickle my feet.

Laugh, his fingers were going in and out like lightening! So fast! He had a great touch! Laugh, I was falling in bits, crying I was. I nearly had a heart attack; the whole wing must've been laughing. One day the terrorist has a grenade in his hand and the next day he's got Bronson's toes. You just couldn't make this up could ya! I hadn't had my toes tickled for years.

For 12 hours we was in that cell together, 12 hours of insanity! But fuck me, I was getting to like them, except old shitty pants under the bed. Some people have just got no social skills, farting's bad enough, but shitting – it's just not on. I gave shitty arse a bloody good crack over the crust with the steel dinner tray, dirty bastard. He might crap his pants over in Iraq, but not in Belmarsh he doesn't.

Would you believe I got seven years added on for that? Seven years added on, would you believe that they got less time for the hijacking, but it's who you know in governments that's important. British justice makes me puke up – seven years for getting my toes tickled! If I hijacked a plane could you imagine what I'd get – life. Yet theses Iraqis get away with murder, whilst I have to eat seven more years of porridge, but I never cry about my life, just survive it, 'cos one day I'm gonna walk free. It's a mission of madness at best, the Iraqis wanted Political Asylum but they got the man from the asylum instead!

1995 - Winson Green, not a lot I can say about this one, I just don't like doctors it's as simple as that. A doctor a day keeps the apple away.

1997 – Bullingdon, my brain wasn't ticking over too good, I walked into the special visits room to see my solicitor and walked into a room to a stranger. So I grabbed his pen and held it to his ear. I told the screws 'If you come in I'll poke his brain out!' Why did I even get out of bed this day? It turned out that he was my solicitor's clerk, hell fire, I didn't know that!! Well you know what I say 'if it's gonna happen it's gonna happen' and it happened. Without something happening how can you read this book? The whole thing was smoothed over, as it was all one big misunderstanding, luckily for me.

Sadly I have to end this chapter here as there just isn't enough room to fit it all in. This has only been a very small amount of my experiences given over to you and from that I hope it gives across a message, any message will do. I'm not one for telling other people what to do that's for you to decide what to do with your life. If it gives you solace or comfort from reading this then that's fine, if it gives you restless nights or bad dreams then don't blame me, blame the authorities for making me the way I've become. If it puts you off becoming a criminal or turns you away from crime then send me a fiver for the sound advice I've given you, God knows I need a break from all of this. I was only joking about the fiver. I've given up with the begging letters, any I get are sent on to Sir Paul Getty.

9

I can't finish off without first telling you about some of the great people I've met along the way. Obviously there just isn't room for all of them so that's why I've written 'Legends' and when that one comes out it will be the Who's Who of the people I've met along my pretty colourful path of life. So if you're not in here don't start screaming, be silent, hold on and read Legends when it comes out 'cos that'll blow your socks off. Sorry that I couldn't get it all in here, but you can be assured it will be coming out in other books I've got, waiting to be published.

Frank Fraser – If you don't vote me in for Mayor of London then vote this man in 'cos he deserves it. I first met him in 1975 in Wandsworth dungeon, he was moved there from Chelmsford; he was opposite my cell. I shouted to him through my door, and we've been pals ever since.

I admire him; he's small with a giant heart. No man has absorbed so many beatings, not even me, inside, as Frank has. We all gotta feel pain and suffer and many of us feel it more than others ever do or will.

Rivers of blood flow in jail, Frank's spilled a lake of it – it's why I love the guy. I last met him again at Wandsworth in 1992 and although years had passed he was still the same old Frankie, 'mad' but great.

I bet you never knew he chinned Pierrepoint (Britain's last hangman), he stuck one on that bastard good style, best thing ever in my book to chin such a rat, all them innocent people he hung, lets hope he's now swinging on the end of a rope in hell, I hate that slag! Frank's a legend, tops, and to prove it what man do you know of at 70+ to survive a bullet in his face? Some areshole shot him and Frank just chased after the mug, this tells you what a man he is, anyone else would probably have died of shock, so who's the mug, Frank or the gunman? I'd have gotta hold of the prick, I'd have rammed the gun up his arse, but you know what, he's no longer around, he's six foot under, straight!

Joe Pyle – I'm lucky to have such a great friend, my dad was Joe Peterson, note the same initials 'JP', sometimes I call Joe 'dad' out of respect, as I've never really accepted my dad's death, nor come to terms with it, but if I had to pick another dad it would be Joe Pyle, simply because I idolise him. Joe at times tells me off and puts me right and gives me serious advice and all of it I accept, because he says it straight, 'cos he's right, a good man. Joe's a friend in a million, nothing's too much trouble for him, he's a kind heart, but a solid nature, only a fool would fuck with Joe. This man is pure respect and if you don't respect him then you don't respect yourself, Joe is Joe, he's a one off man.

Kenneth 'Panda' Anderson – If you're from the North and you don't know of him or you've never heard of this guy then you've lived a very sheltered life. I'd say Panda is a legend so if you see him in a bar buy him a drink and tell him I was asking of him. He's another guy who speaks his mind, it's been said he said I'm mad and lost the plot, but he says it in the best of words, you can't knock a man who speaks the truth 'cos I have lost my way. Sometimes I wake up and have to think who I am. One day I'll wake up and just forget and then there'll be trouble.

Dave Courtney – He's a flash fucker, he would've been a big star out in Hollywood, maybe he still can, he's got it all, charisma, style, pull, power, he says he's my pal and says he respects me. There was a time he pissed me off big style, but when I see where he's come up from and he's worked at it then nobody can take that away from the man, he's come up from nothing. Dave was in Belmarsh the same time as me, I'd heard he was a bit jealous of my press-ups, but that was said by a screw that I believe wanted to cause trouble between us. Anyway I like Dave because he's a winner, but like most winners he's had plenty of falls. I only wish him well.

Ron and Reg – I first met the twins in Parkhurst in 1976 on 'C'-wing, which held only twelve cons. From day one I just took to them, but them days I was supercharged and I never lasted a week anywhere. I think I hold the record for chinning the most screws in a month, fifteen. It works out one every other day, but all know that to throw a punch in jail you have to take twenty back so I don't recommend it. I later spent time with Ron on Broadmoor and in Gartree with Reg.

They were both good to me, Ron was special to me and he knew when I was becoming ill. He helped me many times to get over it. Once he stopped me strangling a guy, I was at a terrible all time low and some loon upset me so I was gonna take him out, Ron said 'No, Chas, you can't do that, he can't die over a silly row, best you just chin him'. So I took Ron's advice and smashed the loon's jaw and knocked half his teeth out.

Ron had a magic about him; my mum and dad also loved the twins. My mum feels a lot of sadness for Reg. This system makes me puke up, these slags in Headquarters are more evil than any con I've ever met, I can't but ever speak highly of the twins and I've some great memories of them, I've got a lovely pocket watch they gave me one Christmas and it's my prized possession although I've been asked to sell it many times, I just couldn't. I'd willingly serve Reggie's remaining years for him, even if it meant my life, I'd do that for Reg.

Ron once said to me, 'It's better to be a King for one day than to be a clown forever'. He was a great man was the Colonel, I was in the seg unit up in Frankland Jail on 17th of March 1995 when a con shouted me, I'd just come in from the caged yard were I'd been working out. I was dripping wet with sweat and went to my window and shouted 'What?' 'Have you heard the news, Chas?' 'No', I said. 'Ron's dead'. 'Who?' 'Ron Kray, it's been on the news'. I froze, I closed my eyes and I felt so sad. I never believed it 'til I heard it on the radio for myself. I got so choked up I went to bed, depressed, I felt like attacking the Governor. There won't ever be another Ronnie or Reggie Kray. Lots act the part but they aren't worthy of cleaning Reg's shoes. I'm honoured to have had them in my world – men of steel.

Martin Oldham – He's a top lawyer that actually cares about me. At one time no lawyer wanted to represent me as I once took one hostage in Bullingdon jail in 1997 when I held a pen to his ear and I threatened to poke it into his brain. It was all calmed over and shouldn't have happened, Martin could've turned me down, he didn't – thank fuck! Martin doesn't see me as a threat or a danger, he doesn't fear me, he actually likes me as a human and he actually makes me laugh. Laughter is the best medicine ever.

Lord Longford – I love the old get, he put me in his book 'Prisoner or Patient' I first met him in Wandsworth block. It was down to my pal Eddie Richardson that I was put in the book. Frank Longford has visited me all over England, he would come to the moon to see me, he comes to all my trials, but I'll make it 100% clear now, I don't like his fight for Hindley and all the monsters. Still, it don't matter what he says she ain't getting out, she's safer inside and she knows it. Frank still writes books and makes speeches, but at the end of the day he can't do a lot to change my life. He recently wrote me to say he was horrified at my conditions, but they still continue, Lord or no lord nobody can change my existence.

Joyce Connor – my Princess, she gives me food for thought for some of my projects and she's my girl, she's pretty, she's clever, she's a real sexy hot cookie who wants to get me into bed, she wants to do it for me, to me, the whole lot. She says I'm sex on legs, I personally can't see it nor do I believe it. I don't even know why she's in love with me, but she is. She makes me feel nice and gives me a lot of nice dreams. That's probably all it ever will be, a dream.

Hell, if she was to get me in bed I doubt very much she could take so much madness, plus I told her apple pies were my first love, but she wants to eat me, love me and to be my Princess. She calls me her madman, so we've created a cartoon book called "Th Princess and the Madman'. Yes, I love her dearly and maybe one day I'll jump into bed with her. It would be lovely just to smell her hair.

If dreams come true I'd say she would be sore for a week after a session in bed with me, what a session that would be. Maybe we could video it like that Pamela Anderson and her Diego did and make a million. My favourite position is doggy, so I can polish off a few apple pies while we're banging away and any crumbs landing on her back I'd lick off later. A guy's gotta eat to survive, yes I do love her, but my love is not like most loves, she accepts it.

Dr Ghosh – All 5'-2" of her, fearless. She was my psychiatrist in the max secure asylums and helped me at Belmarsh. Once I got up on Walton jail roof, I ripped 'H'-wing's roof off; they got Dr Ghosh in to talk me down after a week. I love her, as she's so kind and honest. If they were all like her I'd probably not be in jail today 'cos she treats me like a human. She's got compassion and understanding, I feel a warm sensation when I'm with her, like she's coming to save me, to pour in some feelings and humanity. I just admire her totally and see her as a friend. I fucking despise 99% of prison doctors, but Dr Ghosh is wonderful.

Linda Calvey 'The Black Rose' – Recently she was transferred from Durham's notorious 'H'-wing to Holloway for legal visits to prepare her case for appeal. She's always moved, as she's a high-risk prisoner so she travels in a secure van with a heavy escort. On her journey back to Durham some days later the van pulls up at Leicester jail. This jail has no wing for female prisoners so they locked the black Rose in a prison cell over lunchtime whilst her escort could get a meal before continuing on the remainder of the journey.

In this cell she sat alone thinking when she was struck dumb with shock, facing her written on the wall in big capital letters was 'CHARLES BRONSON – ALIVE AND WELL'. She was sitting in my old cell. She could sense my presence, here is the Black Rose in an all male jail, locked up in the block in the cell I once lived in, what's the odds on this happening, a million to one I'd say. Like I say, she's a true legend. When she wrote and told me this incredible story I was also in a state of shock, it's so unreal it's just incredible, but that's what legends do, they make history.

Linda and me had something going years ago and although we haven't written to each other of late I've still got a soft spot in my heart for her. She's been convicted of conspiring to murder her man; she says she's innocent of this conviction and has been fighting it for a number of years. I'm not a one to say who is innocent or who is guilty, but I wish her the best of luck.

Ray Williams – He's been a good pal of mine for three decades, but he's a double legend to have found my son, Mike, for me. Ray's had his ups and downs in life but he's managed to stay up thanks to a good wife and some great kids. He's now a successful businessman with his own furniture shop, he's brother until the end of time.

Harley – All one foot nothing of him, a bundle of fluff and fun. I'd like to give some acknowledgement to my mascot 'Harley the wonder dog'. Harley rhymes with Charlie, he's been given the title of wonder dog out of respect for 'Fanny the wonder dog who passed away recently. Seriously! Julian Clary that happy and gay comedian's dog died aged about 100+, in human years that is. This has gotta be proof that I'm not anti-gay, although I don't speak from their side of the track.

You'll see Harley's photographed with a lot of the people who are close to me and 'til I'm released then he's deputising for me, book signings the lot. I've grown quite fond of him and I hear he's doing alright on a diet of Pepsi Max and McDonalds French fries. Hell, he's got a good life for a dog and after all I've said about dogs I take it all back, can I be a dog for a day? Although I know Harley goes out training doing the miles to keep that fat off and keep fit for when I get out and take him on long walks.

Although we haven't met yet I'm sure we will and in the meantime Harley will be doing charity work for a Babies Hospice I'm helping out. He's a 'Pet's As Therapy' dog and I myself give help to good causes. In fact I donated £400 from the sale of a winning Koestler Award entry to a Children's Hospice in Merseyside and then had a further £750 worth of toys sent there to Claire House. But you know what, they didn't even acknowledge receiving them and it was only when they were pushed that they wrote saying 'thanks' so I've shifted my help to a Babies' Hospice called 'Zöe's Place'.

I read that one of them teachers' unions wants dogs to be used as classroom assistants. They could help round up children and look for lost gym shoes. Would you believe it was the Professional Association of Teachers that backed this idea at a conference in Southport, I'm fucking serious! And what about the Queen's footman who was spiking Her Majesty's dogs with booze and they laughed when the poor little bleeders were bumping into the walls, blind drunk. I'd have the footman's head chopped off 'cos my landlady, Elizabeth, can do that as she's the Queen – "Off with his head".

Stephen Hill – Hell, he won the 'Bronson' Creative Arts Competition, which is gonna be run every year by 'Inside Time' Prison Newspaper, from what I hear. Stephen is the outright winner from all of the entries received and here's a little bit about him. Stephen's spent 26 years in and out of institutions, which puts him on par with my record! He's had very little education, but he reads a lot and writes the odd poem. He hopes his entry will be shown to me and that I'll see the funny side of it. Laugh, my sides are bustin'. Here's his winning poem, a blinder.

THE SYSTEM

Can our prison system reform this man

High and mighty governors think no one can

Already he's spent 26 years inside

Respected by criminals he's lots of pride

Long days and nights alone in his cell

Even the sanest person would think its hell

So no wonder the system thinks he's mad

Bronson the poet isn't that bad

Reformists and psychologists know this is true

Only your records and adjudication's stick like glue

Now is the time to set Charles free

So long in the system's a liberty

Our prison system has went from bad to worse

Now for Charles remove a political curse

Stephen was released on 12th August, I just hope you manage to stay out of trouble, make peace with yourself and I know you'll crack it, best of luck Stephen.

Loraine – An angel if ever there was one. She's my beautiful cousin, her love and loyalty to me is beyond any I know, it's second to none. I'm convinced I'd be long dead if it wasn't for her. She has stood by through thick and thin, given me strength, given me hope, given me love and given me trust and that's on top of all of that she's come through with her own battle against illness in a big way. Put all her help together that she's given me and she's given me my future.

Andy - He's my cousin Loraine's husband and a good friend of mine too, he stood by me through thick and thin and there was a point where I could do no wrong in his eyes. Andy got right onto the case when the Scrub's screws beat me up. I had to cool Andy down over this situation. I've given Loraine and Andy some grief over the time in the things I've done and when I turned around they were always there for me, thanks.

Graham Kitchen the Education Officer at Hull jail worked with me setting out my latest Koestler entry with an anti-bullying theme. He's a civilian, a great guy and out of this world. It was the first time I'd had this sort of help to set out my entry on a computer. Graham's one of those guys that puts you in charge of yourself and gives you the confidence to go on, I miss this wonderful human being, thanks for all of your help my friend.

I stand accused of taking my latest hostage at Hull prison when I was there in February of 1999. You see my grandmother had died and I was refused leave to attend her funeral and was told by a Home Office employee, *John Golds,* that I'd never be released on parole.

I'm then told that Hull Secure Unit is to close down after I was told that I'd be there for at least another five years by the same man and that I've to get my kit together as I'm likely to be going to HM prison Durham. But a few days before the move I'm told that Durham prison can't take me until April and that I'll have to go into cold storage (solitary confinement) 'til then! You can imagine how I felt after years of being abused by the people in the system that stuck needles into me (Liquid Cosh) filling my veins full of psychotropic drugs.

I was moved to Whitemoor prison in Cambridgeshire after that incident, I intend to plead 'not guilty' to, where I was thrown into a bare cell with nothing but the four walls to look at. In fact when I arrived at Whitemoor the van doors wouldn't open and even an angle grinder wouldn't open the door, the guards politely asked me if I'd kick them open, please, I obliged. I had all of my art materials confiscated and then I was told that no poems would be allowed out! Can you believe the mentally of the prison authorities?

Eventually I was moved to Woodhill prison after my solicitor made representation due to Whitemoor withholding information from him as to my welfare, we've got the proof.

While here at Woodhill prison I received a letter from one of my nemesis, Michael Sams or peg leg as I call him. I fell out with him after he was found guilty of murdering Julie Dart after he told me he hadn't killed her. Anyway for some reason he wrote to me with some vital evidence that could help my case. To cut a long story short the letter was handled by governor Donaldson. He said he'd post it out for me to the person I wanted to have it, guess what? They didn't receive it and when Donaldson was contacted by a film company to find out what had happened to it he said that the 'Press Liaison' officer would contact them about it. This was over a month and a half ago and this press officer guy hasn't even bothered to contact them!

The Prison Media Service were contacted by this company doing a documentary on me and they were turned down for to film me inside Woodhill or any other prison for that matter yet people like Hindley have been covered? They were asked about the Wormwood Scrubs attack on me, about John Golds telling me all those things and about the missing Sams letter. That was one month ago and they heard that Brodie Clark, Head of CSC, was to investigate the matter – when he was back from holiday.

So here I am stuck in a cell on £2.50 a week wages while Sams is getting £10 a week wages and £10 to spend from his private cash, he's in a cushy cell while I'm in a crap one. He gets two hours of visits a month I'm only allowed 2 X ½ hour visits? Tell me that's right for fuck sake? I can only buy one phone card and that's it. I'm being treat like am dog, sorry Harley, I mean even Harley hasn't got it that bad. So you can see how them at the top are treating me, these here at Woodhill want me to have better conditions, but it's them in Prison HQ that are stopping it from happening.

I've just gotta tell you this one before I forget. I told Serial Sex Killer Fred West that the police had found another skeleton up his chimney, but it was only an "old flame". Fred shouted back that he didn't have a chance and later hung himself. He just looked like one of them 'Wurzel' characters, his hair was like tangled fuse wire, all we need now is for Rose to follow his example. What a great guy he was saving you the taxpayer all that money on a long trial and having to keep him in prison afterwards. Here's me costing the taxpayer about £5 a week for the facilities I get and people like them get fucking hundreds of £'s spent on them for special this and special that.

I also challenged Carlos the Jackal to a chess match by post; he's that International Assassin fella, supposed to only have one ball down below! He didn't reply.

Summing up

Dr Chandara Ghosh – Consultant Psychiatrist, M.B.B.S., DPM, MRC Psych.

My involvement with Charlie is a professional one having met him through my work at Ashworth. One of the governors of Belmarsh prison was also working with him.

A care plan was put together at Belmarsh and the Governor invited me there to go and see Charlie and I felt that they were doing excellent work that was of course until Charlie took the Iraqi hostages and that meant they had no other option but to move him according to the prison rules.

The Governor and the prison officers had put so much into Charlie and the care plan seemed to be working so I wrote to the Director of Prison Medical Services and suggested that this kind of care plan should be carried on with if Charlie was ever going to have a chance of moving to a psychiatric hospital. Anyway I wrote to two people and I received a reply saying that they hoped to get him to where he is now, Woodhill. (Coincidentally that took four years and was by accident.) Woodhill was going to be purpose built to manage people like him, if you like, who had personality problems.

The key things of the care plan are very important. It recognises the damage the institutions have done to Charlie and the fact that he is socially phobic and that they clearly recognised that he would have to be reintroduced into society in a very gradual manner, and that is what they where doing.

If you notice he has been managed on his own in virtual solitary confinement and what the Governor had done there was not only to spend a lot of time with Charlie, he also saw Charlie every day, which I thought was quite remarkable. There were prison officers that Charlie would get on with and they would then work with him in terms of introducing him to his art, he's a very talented artist and doing his press ups and so on, but also gradually introducing him back to being with people and I felt that was one of the most important things in terms of if he was ever to get back, to the question he was asking me, and that was to go back to Broadmoor. (Broadmoor has changed over the years and, allegedly, has to act more responsibly towards the patients being treated there and the staff are more accountable for their actions.)

But the only way that you could do that was to gradually get him used to being people because most of the wards in psychiatric hospitals had 20-25 men. The special hospitals now though let the men have their own rooms, but they still didn't have the type of facilities that he had, which was virtually his own apartment and that was the problem. Because of the way he had his original prison sentence extended and extended and extended by the way he reacted he could only be managed in maximum security so it had to be a Special Hospital.

He had a very good lawyer working with him at that time who I had lot of time for, but then Charlie took the Iraqi hostages but then unfortunately he also took a solicitor hostage as well, he made him lie down on the floor and made him take off his shoes and so on and so on.

I believe that Charlie takes hostages to attract attention to himself and to his plight, but I think he wasn't happy and would become quite distorted because he does want attention when he does that, but the attention doesn't help him in any way because it doesn't deliver what he wants, which is to one day return to society and lead a normal life.

There is another thing that is going to be difficult in terms of Charlie Bronson and that is he has a very idealised notion of people in authority. He can't cope with anything that he sees as lies. It may just be the person not being able to meet Charlie's standards. The first governor Charlie took hostage, I remember Charlie saying that he'd promised him something and not delivered. It's almost as if Charlie does not understand that these are ordinary human beings who work within the system and might be trying to do their best but might not always be able to deliver.

Charlie's very bright so I don't think he necessarily misconstrues what people say to him, he knows exactly what people are saying to him. I think what he doesn't understand is that sometimes people with the best intentions in the world cannot deliver. For example, for some odd reason, he allows me that which he won't allow to, say, someone like a governor. When I say to him I cannot get you to a maximum secure hospital unless you do this, this and this, he accepts that, but from other people he won't you see. He will expect them somehow to jump through the hoops for him and to deliver and when they can't do that he says they're lying to him. And they are not lying to him, they're simply saying I would like to deliver this but I can't because the prison system for example or some other system doesn't allow it.

I think Charlie is looking for help in someone being a lifeline for him and maybe that is the way he sees me, which will then lead to Ashworth or Broadmoor being available to him. It will be there that he will find this person that is going to sit down and find the Charlie Bronson that nobody else has been able to find. I think people have found Charlie Bronson, but I think the problem with Charlie is Charlie that he can't sustain it there.

Lots of people have a lot of affection for him, you should have seen people in how upset they were when he took the hostages at Belmarsh because they seen it as a personal failure on their part. That they couldn't sustain things that he needed, and he makes people feel like that. When he's feeling good he makes other people feel very good, but when he's feeling bad he actually makes people feel almost as if he's destroyed them and that happened with the Governor that was working with him.

I don't think he sets out to upset people but he likes the sense of power that people get so involved. I mean look at me, for so many years, every time he's written to me I've went to see him or he's written to other people persuading them to get in touch with me. It's a peculiar feeling that you feel as if you're betraying him if you don't turn around, but actually what we can deliver is very limited, because when you try to deliver he doesn't want it.

I think what people have done is try to work with him, recognise the damage what the institution has done and mistakes that have been done in the past. People have tried to repair that, but because the damage is great and also because of the system and of because individuals within the system need to deliver so much. Everybody's perception of Charlie is very warm hearted, extremely generous, very honest and upright individual. Unfortunately he's stuck in the most punitive and degrading criminal justice system that I think exists. So people that work within that system when they do come across a Charlie Bronson they say 'here's somebody we can do something with, it will give me a purpose'. And I think that's what the prison officers and prison governors and maybe even myself when I was working with him thought we could do something with.

What should happen, and nobody will be able to deliver that, but what should happen is that if I had my way and what I would like to do is, say for example, there is a friend of mine, an excellent psychologist, who has worked with people like Charlie in the past, perhaps, not damaged to the same degree.

Charlie would need somebody like that, but outside the prison system, he must be allowed to come out and into a hospital, but a one outside the Prison Service, within the Health Service, if you like, where he could work with psychologists who will be more sophisticated and be able to understand the fact that he's so frightened. That's the one thing that we don't recognise about Charles Bronson, because he's so big and overawing, but inside there's a very frightened person who can't cope with prison! The degree of consistency he expects of people, who are in authority, most of them can't deliver.

I think when he takes people hostage he feels frightened and he reacts very badly to his fear, I don't think he takes advantage of taking people hostage. And that is something that is almost impossible to get people to recognise. He's actually frightened of people, that's the damage that has been done to him because he's been in solitary confinement for so long, it has actually made him frightened of people and that Governor in Belmarsh recognised that, their whole care plan recognised that.

They may not have used sophisticated language to say it, but what they recognised that here was a man who had been damaged so much that he had become socially dysfunctional and the only way to reintroduce him to society was to slowly address that fear and make him more use to having people around him, but also a feeling of trust.

I know he wants to get out, I see him as needing help from the mental health profession. The solution has to be quite radical and I don't think the prison system or the health service has that kind of, almost, radical approach.

I work with women now but for 21 years I worked with men. I think Charlie is unique in the sense that a lot of prison officers can identify with him. Charlie's not a sex offender, Charlie's not a person who harms people just for the heck of it, Charlie's not a drug addict, Charlie's not considered as a waster and in fact to some prison officers they could actually see him as someone they could identify with and accept that he's went the wrong way.

I think what we're looking at is a system that cannot manage him, I don't know if they have the will to step back or whether the politicians will be able to cope with Charlie Bronson coming out of Woodhill prison and being transferred to another unit to undergo therapy, they may find that very difficult especially when he's got a court case. (Hostage taking at Hull prison in February of 1999, case pending now, late '99.) He needs to be in a medium secure facility and given therapy. They don't recognise that they've produced Charlie.

The Belmarsh care plan was at a very crucial time and what they should have done was to have allowed him to stay on it. To be fair to the prison staff, some of the prison officers and senior staff did allow him to stay on for a while, normally for an offence like that he would've been moved the next day.

I remember when he got on the roof in Walton prison, he got the Governor to go up and pray with him or something, he rang me up. The history of Charlie is that he gets into trouble every three years or so.

Charlie has an idealised notion of the world. He expects people to be absolutely honest and totally consistent. I don't know if people could have the sort of relationship with him where they wouldn't be frightened of him and if they would be able to recognise that Charlie had these problems. Because of this idealised notion my biggest fear is that if he ever did go out and he saw somebody that was a drug addict, for example, who he saw mugging a woman or something, can you imagine, Charlie would want to kill the man and he'd end up a murderer, as far as he's concerned you don't do things like that. And because of his enormous strength and great size he could break the perpetrator's back or something.

We have given the standards to Charlie, we've promised him things, and we've shown him the idealised world exists. We've said to him 'you've broken the law and are being punished'. Other people who break the law and do far more damage go unpunished. So as far as he's concerned we've told him certain things and given him certain things and then when he tries to operate on it we tell him he's done wrong! I think we do that all the time. I think we're all hypocrites.

I think if anyone is going to do anything for Charlie then they need to recognise that behind that huge body is a very frightened person and that fear of people and people failing him will compound itself repeatedly and then punishing him for our failures by locking him up, putting him a cage when he has reacted quite violently to the fact that he in fact has been given a double messages we have reacted in an even more punitive manner.

And I think until we acknowledge that we are given him double messages with the best intentions in the world and all of our weaknesses we need to recognise that when we put him in a cage in a democratic so called civilized society and increasing Charlie Bronson's sentence and locking him up it will go on.

They created him, call them human beings, it's appalling!

(Charlie currently awaits trial at Luton Crown Court after being committed from Luton magistrates at the end of August, he intends submitting a 'not guilty' plea. For obvious reasons Charlie's defence cannot be gone into at this stage, but you can be assured of a very interesting trial that will hold the British Penal System responsible and hopefully there will be a reckoning of some sorts. Don't wait for the ink to dry as the Charles Bronson story has not yet finished by a long chalk.

Charlie says: 'Come grow old with me for the best is yet to come. One good thing's come out of this and that's my Poem, Short Story, Cartoon and Drawing/Painting Competition for all prisoners of the UK run by Inside Time, the newspaper for prisoners. My special thanks go to John Bowers for organising this

OTHER TITLES FROM MIRAGE

All of our titles can be ordered from any good bookstore by quoting the ISBN number. But in case of difficulty you can order directly from the publisher. Send cheque or Postal Order (P+P free in the UK) Europe send payment drawn against UK bank or International Money order + 20% for P+P. Rest of the world send + 50%. Always try your local bookstore as we have accounts with all of the major bookstores in the UK and our book wholesaler exports to 106 different countries.

Viv (Graham) – 'Simply the Best'

True Crime paperback 242 pages. Foreword by Gazza. ISBN No: 1–902578-00–7. A Local Best Seller, fast becoming a nation-wide read book. £7.99

New Year's Eve 1993 Viv Graham's life came to a violent end. His involvement with the Geordie Mafia is unfolded. The truth, pain and anguish are revealed in this action packed book alongside a gripping catalogue of crime never before compiled. Feared gangland reprisals abruptly end academic views. Spine Chilling real life hitman presently based in Manchester gives his professional opinion on the gangland assassination of Viv. Manchester and Newcastle Super City comparisons. An insight into events that triggered riots across the North East of England that eventually dominoes throughout the UK. The Criminal Underworld of the North explored. Murders, Kneecappings, Shootings, Drug Dealing, Protection Rackets, Blackmailing, Robberies, Torturing and more. Microscopic and graphic details of Viv's murder and funeral visited by Tenerife's underworld. Viv's prophecy of his own death, his involvement with the stars Tim Healy and Gazza. Personal details of Viv's family life from insiders. Gazza – "My comments on Viv." Tyneside's own 4th Emergency Service. Loved by 1,000's, murdered by the jealous few.

Viv – and the Geordie Mafia (Vol 2)

The follow up to 'Viv (Graham) – 'Simply the Best' Much bigger with 326 pages and 13 prelim pages. Another Local Best Seller. ISBN No: 1-902578-01-5. RRP£9.99 Foreword by John Davison World Champ Boxer.

Police Seize computer & disks from the author and feign disinterest in the previous 'Viv' book. The author and two researchers arrested, later released without charge after answering bail for many months while police look through research items looking for clues to help find killers. The Candy Rock Resort of Blackpool is looked at in detail – Drug Dealing, Kidnapping, a beach murder and the club doorman scene. A convicted Beach Murderer alleges, the now dead, Viv was his alibi. Clairvoyant Spiritualist visits the death site of Viv and reveals that she has made contact with him. More Murders, Kneecappings, Shootings, Drug Dealing, Protection Rackets, Torturing and Scams. Liverpool's doormen scene is looked at - Home Office reports show connection to Sunderland's drug scene. Viv's three lovers fight over insurance payouts withheld when his insurers describe his death as 'self inflicted'. Intimate details from the three women in his life, love 'em and leave 'em, not likely they became his possessions. What really happened when Reg Kray visited Newcastle all of those years ago, was he kicked out like they say – an Original Geordie Mafia member reveals all? Did alleged Jury Rigging help convict alleged pliers torturer Paddy Conroy when he went on the rampage after his dead father's headstone was vandalised. The culprit got off scot-free and Paddy got eleven years. First ever interview with all of those close to Viv including an exclusive interview with his mother and father. One of the murder suspects gives an interview for the first time ever! Free guide to some of Tyneside's better known Pubs 'n' Clubs. The book has been written into a film script.

'Viv' update chapter – not available in shops!

An addendum chapter that could not be published in the above books is on sale at £2.99 (includes P+P in UK only) and covers a further 80+ pages of crime. The truth that will startle and shock you all, not to be missed. Only available directly from the publisher.

Viv Graham books converted into film script
'Gangsters' Paradise'

James DeMarco and Zahra Zomorrodian assisted by the author and advised by Kenneth 'Panda' Anderson have successfully converted the successful range of Viv books into a movie script.

Said to equal, if not better, 'Get Carter' this script based on real life is now available in loose-leaf form. Only available from Mirage £8.99.

The Charles Bronson Book of Poems
'Birdman Opens His Mind' Book one.

The first in a series of colour illustrated books bound in hardback cover. Laughing all the way to the crematorium written and illustrated by the Poet from Hell. ISBN No: 1-902578-03-1. £7.99, get one if you can

The book is an adult humour type poetry book like no other that has been produced and in Charlie's own inimitable style he will make you laugh and maybe even cry.

Charles Bronson – *Sincerely Yours* - Documentary

An explosive 3 hour+ documentary only available on video. All about Charlie and his life inside. This documentary will not be shown on television as the director has refused to cut it to any less than three hours! It is hoped that by the time you get to reach this that agreement has been reached between the director and London Weekend Television (LWT) for them to use certain material from this most revealing documentary, which if approved you'll have the thrill of seeing some very entertaining items that will be covered in ultimate detail in this production that will show exclusive footage never ever before seen by the public.

Contributors include: Joe Pyle, Lord Longford, Kenneth 'Panda' Anderson (the original Geordie Mafia), Andy Jones (owner of Crime Through Time museum), Tony Lambrianou, Charlie's mother; Eira (Worldwide exclusive first time interview), James DeMarco (USA playwright), Loraine; Charlie's cousin, Ray Williams; long time civilian friend of 30+ years, Jan Lamb and by no means least that flash showbizz character Dave Courtney. Includes footage not ever before seen and audio action of an actual prison hostage taking situation involving Charlie!!!! Unbelievable!

There will be a few surprises in there as well including the rock group 'Garrison Damn' who give a rendition of 'Desperate Avenue', it's out of this world and with a touch of magic we see inside of Charlie's head and how he sees it all. Garrison Damn have been chosen to provide the music and songs for the Charlie Bronson movie, they are the best band to come out of the UK since AC/DC and are already established in the USA. 'Desperate Avenue' just has to be heard and a number of other tracks. Filmed in the grounds of 'Crime Through Time' museum as a backdrop. Includes Charlie's voiceover. Watch out for 'Harley', Charlie's gangster dog.

You get to see Charlie boxing in an unlicensed fight, watch a gun fall to the floor from someone's coat pocket when one hell of a fight breaks out as the crowd at ringside spill into the ring to pull Charlie off his victim. This hopefully will be available from outlets of big bookstores and High Street chains of newsagents. Price £15.99 and will be available on sale immediately after LWT show their documentary in early 2,000. Should you have any difficulty at all in obtaining a copy of this very controversial documentary then apply directly to the publisher, add £2.00 for P+P in UK. (USA compatible format will be produced, add 50% for P+P, pay by Int. Money Order in £ Sterling.)

PUBLIC *consumer* ENEMY
'The A-Z Handbook of how to complain and Win!'
Another Investigative book from Mirage. Shows how the consumer is being ripped off. Paperback, ISBN 1-902578-02-3, RRP £5.99 (P+P free in UK others add 50%)

The author and two of his researchers are arrested by the police for alleged deception after national food and drinks companies complain to the police about the amount of complaints they're receiving. This incenses the author so much that he really goes to town on hundreds of companies, all is revealed within. Never take 'no' for an answer again after reading this handy sized book. Full of guidance notes and even copy letters prepared by lawyers for you to use. Read about secret undercover work at a Kebab factory in Leèds, which is still going to date in Sept '99 after national and local newspapers were informed of it and how it was producing meat kebabs that can kill, the company and its dodgy contacts are revealed. Too much to list here, simply put it's a complainer's bible. **Read how consumer goods manufacturers wouldn't co-operate, out of fear! And more and more and more!!!**

<u>Looking at Life</u>

By Joe Pyle, Foreword by Ray Winstone (Star of many feature films.) *A5 size *Hardback *ISBN: 1-902578–09-0 RRP: £8.99

This has to be the charity book of the year. Joe, a London businessman, ex-pro boxer, recording manager and film producer has waived his fee for this book. He has nominated ZÖe's Place Baby Hospice (the only hospice for babies in the whole world) to receive most of the proceeds from the sale of this book. You must have heard of the 'Sunscreen' chart topping No: 1 hit, full of advice. Joe compiled this book as a tribute to his family and friends for standing by him through some bad times. It wasn't ever intended for resale or publication, but through a bizarre set of circumstances this has come about.

This book can be classed as the written version of the 'Sunscreen' hit. The pages are packed with all sorts of help contributed by stars of showbizz and sport. Here's a list of some of the contributors, some of whom interpret Joe's advices. Bruce Reynolds, Sir Elton John, Billy Murray (The Bill), Charlie Richardson, Peter Brayham (Stunt Co-ordinator from Bond movies), Mohamed Al Fayed, Michael Winner, Samantha Janus, Elizabeth Hurley, Torvill & Dean, Cilla Black, Charlie Bronson, Kenny Dalglish, The Marquess of Bath, Roy Shaw, Barbara Cartland, Freddie Foreman, Richard Branson, Chris Tarrant, Jeffrey Archer, Ruby Wax, Frank Maloney, Kevin Keegan, Lilly Savage, Benjamin Zephaniah and more. This is your chance to support a charity that gets absolutely no help from the UK Government and only works on donations. Let's change that! For those large companies and stars that refused to help, all what we can say is that you're a heartless lot! If wasn't for bringing disrepute and shame to the human race we would name the whole sorry lot of you, but the babies are bigger than that and these babies are above begging

<u>TITLES DUE FOR FUTURE RELEASE</u>

RAMRAIDERS (NORTH EAST) UK LTD
Should be on general sale in January/February 2000.
ISBN: 1-902578-10-4 Paperback £8.99 _

A Ramraiding spectacular. A new word added to the English Dictionary. Invented in the North East of England and exported around the world. (Ramraiders) A true story that can only show the daring of how these criminals drove into premises right through the doors and windows in top of the range vehicles even while security men looked on in disbelief. How a young single mother grassed them all up, all because her catalogue payments were late. Read how the modern day 'stand and deliver' criminals outfoxed them all. Since we told you about this in 1998 you've been going mad for it, sorry for the delay but this year has been devoted to Charlie Bronson.

STAMPS

This book completely blows the lid off stamp fraud and shows how the Post Office were stopped from being sold off in the early 1990's and again of late. As predicted in a book published in 1998. You will never lick a stamp with the same respect ever again after reading this book. An exposé full of sex and violence, bed hopping and wife swapping. A true story that shows how the Post Office were duped out of £millions and are still losing revenue because of it. Sure to be another best seller from Mirage Publishing who are not frightened to tackle problems head on. It all ended in tragedy and lives were ruined over the build up to the trial that culminates to a climax that will sit you on a razor edge. Read how the Mafia in the USA also dupe their postal system out of $millions. Nothing can be done to prevent it, not here, not anywhere. The problem will not go away in the foreseeable future. No firm release date as of yet, hoped for 2,000 (Late).

Murderers Square Mile

A square mile of avenues and streets suddenly becomes a 'Bermuda Triangle' of death. What is the cause of this real life horror in such a small area? The area is the heart of evil, what happened to make it so? What sort of evil and darkness takes hold of victims in such a sudden terror stricken way? Another murder recently in August '99 proves this! (Shooting). Hopefully summer 2,000 this will be released, already in demand.

'LEGENDS'

ISBN 1-902578-11-2 Should be ready for early to mid 2,000 Possibly in Hardback format £16.99

Legends that Charlie feels deserves space in this Who's Who of Criminals and those connected in some way to them. You will not be able to put this book down, what a read it is. Short succinct and to the point write-ups. This book is already in demand and it isn't even in print yet!

BRONSON SERIES OF BOOKS DUE FOR RELEASE
(All were planned for release this year 1999, look out for them in 2,000)

Hostage of my Past Vol 1
Unbelievable colour illustrations of some of Charlie's hostage situations with his comments. (Book two) ISBN 1-902578-04-X
Hostage of my Past Vol 2
As above but too much for one book so it has been split. (Book three) ISBN 1-902578-05-8
Birdman Blows His Mind
Further insight into his mind via illustrated poems. (Book four) ISBN 1-902578-06-6
Bronson Rides Again
See the funny side of Charlie, or else!
Mission of Madness
A magnificent piece of work, not to be missed
Insanity – 'Laughing all the way to the Padded Cell Block'
Truly Insane – ISBN 1-902578-07-4
The Christmas Cracker Mad Millennium Book
A bumper Christmas Edition filled with Yuletide fun. (Possibly?)
Solitary Fitness
Bedsit Biceps. How did Charlie get to be so fit and strong on all that yuk they feed him inside the Grey Bar Hotel, find out the secrets of his feats of strength and endurance.

ORDER FORM   AMOUNT

Viv (Graham) – 'Simply the Best' £7.99...

Viv – And the Geordie Mafia (Vol 2) £8.99...

Viv – Update Chapter (Loose leaf format) £2.99...........................

Gangsters' Paradise Movie Script based on above £8.99...............

Viv Poster (A3 size – not shown in this book) £1.99.....................

PUBLIC *consumer* **ENEMY £5.99**...

The Charles Bronson Book of Poems (Book One)
           'Birdman Opens His Mind' £7.99...............................

Charles Bronson – *Sincerely Yours* (Documentary) £15.99............

Looking at Life £8.99...

Ramraiders (North East) UK Ltd £8.99.................................

Legends £16.99 (Early to mid 2,000)..
'Bronson' Pen £1.00 each (not illustrated)................................
Posters 'A' & 'B' (A3 size) £2.49 each..
(shown in this book)

Payment to be made to: Mirage Publishing. **Total   £**............
P+P for all books/posters/script is free in the UK. Video
documentary **add £2.00 for P+P** in UK. Overseas please see
appropriate costings for shipping in write ups. All prisoners
qualify for 50% discount and free shipping in the UK. Overseas
prisoners pay full price, but qualify for free shipping.

We do not accept credit cards due to increase in credit card fraud

Title: Mr/Mrs/Miss/Ms Forename:......................................

Last Name:...

Delivery address:...

....

If we can get book signed and dedicated by the author who
to:...

Post to: Mirage Publishing, PO Box 161, Gateshead, NE8 4WW, England

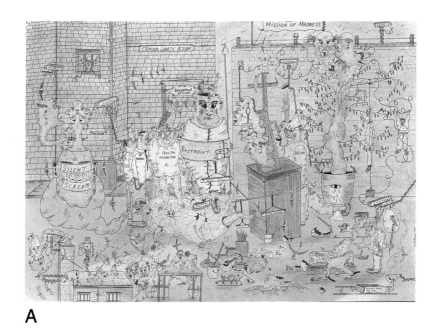

A

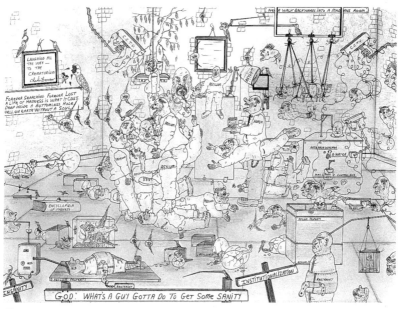

B